THE PARABLES OF JESUS

E H SEQUEIRA

I would like to dedicate this book to my wife, Jean and my children Jenny & Christopher.

Contents

Acknowledgements

I would thank many people in my life for helping in coming up with this book.

*First and foremost, my wife, **Jean**. She has ever been a great support and encouragement to me. Without her constant help, things would have been tough.*

*My children, **Jenny** & **Christopher**, for teaching me love.*

*Elder **Robert J. Wieland**, for his guidance and theological support. His presentations have always been clear & Jesus-centric.*

Church Menbers at Walla Walla City Church. They have been a great support to the Ministry.

*And mainly, **God**, for His love, grace, mercy kindness. Without Him, nothing would ever be in its place. He is the very reason for this material. His care demonstrates us this Message, to which He calls us back to Himself.*

About The Author

Pastor E. H. (Jack) Sequeira was born in Nairobi, Kenya. He joined the Seventh-day Adventist Church through evangelism in 1957. Feeling called to the ministry, he rode to England from Nairobi on his motorcycle in 1958 and spent 14 months working as a literature evangelist before enrolling at Newbold College (England). He graduated with a B.A. in theology in 1963. He earned an M.A. in systematic theology at Andrews University (Berrien Springs, Michigan, U.S.A.) in 1965. Pastor Sequeira earned his M.Div. at Andrews University in 1970.

Pastor E. H. Sequeira got married to Jean on New Year's Day, 1964. They served as missionaries for 17 years in Uganda, Kenya, and Ethiopia. He served in various capacities as Bible teacher, departmental director, university chaplain, union ministerial director, and college president.

In 1982, the Sequeiras moved to the United States. Jack served as pastor for the Kuna and Nampa churches in the Idaho Conference, then as senior pastor of the Walla Walla City Church in Washington State. In 1991, he became senior pastor of the Capital Memorial Church in Washington, D.C. Pastor Jack retired in January 2001 but still ministers to others. He has enjoyed a lifetime of preaching and seminar appointments. Jack enjoys the beautiful Pacific Northwest.

Jack and Jean have two children. Jenny (born in Uganda), was a Peace Corps Volunteer in The Gambia. Christopher (born in Kenya) is married to Nenette.

Jack and Jean live in Oregon and began JackSequeira.org in 2002 to share the Good News of the Gospel and give hope to God's children everywhere.

THE PARABLE OF THE PERILS OF AN EMPTY HEART

Turn in your Bible to Luke 11:24-26. This is one of the short parables of Christ. Jesus said,

When an evil spirit comes out of a man, it goes through arid places seeking rest and does not find it. Then it says, "I will return to the house I left." When it arrives, it finds the house swept clean and put in order. Then it goes and takes seven other spirits more wicked than itself, and they go in and live there. And the final condition of that man is worse than the first.

I would like to start by giving you a little bit of introduction regarding the parables of Christ. Over one third of the recorded teachings of Christ consist of parables. Why did Christ teach in parables? Well, parables in the days of Christ were equivalent to what we would call today visual aids. It has been discovered that visual aids — what the eye sees — leaves a much deeper impression than what one simply hears. Parables are simply word pictures. Jesus took incidences in life, He took things from nature, He took things that people were familiar with and He gave them some wonderful spiritual truths.

In other words, Jesus taught in parables to communicate to His hearers the message of salvation in a clear and simple manner. Through these parables the people could understand Christ, His mission, and His kingdom which He had come to establish.

Now it is very interesting that to those who accepted Christ as the Messiah, the parable became a means of clarifying His message and His truth. To those who rejected Christ, the very same parables obscured the truth from them. It is the same today. The parables were given by Christ to help us understand His redemptive activity, His mission, His kingdom, and what our response should be.

I have chosen for our very first study this short parable because when we realize what Christ is trying to say, we realize that it is a parable that is very fitting for us as we begin this study. It is also fitting for us in terms of our Christian experience.

Six months before Christ began His ministry, God sent John the Baptist to prepare the way for Christ. We know from the Biblical record that John the Baptist had tremendous success. People from the cities and from the country flocked to hear him. There was a revival among the Jews and they were baptized, the baptism of repentance. But, sad to say, six months later when Christ, to whom John pointed, came on the scene, many of the hearts of these people had gone cold. They had lost that experience so that not only did they reject Christ but some of them became His bitterest enemies. Jesus told this parable in which He touched the core of the problem.

One of the things that faces the Christian church is this very thing. How can we maintain the blessings we receive? Look at Pentecost. It was a wonderful blessing that the early church received but it was short-lived. Or look at the Reformation when there was a tremendous revival in Europe but within a few years the theologians went liberal and the power of the gospel was almost made null and void. Look at the great revival in England in the 19th century under John Wesley. When he died it all fizzled away.

I was at Andrews University in 1970 and the campuses of the colleges in the United States at that time were facing a tremendous revival. There was a revival among our young people. Some of you may remember that. I came back from mission service in 1975 on furlough and it was all gone. I am sure that you all have had the same experience. You have received blessings, maybe at camp meetings or at other times, but the problem is, how do we maintain that blessing? I hope that our study of this parable will help us.

First of all, let's look at the context. It is important to realize what Jesus had to say to the people to whom He spoke. If you look at Luke 11:14, you will discover that Jesus was casting out demons, manifesting His power over the devil.

Jesus was driving out a demon that was mute. When the demon left, the man who had been mute spoke, and the crowd was amazed.

But some of those who saw that miracle accused Him of casting out the demons through Beelzebub, who was the leader of the devils. Luke 11:15:

But some of them said, "By Beelzebub, the prince of demons, he is driving out demons."

Then there were others in verse 16 who insisted that He give a sign from heaven so that they could believe:

Others tested him by asking for a sign from heaven.

Then in verse 17 to about 20, Jesus responds to this:

Jesus knew their thoughts and said to them, "Any kingdom divided against itself will be ruined, and a house divided against itself will fall. If Satan is divided against himself, how can his kingdom stand? I say this because you claim that I drive out demons by Beelzebub. Now if I drive out demons by Beelzebub, by whom do your followers drive them out? So then, they will be your judges. But if I drive out demons by the finger of God, then the kingdom of God has come to you."

"If I am casting out devils by the power of the devil, then the devil is divided and a house that is divided will not be able to stand."

Now I know He said the devil is crazy but he's not that stupid. He said, "It is foolishness what you are saying. It makes no sense. If I am casting out devils by the power of the devil, what about your leaders? Whose power are they using?"

Then in verse 21 and 22, He tells us something very significant. He says in verse 21:

When a strong man, fully armed [that is referring to Satan, Satan is the strong man, fully armed], guards his own house, his possessions are safe.

When Satan succeeded in knocking down Adam and Eve, he took the whole world in his control. Since the fall, Satan has had man under his domination and no human being has been able to overcome the devil.

But (there is a "but" in verse 22) when one stronger than he comes, and that is Christ, when Christ came He came to defeat the enemy of souls. When Christ came, it says,

But when someone stronger attacks and overpowers him, he takes away the armor in which the man trusted and divides up the spoils.

In other words, when Christ came, He came to set us captives free. And that's what He did.

But Luke 11:23 says that, unfortunately, there were some who did not accept that liberation and so Jesus makes this statement to those who had turned their backs to the Messiah, to those who had become cold:

He who is not with me is against me....

You are either for Christ or you are against Christ.

He who is not with me is against me, and he who does not gather with me, scatters.

When Jesus died on the cross there were two thieves who were nailed with Him. Those two thieves both were sinners. Those two thieves represented the world but the difference is that one thief accepted Christ; the other rejected Him. Jesus is saying that, "If you reject Me, you are against Me." You are either for Him or you are against Him. You are either crucified with Christ or you shout, "Crucify Him." It is in this context Jesus gave this parable.

Now what is the parable saying? First of all, Jesus says,

When an evil spirit comes out of a man....

The term "evil spirit" (or "unclean spirit" in some translations) is a Jewish expression which is synonymous with what we would call the devil. That is the term they often used for the devil. When does the devil leave you? When one stronger than he comes and dwells in you. When you accept Christ and Christ comes through His Holy Spirit and dwells in you, the devil has to leave because Jesus is stronger and His Spirit is stronger than the devil.

What happened to the devil? He goes and looks for rest somewhere else. The words "arid places" is another expression which the Jews used to refer to the desert and the desert has very little to offer. In 1980, after conducting some worker's meetings in Egypt, out of kindness they took me on a trip to Mount Sinai. Those were the days when Israel and Egypt were not friends but they had made some sort of peace. We drove miles and miles of desert and there was nothing attractive in that desert. It was dry and my thoughts went back to the Exodus and I said, "The Jews would never have made it if it weren't for the grace of our Lord Jesus Christ."

He gave them heat at night because it was quite cold at night, but it was very hot — unbearably hot — in the daytime, so hot that even when we had the windows rolled down the air was hotter than what it was in the car. So we had to roll the windows up even though none of those cars had air conditioning. That's how hot it was. Somebody told me it was 122 degrees. That seems high but it was very hot.

The devil wants to find rest. When we read that expression "seeking rest," we must not project our ideas of rest. When I want to seek rest I lie down on those "lazy boy" chairs that lift up your legs, only America has them, wonderful chairs, you just relax. That's my idea of seeking rest. Some, of course, find rest sitting by a stream with a fishing rod; that's rest to them until they catch the fish. But when the devil seeks rest it means something very different. I want to give you a text to show what it means when the devil is seeking rest.

Turn to 1 Peter 5:8. There the apostle Peter tells us what it means when the devil goes about seeking rest. This is a very relevant statement in terms of our parable.

Be self-controlled and alert. Your enemy the devil prowls around like a roaring lion looking for someone to devour.

That's Satan's idea of seeking rest. He wants you. He's mad because Christ has driven him out of his abode and he cannot find rest, according to this parable.

So what does he say? He says in Luke 11:24:

...“I will return to the house I left.”

The word “house” is often used to refer to human beings. We are a house. God created us as a house but He created us to be indwelt by the Holy Spirit, not by the devil. It is because of the fall we are in this predicament.

...“I will return to the house I left.”

He came out of a man; he wants to return back. Well, he does come back and guess what he finds? Verse 25:

When it arrives, it finds the house swept clean and put in order.

Now what does the parable mean by that? You see, when you come to Christ, what do you do? Well, I read in 1 John 1:9, if you come to Christ you confess your sins, He is faithful to cleanse you, to sweep away all your filth:

If we confess our sins, he is faithful and just and will forgive us our sins and purify us from all unrighteousness.

So here is a Christian who has accepted Christ, who has swept away all the filth; you have given up all your bad habits; you have decided to walk a new life and you have garnished your house with new resolutions.

Very often when I visit houses, there are placards, “Christ is the Head of this house,” and so on. Some of you have placards and this is what you have done with yourself. You have garnished yourself with promises, with resolutions, and very often we do that at the beginning of the year. We make resolutions. We say, “Last year I was a failure but this year I'm determined to spend more time studying the Bible, more time in prayer, more time in witnessing.” And the devil comes and sees your clean house and he sees your wonderful placards and your promises and what does he do? He says, "I need help. This fellow is a little bit stronger than he was when I left him."

The text says, verse 26,

Then it goes and takes seven other spirits more wicked than itself, and they go in and live there.

Apparently they have degrees of wickedness among the fallen angels. But the word "seven" signifies that he comes back with full, complete force because the word "seven" means completeness. The question is, "Does he enter in?" and the parable says, "Yes." They not only enter but they dwell there.

And the final condition of that man is worse than the first.

Where is the problem? Why is it that the devil was able to enter in? I thought, in verse 21, that the Spirit and Christ are stronger than the devil. How is it that the devil could enter in? Where was the problem? Well, the answer is not found in Luke; it is found in Matthew. So I'll tell you what I'm going to do. I'm going to read the parable in Luke once again. The same parable is repeated in Matthew, except in Matthew there is one more word that Matthew uses that Luke has somehow omitted. In that one word we have the answer to the problem.

Turn to Matthew 12:43 and I want you to keep your finger there. It's a short parable so I can read Luke 11:24-26 again. I want you to listen very carefully. The only difference is one word.

When an evil spirit comes out of a man, it goes through arid places seeking rest and does not find it. Then it says, "I will return to the house I left." When it arrives, it finds the house swept clean and put in order. Then it goes and takes seven other spirits more wicked than itself, and they go in and live there. And the final condition of that man is worse than the first.

Now listen to Matthew 12:43-45:

When an evil spirit comes out of a man, it goes through arid places seeking rest and does not find it. Then it says, "I will return to the house I left." When it arrives, it finds the house unoccupied, swept clean and put in order. Then it goes and takes seven other spirits more wicked than itself, and they go in and live there. And the final condition of that man is worse than the first.

One word that Matthew adds that is not found in Luke, the word "unoccupied" or "empty." The word "empty" makes the world of difference. It is swept; it is clean; it is full of promises and resolutions but it is empty. And when the devil finds that it is empty, it makes it possible for him to go in and dwell there. And when he dwells there he makes sure that he secures himself much stronger than he did in the past so that your last state is worse than the first.

Why was it empty? Well, it's a human problem. According to the gospel of Jesus Christ, salvation is by faith in Christ from beginning to end. Jesus said in John 15:5,

I am the vine; you are the branches. If a man remains in me and I in him, he will bear much fruit; apart from me you can do nothing.

"Without me, you can do nothing."

But, you see, we human beings are born egocentric. We are born naturally to depend on ourselves and the moment we relax, we forget that we have a Holy Spirit who has been sent to be our Comforter, our strength, our Guide, and we become self-dependent. The moment you become self-dependent, the moment you try to fulfill what is the work of God, you are in trouble.

Let me give you a couple of examples. Turn to Galatians 3. Now the churches of Galatia had received the gospel; they had accepted Christ through the preaching of Christ our righteousness by Paul himself. But somehow these Galatian Christians were convinced that the gospel is not "not I, but Christ," but "Christ plus me." Somehow they turned from the pure gospel to self.

So in Galatians 3 Paul uses some very strong words. The King James version kindly uses the word "foolish." The Greek word is much stronger than that. It is closer to the word "stupid." Paul was angry because these Galatian Christians were deceived and he said in Galatians 3:1-2:

You foolish [or stupid] Galatians! Who has bewitched [or cast a spell on] you? Before your very eyes Jesus Christ was clearly portrayed as crucified. I would like to learn just one thing from you:

Did you receive the Spirit [experience the new birth] by observing the law [by being good], or by believing what you heard?

How did you receive the Spirit? By faith. How do you maintain the Spirit? By faith.

You and I are no match for the devil. You and I are no match for the flesh, but the Spirit is. And Paul is asking the Galatian Christians, "How did you receive the Spirit?" And the answer is obvious. Galatians 3:3:

Are you so foolish? After beginning with the Spirit, are you now trying to attain your goal by human effort?

"Are you trying now to improve your standing before God by your own performance? How can you be so stupid?" he says. "Who has cast a spell on you?" But I tell you, it was the devil who cast a spell on them. Why am I saying that? Because when he says, "Who has bewitched you," Paul is using the singular term. The people who deceived them were the Judaizers. They were more than one. But behind the Judaizers was one person, the devil. He first deceived them that you can live without Christ; you can be good through the willpower, by making resolutions and promises and they fell for it. Then the devil came in and the last state of them was worse than the first.

Let us be very clear. In Romans 7, Paul points to a very important problem that we face and the problem is what he calls the "law of sin at work in my members" (Romans 7:23). Notice he calls it a law and by that he means it is a principle or a force as we use the term "law of gravity."

The law of gravity is a constant unending force and in every sinful, fallen human being there is this law of sin and death which is pulling us down. Paul says, "Even if I choose not to obey the law of sin I find that I cannot keep my choice; fulfill my choice. I try and I fail." At the end of this battle he cries out in desperation [Romans 8:24],

What a wretched man I am! Who will rescue me from this body of death?

"Who will deliver me from this body controlled by the law of sin which is taking me to death?" And he says [Romans 8:25],

Thanks be to God — through Jesus Christ our Lord!

"I am no match for him; he is the strong man and I am the captive but I thank God through Jesus Christ."

Incidentally, the word "wretched" appears only twice in the whole of the New Testament, at least in the original. This is the first time. The second time it is found in Revelation 3 to the Laodicean church where Jesus, the True Witness, says [Revelation 3:7],

But you do not realize that you are wretched, pitiful, poor, blind and naked.

That is why God wants to give us eye-salve that we may realize what Paul discovered and what he declared in Romans 7:18,

I know that nothing good lives in me, that is, in my sinful nature. For I have the desire to do what is good, but I cannot carry it out.

But Paul doesn't end by simply saying,

Thanks be to God — through Jesus Christ our Lord!

In Romans 8:1-2, he tells us where the power comes from, where the source of our victory is.

Therefore, there is now no condemnation for those who are in Christ Jesus, because through Christ Jesus the law of the Spirit of life set me free from the law of sin and death.

"For the law of the Spirit of life in Christ Jesus has made me free from the law of sin and death."

Here are two forces: the law of the Spirit and the law of sin. Both are constant. My willpower is not a law; it is a force but it is never constant. It is strong sometimes, weak other times, but the law of the Spirit is a constant force and the law of sin is a constant force and these two met in Jesus Christ. These two forces met in Jesus Christ and guess who won? The law of the Spirit in Christ Jesus and that Spirit is now made available to us.

Paul says in Romans 8:9-10 that if the Spirit is not dwelling in you, you do not belong to Him:

You, however, are controlled not by the sinful nature but by the Spirit, if the Spirit of God lives in you. And if anyone does not have the Spirit of Christ, he does not belong to Christ. But if Christ is in you, your body is dead because of sin, yet your spirit is alive because of righteousness.

But he also goes on in Romans 8 that this Spirit is able to suppress — to keep down — your mortal body and produce righteousness in you.

There are some here who believe that I do not teach sanctification. I have the same desire as any of you who wants to see Christ's character reproduced in the church. Where we may disagree is the method. I believe that both justification and sanctification are by faith alone. I cannot contribute one iota before justification nor after justification towards righteousness. All I can produce is self-righteousness, which outwardly may look beautiful but inwardly it is polluted with self.

But when the Spirit dwells in me, the devil cannot touch me. I read in 1 John 4:4 that greater is he that is in me than he that is in the world:

You, dear children, are from God and have overcome them, because the one who is in you is greater than the one who is in the world.

But the question is that the Holy Spirit does not work in us automatically. I read in Galatians 5:16:

So I say, live by the Spirit, and you will not gratify the desires of the sinful nature.

But, as I mentioned, the Holy Spirit does not work in us automatically. I wish He did. All I have to do is press a button like I do the dishwasher. No problem washing dishes in America except in our church kitchen because we are not supposed to wash them by hand because of some crazy rule that we have to buy some expensive equipment because it is a public place. I see no difference why I can wash my dishes in my house and invite guests and I can't use a normal dishwasher in the church. Anyway, I will never understand all the rules of this country but here it is. But this one thing I do know, that the Holy Spirit does not live in me automatically. I have to keep constantly having a walk with

Him. As Paul says, I need to pray without ceasing; I need to keep Him constantly in contact because the Holy Spirit will do nothing against your will. He is not a dictator.

So I read in Ephesians 4:30,

And do not grieve the Holy Spirit of God, with whom you were sealed for the day of redemption.

Don't drive the Holy Spirit out. I read in 1 Thessalonians 5:19:

Do not put out the Spirit's fire....

I can drink a glass of water and I say, "That's enough. I've had enough." There will never come a time when you will say to the Holy Spirit, "I don't need You any more."

There was a time when there were some dear brethren in this church who produced an off-shoot movement called "The Awakening" who taught that when probation is closed we will have to live without a Mediator, perverting the statement of Ellen G. White. Yes, we will have to live without a Mediator because we don't need an advocate after the verdict of a Judgment. You needed it before the verdict but the statement does not say that we will live without a Saviour. The statement does not teach that we will live without the Holy Spirit. In fact, we will be sealed by the Holy Spirit. He will be there to take us through the time of trouble.

The devil wants you. The moment you allow Christ to come and dwell in you and the devil is driven out of you, that is not the end of the problem. May I take you back to Luke 4 where we have recorded for us the three temptations that Jesus experienced after His baptism. You are familiar with the temptations [Luke 4:1-12] but I want you to notice two things that followed the temptations. Luke 4:13:

When the devil had finished all this tempting, he left him until an opportune time.

By the way, did the devil succeed? No. He tried to enter into Christ but he failed. Did he say, "It is no use trying." No. He departed from him "until an opportune time."

So when you have a tremendous experience and, through the grace of God, you are able to drive the devil out of you, I can guarantee he says, "I'll wait till he goes home and goes back to his normal schedule. I'll wait till he is exhausted and tired and in a weak moment, then I'll come in." And, unfortunately, too often he succeeds. He left Jesus for a season. Did he come back? Yes. How often? Well, Hebrews 4:15 says he was tempted in all points like us:

For we do not have a high priest who is unable to sympathize with our weaknesses, but we have one who has been tempted in every way, just as we are — yet was without sin.

Is there any time when the devil doesn't tempt you? No. He's always trying to come back.

So I want to go to the next verse. Luke 4:14:

Jesus returned to Galilee in the power of the Spirit, and news about him spread through the whole countryside.

And I pray that you, when you end this study, will leave in the power of the Spirit. Don't leave Him behind. We need Him 24 hours a day, seven days a week.

Well, the parable is over but I want to close with looking at what happened after Jesus gave the parable. Back to Luke 11:27:

As Jesus was saying these things, a woman in the crowd called out, "Blessed is the mother who gave you birth and nursed you."

The New King James Version says, "What a lucky woman" I don't think she felt lucky at the cross. Jesus responds in Luke 11:28:

He replied, "Blessed rather are those who hear the word of God and obey it."

May God bless you.

CHAPTER TWO

The Parable of New Wine in Old Bottles

In Luke 5:27-28 we have the call of Matthew or Levi, who was a tax collector (or publican):

After this, Jesus went out and saw a tax collector by the name of Levi sitting at his tax booth. "Follow me," Jesus said to him, and Levi got up, left everything and followed him.

Now I want you to get the picture. Matthew was a tax collector. A tax collector was despised. He was looked upon as a sinner, as a traitor to the Jewish cause and he was looked upon as out of reach of salvation. The Pharisees, the religious leaders of Christ's day gave the tax collectors no hope of salvation. By this time Jesus' name was quite famous and Jesus comes and says to Matthew, "I want you to be one of my disciples."

Can you imagine what that must have done to Matthew? He was so excited that not only did he leave everything and follow Christ but the next verse (29) says:

Then Levi held a great banquet for Jesus at his house, and a large crowd of tax collectors and others were eating with them.

He had a big party. Of course, he wouldn't invite the scribes and Pharisees; they wouldn't come, I suppose. The "others" were "sinners" like them. Here was a big feast where all the publicans and sinners came — and Jesus was with them — rejoicing that Jesus had given them hope.

But now look at verse 30:

But the Pharisees and the teachers of the law who belonged to their sect complained to this disciples, "Why do you eat and drink with tax collectors and 'sinners'?"

Now remember, in the Jewish culture eating and drinking with somebody was more than a social event. When Jesus ate with publicans and sinners, He was simply saying that, "I accept you; I welcome you." And that was completely in contradiction to the Jewish teaching.

So they began to murmur and Jesus answered in verse 31:

Jesus answered them, "It is not the healthy who need a doctor, but the sick."

Then in verse 32 (I want you to keep this in mind):

"I have not come to call the righteous, but sinners to repentance."

In other words, "I came to save sinners." Judaism only saved the righteous. Christ came to save sinners. So there was a complete contrast of these two positions.

Verse 33 says,

They said to him, "John's disciples often fast and pray, and so do the disciples of the Pharisees, but yours go on eating and drinking."

They could not answer back, so they turned around to something else. Jesus said something very interesting in reply in verse 34:

Jesus answered, "Can you make the guests of the bridegroom fast while he is with them?"

Now this may mean nothing to you, but the Jews were very familiar with Psalms 19:1-6 which identified the coming of the Messiah with the bridegroom:

The heavens declare the glory of God; the skies proclaim the work of his hands. Day after day they pour forth speech; night after night they display knowledge. There is no speech or language where their voice is not heard. Their voice goes out into all the earth, their words to the ends of the world. In the heavens he has pitched a tent for the sun, which is like a bridegroom coming forth from his pavilion, like a champion rejoicing to run his course. It rises at one end of the heavens and makes its circuit to the other; nothing is hidden from its heat.

So what He was telling the Pharisees and scribes was, "Why should my disciples fast when the Messiah is here?" But, He said (verse 35):

"But the time will come when the bridegroom will be taken from them; in those days they will fast."

It was in this context that He gave these two parables. Now Christ's parables were taken from the daily life experiences. Unfortunately, we are living 2,000 years later so I need to explain to you what those two illustrations were in order to understand the significance.

Verse 36:

He told them this parable: " No one tears a patch from a new garment and sews on an old one. If he does, he will have torn that new garment, and the patch from the new will not match the old."

Remember, that is the first parable. In the days of Christ there were only two kinds of material — cotton and wool — and neither of them had the advantages of the synthetic material that we have today. They all shrink when you wash them for the first time. Of course, today we have pre-shrunk wool and pre-shrunk cotton but in those days they did not have pre-shrunk material.

I remember when I was at Newbold [College, U.K.], a young lady who was sweet on me made me a jumper [sweater]. She finally won because she's my wife today. We were allowed a quota of how many clothes we could give to the school for washing. The school would wash a certain amount of clothes. It was part of the allowance like the cafeteria allowance in school here. So, after wearing it for a while, I gave this jumper to be washed and the girl who did it forgot that it was wool and so when it came back it was three times smaller than when it went in. There was no way I could wear it. And I looked and I looked and I looked and I finally found a student who was small enough so it would fit and I gave it to him.

Let's say you have a coat and the elbow is worn out. The coat has been washed several times and has shrunk to its maximum shrinkage condition. If you put a new patch of cloth on it and you wash it, what happens to the new patch? It shrinks; the old doesn't shrink any more, it has shrunk as much as it can. So the new patch tears away. In other words the two materials are incompatible. That is what Christ is trying to get across:

"If he does, he will have torn that new garment, and the patch from the new will not match the old."

The second parable, verses 37-38:

"And no one pours new wine into old wineskins. If he does, the new wine will burst the skins, the wine will run out and the wineskins will be ruined. No, new wine must be poured into new wineskins."

The wine makers used sheepskin or goatskin for bottles. When you look at them it looks horrifying when you first see it. In the Middle East they use it for water, too. Have you ever seen a dead animal bloated up? That's what it looks like. When they slaughter an animal they cut it open and then they stitch the whole animal back to its position, the front legs and back legs, and the neck is the opening part.

When they made wine they put this wine in and they allowed it to ferment in the skin. Now new skin is flexible; it's soft, and, when the wine fermented, it expanded and the skin expanded with it. No problem. Then, after so many days, it was mature; it was ready for selling. They would sell it gradually or use it and when the wine was finished the skin was no longer usable to make new wine. The reasons were, number one, the wineskin had stretched to its maximum capacity. Number two, when the wine was gone it did not shrink back. It remained stretched and it dried. So if you put new wine into it, it would have to expand further and the skin would not take it. It would burst and he would lose the bottle and the wine at the same time.

What was Jesus trying to get across to the people with whom He spoke? Remember, He was responding to the scribes and Pharisees. What was their religion? Their religion was a religion of dos and don'ts. Religion to them was not a joyous expression of God's blessings on them. Religion to them was dos and don'ts; they had long faces; they looked miserable.

For example, Moses commanded that they should fast once a year. By the time of Christ, tradition had made it twice a week so they would fast twice a week. Remember the Sermon on the Mount? They had ashes on their faces, rags, long faces. To them salvation was very hard, very difficult. In a nutshell, the religion of the scribes and Pharisees was called the Old Covenant.

The message that Christ brought was radical; it was revolutionary; it was so contradictory to the traditional Judaism that the two were incompatible. And the two that are incompatible are the Old Covenant and the New Covenant. Here you have two covenants; one was taught by the Pharisees, the other by the scribes.

Before I turn to these covenants, let me give you a couple of verses to show you to what I am referring. Please turn in your Bible to Romans 4. Romans 4:14:

For if those who live by law are heirs...

What does he mean by that? "Those of you who are trying to go to heaven by the works of the law"; that's what he's means. He is not talking here about the law as a standard of Christian living; He is talking here of the law as a method of going to heaven.

For if those who live by law are heirs, faith has no value and the promise is worthless....

You cannot have it both ways. It's either one or the other. You cannot mix the two. You cannot put a new patch on an old garment. You can't put new wine in an old bottle. They are incompatible.

Another text that I would like you to turn to is Galatians 3:18 and Paul is saying the same thing here:

For if the inheritance depends on the law, then it no longer depends on a promise; but God in his grace gave it to Abraham through a promise.

You can't have it both ways, says Paul. Now, what is the difference between the Old and the New Covenants? There are many Christians who say that the difference between the Old and the New Covenants has to do with time. No, it has nothing to do with time. They teach — and this is the Dispensational teaching — that from Moses to Christ was the dispensation of the Old Covenant and from Christ to us, to the end of time is the dispensation of the New Covenant.

The Bible does not teach such nonsense. The Bible teaches that men were only saved by one covenant, the New Covenant, often called the Everlasting Covenant. Then what is the difference? I'll give you several differences.

The Old Covenant was based on man's promise, "All that you say, we will do." The New Covenant is based on God's promise. That is why the book of Hebrews calls it a better promise.

The Old Covenant depends on human ability. The New Covenant is based on God's provision. Two opposite concepts. In other words, the Old Covenant is a covenant of works. The New Covenant is a covenant of grace. This is the distinction between the two.

What Christ is saying in these two parables is that legalism and salvation by grace are incompatible. You cannot mix them together. They do not go together. You cannot synthesize them. They are two opposite, contradictory ways of salvation. One is man-made, the basis of all pagan religions. The other is from above.

I want to make it very clear what the Bible says. Turn to Hebrews 8. When Christ came to this world, He did not come to refine Judaism. He did not come to improve it. He came to take it away and replace it with the new. Hebrews 8:13:

By calling this convenant "new," he has made the first one obsolete; and what is obsolete and aging will soon disappear.

In Hebrews 10:9, he goes on to say:

Then he said, "Here I am, I have come to do your will." He sets aside the first to establish the second.

Hebrews 8:6-9:

But the ministry Jesus has received is as superior to theirs as the covenant of which he is mediator is superior to the old one, and it is founded on better promises. For if there had been nothing wrong with that first covenant, no place would have been sought for another. But God found fault with the people [please notice where the fault was; it was with them] and said: "The time is coming, declares the Lord, when I will make a new covenant with the house of Israel and with the house of Judah. It will not be like the covenant I made with their forefathers when I took them by the hand to lead them out of Egypt, because they did not remain faithful to my covenant, and I turned away from them, declares the Lord...."

The Old Covenant failed not because the law was faulty but the fault was with the people. The people could not keep the promise. Their ability was insufficient to fulfill the law of God. In the New Covenant, Christ is our righteousness, both in terms of our standing before God and in terms of our daily living. It is always, "Not I, but Christ."

The reason I have chosen this parable is that we are facing a similar crisis. Some years ago there was an excellent article in the Review and Herald. The title of the article was, "From Sinai to Golgotha." It was well documented. It presented — the document proved — that Ellen G. White used more and more grace terms and less and less law as she progressed in life. The idea was her knowledge of the gospel was increasing as she went along. While I see eye-to-eye with the research work, I myself feel that Ellen G. White understood the gospel right from the beginning. But I'll give you the reason I believe why she changed: she began to use more grace terms. It's not because her knowledge of the gospel was increasing but because a problem was creeping into our church that had to be solved.

In our attempt as a people to fight against the Dispensational teaching which was doing away with the law, we got into the tendency of going to the other extreme and preaching the law and the law until we were as dry as the hills of Gilboa. I'll give you some evidence. In 1874, 17 August to 19 December, Uriah Smith published a series of articles called "The Leading Doctrines of the Review" with no mention of justification by faith. In 1877, Uriah Smith and James White conducted jointly a Bible Institute for pastors. The studies published, called "Bible Institute," had no mention of righteousness by faith. In 1878, Uriah Smith published a book called Synopsis of Present Truth, 336 pages long, which contained no mention of righteousness or justification by faith.

So we were becoming so heavy on the law that I think Sister White realized that we were out of balance. In fact, if you read the book Faith and Works, she makes the statement, "On the one hand, religionists [and I think she was referring to Dispensationalists] generally have divorced the law and the gospel while we [that is, we SDAs] have, on the other hand, almost done the same thing from another standpoint. We have not upheld before the people the righteousness and the full significance of His great plan of salvation."

I think that she saw this danger and so she began to try to correct it, because I read this statement in the later years (1890): "For nearly two years we have been urging the people to come and accept the light and the truth concerning the righteousness of Christ and they do not know whether to come and take hold of this precious truth or not. [That new wine was too much for them.] They are bound about their own ideas." Remember how the parable goes? The old wine tastes better than the new.

Then she goes on to say this is the Review and Herald, 11 March 1890: "You will meet with those who will say, 'You are too much excited over this matter. You are too much in earnest. You should not be reaching for the righteousness of Christ and making so much of that. You should preach the law.' [And she responds] As a people we have preached the law until we are as dry as the hills of Gilboa that had neither dew or rain. We must preach Christ in the law and there will be sup and nourishment in the preaching that will be as food for the famishing flock of God."

In Gospel Workers, page 301, I have a statement in the very back of my Bible to remind myself. She makes this statement over the argument they had in those days over the gospel: "This I do know [you may be fighting among yourselves] that our churches are dying for the want of the teaching on the subject of righteousness by faith in Christ, and on kindred truths."

We cannot mix the two together. But now comes the problem. There are many who feel that if you preach righteousness by faith you are doing away with the law; you are doing away with Christian living. No, true justification by faith always produces holiness of living. A group of us met with deep concerns because our church is polarizing into camps. There are three major camps and all the camps are very sincere. They all have a burden for God's people.

We analyzed that. "What can we do?" we said, and we discovered something very interesting that I would like to share with you. First of all, we looked at their objectives and we discovered that all three objectives of the three camps were genuine, were legitimate, and were essential to our needs today. One camp has a great burden that our people realize that God is love. Our people desperately need to know that. There are many who look at God as a vindictive tyrant ready to push you in the fire every mistake you have done. So their great burden is that God is love. No one can complain with that objective.

The problem we faced was the method. They lean very heavily on what we call the "moral influence theory," which does present God as love but at the expense of God's justice. You cannot present one truth at the expense of another. That is not the gospel. At the cross, love and justice met together. You see, the moral influence theory is heretical not because of what it teaches but what it denies. It denies the legal framework of the atonement. It teaches that Christ did not have to die to pay any price to save us. He died only to demonstrate that He loves us. So while we shared the objectives, the answer was, "No," we cannot agree with the method.

Then we went to the second group's position. Their greatest burden is that our people have security of salvation, assurance of salvation. In 1975, the Personal Ministry Department of the General Conference at Vienna reported that only 10 percent, 10 out of every 100 — and this is the world field, including Africa and Inter America where we have tremendous witnessing — only 10 percent of the world field membership is involved in any form of witnessing; 90 percent are simply sitting down and doing nothing.

The question was raised, "What can we do about it?" One man stood up and said, "Brethren, it is not because we lack programs. We have enough programs in our files to fill this auditorium but our people will not witness unless they are sure of their own salvation. You cannot witness something you are not sure about yourself." We all felt that burden was legitimate, but to use the evangelical gospel which leads to cheap grace is where the problem was, we felt. You can't lift up justification and say it is all that righteousness by faith is about and that sanctification doesn't belong to it. From beginning to end it is by faith alone. It is justification by faith, it is sanctification by faith, and my glorification will be the result of faith alone.

Then we went to the third group. Their objectives are very good, very legitimate. Their great concern is victorious living, character perfection. Do we need that today? I'll tell you, we are living in a scientific age and science will not believe anything without a demonstration. As the famous pagan philosopher Nietzche who was the son of a pastor (he was a Pastor's kid who became an atheist) said to the Christian church, "If you expect me to believe in your Redeemer, you Christians will have to look a lot more redeemed."

Brethren, before the end comes, God is going to lighten this earth with His glory. We shared that burden, we agreed with that burden, but you cannot produce victorious living by hammering at victorious living. That is not where "the rubber meets the road." That is not where it is because holiness of living is the fruit of justification by faith. I believe that the message that God brought to this church 100 years ago, the message of Christ our righteousness, correctly understood, and faith, correctly understood, will produce a people who believe in a loving God and who will serve Him not because they are afraid of Him; they will serve Him because He first loved them and gave Himself for them.

I believe that message will produce a people who will want to vindicate God, who will say with Paul, "Take me God; use me. I want to be Yours fully and completely." There will be a people who will not be afraid to die because they know in whom they believe. They know that in Christ they stand secure. They have built their house on the rock, Jesus Christ.

But here is the problem. This message is radical. You cannot put it in your legalistic mind. It does not make sense. You have to come to this message with an open mind like the disciples had to do. The disciples were like rest of the Jews; they had preconceived ideas. Jesus spent almost three years with them and at the end of the three years they still had not understood the gospel. Why? Was it because the teaching of Jesus was hard? No. It is because they were trying to put new wine into the old bottles and it could not match. They could not handle the teaching of Christ.

So God had to undo what they had learned all their lifetime. It took more than three years for that to happen. When Paul was called to be an apostle of Christ, when he was converted, God could not fully use him straightway. God had to take him to the desert of Arabia and undo his false theology because his old theology could not take the new theology of Christ.

So, I want you to go to scripture and study for yourselves. Come with an open mind. Forget your upbringing. Forget the things that you were taught and ask yourself — be prayerful — "Is this of God or is this heresy?" In other words, don't condemn anything that you hear just because it does not agree with what you were taught.

I would like to conclude by a statement that is found in Ellen G. White's Counsels to Writers and Editors, page 35: "Let us come to the word of God with open minds that we may learn from God what is truth." (This statement was made regarding those who were opposing righteousness by faith.) "There is no excuse for anyone in taking the position that there is no more truth to be revealed, and that all our expositions of Scripture are without an error. The fact that certain doctrines have been held as truth for many years by our people is not a proof that our ideas are infallible. Age will not make error into truth, and truth can afford to be fair. No true doctrine will lose anything by close investigation."

I want you to investigate. Let me explain the background of this. The Adventist church came out of the Millerite movement. When Miller first began his studies on the book of Daniel, one of the questions that he asked himself was, "What did Daniel mean by the word 'sanctuary'?" There were six views in those days. It could mean the heavenly sanctuary; it could mean the earthly sanctuary; it could mean the Jews; it could mean the earth; it could mean the Christian church; and there was one other. He sat down and he came to the conclusion that the sanctuary that Daniel had in mind was the earth and the Christian church. He rejected the others.

When the disappointment came, God revealed that it was the heavenly sanctuary that Daniel had in mind. A few years later when Waggoner and Jones came up with the idea that the cleansing of the sanctuary includes the church, it was thought that they were going back to Millerite teaching. You see, Miller believed that because the sanctuary was the earth and the church, the coming of Christ would be the cleansing of the sanctuary. The earth would be cleansed by fire. The church would be cleansed by this corruption putting on incorruption.

When Waggoner and Jones said the heavenly is the church also they said, "No, you are going back to Millerite." But his interpretation was different from the Millerite interpretation and so they argued. It was the same over the law of Galatians. It was the same over righteousness by faith. So Sister White said, "Don't condemn these men until you study for yourselves."

If you hear anything new, go to the word of God. Please make this the measuring stick. Come with an open mind, because those Pharisees lost a blessing by rejecting Jesus Christ just because what He taught, what He did, did not agree with their traditional teaching. We must remember that we can be in the same boat. Never say that we cannot make the same mistakes as the Jews because we have done it many times.

In closing, please remember what Jesus said in the parable. As He concludes this parable, He says:

"And no one after drinking old wine wants the new, for he says, 'The old is better.'"

When you hear something new, it is hard for you to simply say, "Yes"? It does take time. We have to be patient. Why doesn't he take it straightway? Because the old is better than the new. Whenever anything new is introduced — like a new worship format — you have the same problem; with new theology you have the same problem. But never judge truth by your old teachings. The Bible is the measuring stick of truth. Study for yourself. This is the new wine.

It is my prayer that we will become a church that will study and will grow together and, as we deal with the parables of Christ, that we will not act like the Pharisees, that we will accept the new wine and produce new fruit. That will be glory to His name. That's my prayer in Jesus' name.

CHAPTER THREE

THE PARABLE OF THE ROYAL MARRIAGE FEAST

Matthew 22:1-14:

Jesus spoke to them again in parables, saying: "The kingdom of heaven is like a king who prepared a wedding banquet for his son. He sent his servants to those who had been invited to the banquet to tell them to come, but they refused to come.

"Then he sent some more servants and said, 'Tell those who have been invited that I have prepared my dinner: My oxen and fattened cattle have been butchered, and everything is ready. Come to the wedding banquet.'

"But they paid no attention and went off — one to his field, another to his business. The rest seized his servants, mistreated them and killed them. The king was enraged. He sent his army and destroyed those murderers and burned their city.

"Then he said to this servants, 'The wedding banquet is ready, but those I invited did not deserve to come. Go the street corners and invite to the banquet anyone you find.' So the servants went out into the streets and gathered all the people they could find, both good and bad, and the wedding hall was filled with guests.

"But when the king came in to see the guests, he noticed a man there who was not wearing wedding clothes. 'Friend,' he asked, 'how did you get in here without wedding clothes?' The man was speechless.

"Then the king told the attendants, 'Tie him hand and foot, and throw him outside, into the darkness, where there will be weeping and gnashing of teeth.'

"For many are invited, but few are chosen."

Jesus was in the temple preaching and teaching in parables and the parable we just read is one of them. If you turn to Matthew 21:45-46 you will discover who Jesus meant where it says in Matthew 22:1:

Jesus spoke to them again in parables, saying....

In verse 45 and 46 of the previous chapter I read:

When the chief priests and the Pharisees heard Jesus' parables, they knew he was talking about them. They looked for a way to arrest him, but they were afraid of the crowd because the people held that he was a prophet.

It is to them Jesus spoke this parable of the wedding feast.

As we look at the parable, it is not only an important parable but it covers a vast span of time. It begins with the Jews and it takes us right up to the end of time. It includes all mankind, both Jews and Gentiles. We're going to call this parable "The Royal Marriage Feast" because that's what it is. If you look at your Bibles you will discover that very often, especially in the book of Revelation, the Second Coming of Christ and the establishing of His kingdom is often called or referred to as the great wedding feast.

I want to give you one example. Turn to Revelation 19. Keep your finger in Matthew 22 because that is what we are going to cover. We are going to cover verses 1-14, the parable of the wedding garment but in Revelation 19:6-9 you will notice how the second coming of Christ and that great gathering of the saints is referred to as the great wedding feast of the Lamb. Revelation 19:6-9:

Then I heard what sounded like a great multitude, like the roar of rushing waters and like loud peals of thunder, shouting: "Hallelujah!

For our Lord God Almighty reigns. Let us rejoice and be glad and give him glory! For the wedding of the Lamb has come, and his bride has made herself ready. Fine linen, bright and clean, was given her to wear."

(Fine linen stands for the righteous acts of the saints.)

Then the angel said to me, "Write: 'Blessed are those who are invited to the wedding supper of the Lamb!'" And he added, "These are the true words of God."

It is this that Jesus is describing in Matthew 22. Now according to this parable, the chief concern that Christ had is brought out in terms of our human response to the wedding invitation. As we analyze this parable, we can divide it into three parts or three stages. The first part is verses 2-7, where Christ is dealing specifically with those chief priests, the Pharisees, and the people who were under them.

In verse 2, He says:

"The kingdom of heaven is like a king who prepared a wedding banquet for his son."

We know the son is Jesus Christ.

He sent his servants to those who had been invited to the banquet to tell them to come....

Remember, the invitation had already gone long before, but it was the custom in the Eastern world and still is, especially when you have a royal wedding, that the host — the one who has the wedding feast or prepares the wedding feast — sends out his servants to remind the people that have already been invited, to come to the wedding feast.

In verse 3, we are told that he sent forth his servants to call those that were already bidden but the sad fact is that they would not come. But the king was patient; he was longsuffering; there was still a little bit of time and so we read in verse 4:

Then he sent some more servants and said, "Tell those who have been invited that I have prepared my dinner: My oxen and fattened cattle have been butchered, and everything is ready. Come to the wedding banquet."

This first section deals with the Jews. For 1,500 years God had promised the Jews that the Messiah would come and He would establish His kingdom. In fact, that was the message Jesus preached when He came, "The kingdom of God is at hand." But I read in verse 5:

But they paid no attention and went off — one to his field, another to his business. The rest seized his servants, mistreated them and killed them.

They made light of the Messiah, they made light of the gospel, and went their own ways, one to his farm, another to his merchandise. And the remnant (that is, the last generation of the Jews before the Messiah came) took his servants and treated them spitefully, and even killed them.

Then we have in verse 7 the sad story:

The king was enraged. He sent his army and destroyed those murderers and burned their city.

Now, of course, we are living 2,000 years later and we know this is exactly what happened to the Jews as a nation. Remember, it is not God who rejected them but they who rejected the Messiah. As you know, in 70 A.D., Titus' army destroyed Jerusalem and the people were scattered.

But the wedding was not canceled because of this, for, as we go to the second section, verses 8-10, we are told that the king said to his servants,

"The wedding banquet is ready, but those I invited did not deserve to come."

They were not worthy because of the very fact that they deliberately, persistently, and willfully said, "We don't want your gift. We don't want your wedding invitation. We don't want to come to the feast." It is they themselves who made themselves unworthy by their rejection.

Now the gospel goes (verse 9) to the Gentile world:

"Go the street corners and invite to the banquet anyone you find."

Now I want you to look at verse 10:

So the servants went out into the streets and gathered all the people they could find [notice the next statement], both good and bad, and the wedding hall was filled with guests.

Here is the king inviting every person that his servants can find on the streets, both bad and good. Of course, the wedding hall is filled with guests, both bad and good.

Now the king doesn't want to distinguish the two, so he prepares wedding garments for all of them. In England, the schools — elementary and academy [high school] — have what they call school uniforms. I know people in this country frown on it but it has some good points. One good point is that you cannot tell the difference between the children from the rich homes and the children from the poor homes. They all have the same uniform supplied by the school because the parents have to pay out of their school fees. But, of course, in the government schools, it is supplied just like this wedding garment was supplied.

When we stand before God there is no distinction of where you come from. The only thing that qualifies us is the wedding garment. The other day I was listening to a couple of girls. They didn't know I was hearing them and I am not sure where they were from but apparently they were discussing a group of girls who belonged to their own self-made club. Apparently, these girls come from the uppercrust families because they wear the latest fashions. They are "with it" and the other girls can't join them and these two girls were complaining about this class distinction. Well, if they had school uniforms they would not have the problem. When you come to the wedding feast, the only garment that is acceptable before the king is what he has supplied.

As we go on in this story we come to the third part, because this parable involves three kinds of people, three groups of people, three categories. The first group are those who willfully, deliberately, persistently say, "We don't want to come to the wedding feast." I suppose this doesn't apply to any of us here because the fact that we are here is evidence that we have accepted the invitation.

But the other two groups had actually accepted the invitation. They both joined the church; they both accepted the gift of the invitation to come to the wedding feast. But there is a difference, because I read in verse 11:

But when the king came in to see the guests, he noticed a man there who was not wearing wedding clothes.

He accepted the invitation, but he came to the wedding feast on his own terms.

Verse 12:

"Friend," he [the king] asked, "how did you get in here without wedding clothes?" The man was speechless.

Why was he speechless? Because he could not say to the king, "I came but the wedding garments were all taken up and I had none." He could not say that because the king had prepared wedding garments for every single guest, even the ones who refused to come. So there was no reason for saying why he could not wear it. The only reason was his own deliberate refusal to wear the wedding garment.

Now the question is, What is this wedding garment? Both the Old and the New Testament make it very clear that the wedding garment is the righteousness of God fulfilled and prepared for us in Jesus Christ. In the book Christ's Object Lessons, p. 311, Ellen G. White describes this wedding garment: "This robe, woven in the loom of heaven, has in it not one thread of human devising." It's all of God.

Let me give you some texts, one from the Old Testament because it's very likely Jesus had this verse in mind when He told this parable. That is Isaiah 61:10. Listen to what the prophet Isaiah says:

I delight greatly in the Lord [there you have the "In Christ" motif already in the Old Testament]; my soul rejoices in my God. For he has clothed me with garments of salvation and arrayed me in a robe of righteousness, as a bridegroom adorns his head like a priest, and as a bride adorns herself with her jewels.

God has clothed us with the righteousness of His Son.

Turning to the book of Revelation, we have several references. I can give you just two or three. In Revelation 3:5 I read these words:

He who overcomes will, like them, be dressed in white....

Those who come must come and accept God's gift entirely. In Revelation 7:9 I read that a great multitude stands before the throne of God and before the Lamb. What are they clothed with? They are clothed with white robes:

After this I looked and there before me was a great multitude that no one could count, from every nation, tribe, people and language, standing before the throne and in front of the Lamb. They were wearing white robes and were holding palm branches intheir hands.

In Revelation 19:8, they are clothed with the righteousness of Christ which has become theirs because they are wearing it:

"Fine linen, bright and clean, was given her [the bride of the Lamb] to wear." (Fine linen stands for the righteous acts of the saints.)

I am concerned with those who have accepted the invitation but who are not wearing the wedding garment.

Now comes the question, a question which is normally raised up, "Is this wedding garment, which we know is the righteousness of Christ, His imputed righteousness or is it His imparted righteousness?" I would like to suggest that the moment you ask that question, you have told me that you have not understood the truth of Christ our righteousness, because you cannot separate the two; they are linked together. You cannot divide Christ in half. It is true they are distinct, it is true there are differences, but they are inseparable. God doesn't give some imputed righteousness and some imparted. They come together in one parcel, Jesus Christ.

Let me show the distinction. The righteousness that qualifies us for heaven is clear: it is the imputed righteousness of Christ because in that righteousness we stand perfect. We stand perfect in nature because we have been redeemed from that. We stand perfect in character and we stand perfect judicially; in other words, in terms of justice we stand perfect. As Colossians 2:10 says, we are complete in Him:

...And you have been given fullness in Christ, who is the head over every power and authority.

But the evidence that we are actually wearing the garment is the imparted righteousness of Christ. Yes, it is ongoing, it is progressive, but in the judgment ... what does verse 11 refer to? When the king comes and examines his guests, to what does that refer?

But when the king came in to see the guests, he noticed a man there who was not wearing wedding clothes.

It is accepted by most scholars that this refers to the judgment, to the scrutinizing of the lives of the saints. We call it the investigative judgment. In the investigative judgment, God is going to scrutinize and it is very important for us to realize that what will qualify us for heaven in the investigative judgment is the wedding robe. Our works, which is, of course, the righteousness of Christ reproduced in us, is evidence that we have put on the imputed righteousness of Christ. In other words, there has to be a visible, tangible evidence that we have put on the robes. It is true that the imparted righteousness of Christ is not what qualifies us for heaven but it is evidence that we are wearing the righteousness of Christ imputed.

In the investigative judgment, the big question that will come is not whether you have been good or bad but are you in your Christian life reflecting what you have received? In other words, are you wearing the wedding garment or is it simply an idea that you heard about but you are not wearing it?

Now let's go back to a statement of which I reminded you. When the servants go out in verse 8 onwards and invite the people, there are two groups of people who accept the invitation. They are described in verse 10 as bad and good. Is Christ contradicting Himself? Turn to Matthew 19:16-17:

Now a man came up to Jesus and asked, "Teacher, what good thing must I do to get eternal life?"

"Why do you ask me about what is good?" Jesus replied. "There is only One who is good...."

If there is none good, how can Jesus in Matthew 22 say that both good and bad were invited?

If you read Romans 3:10, Paul, quoting from the Old Testament, makes it very clear there is none righteous, there is none good:

As it is written: "There is no one righteous, not even one...."

So who are these good people? Well, they are people who have confidence in their own righteousness. The wedding robe that they want to wear is not the righteousness of Christ but their own self-righteousness and this is what the problem is. They think they are good enough for heaven. In the Sermon on the Mount, Jesus says in Matthew 7:21-23:

"Not everyone who says to me, 'Lord, Lord,' will enter the kingdom of heaven, but only he who does the will of my Father who is in heaven. Many will say to me on that day, 'Lord, Lord, did we not prophesy in your name, and in your name drive out demons and perform many miracles?' Then I will tell them plainly, 'I never knew you. Away from me, you evildoers!'"

The righteousness that qualifies us for heaven is the righteousness of Christ. Whether it is imputed or imparted that we are talking about it is always Christ's righteousness; it is not mine. When I accept the invitation to the wedding feast, the only qualification that will qualify for that wedding feast is, "Am I wearing the righteousness of Christ?"

If you are among the bad group, there is no problem because the bad people are those who are poor in spirit. They recognize that they are sinners. They accept the wedding garment with open arms and say, "God, thank You, not only for the invitation but for covering our filthy rags by taking away our filthy rags and giving us Your wonderful white raiment." The trouble is for those of us who have had some success in our Christian walk. We tend to depend on that for our qualification.

I want to turn to Philippians 3 and show you that it is very costly. When you accept the wedding invitation that is not bad; that is not hard. But when God says to you, "I want to take away your filthy rags and give you the garment of My Son," that becomes hard if you have had any success in your own personal righteousness. So in Philippians we have the story of a man who was very successful in his religious life. His name was Saul and he describes himself before his conversion to the Philippians in Philippians 3:4-6:

...If anyone else thinks he has reasons to put confidence in the flesh, I have more: circumcised on the eighth day, of the people of Israel, of the tribe of Benjamin, a Hebrew of Hebrews; in regard to the law, a Pharisee; as for zeal, persecuting the church; as for legalistic righteousness, faultless.

He tells them, number one, "I was circumcised the eighth day." Number two, "I am a pedigree Jew. I don't have mixed blood in me. I am a Jew of the Jews, a Hebrew of the Hebrews, and — not only that — I am a Pharisee. I have such zeal for the law that I belong to those people called the Pharisees." That is what they were famous for. Then, concerning zeal for God and his mission, "I persecuted the Christian church" and he thought he was doing God a favor. Then, "Touching the righteousness which is in the law, I am blameless." He had a garment that he felt was fit for the wedding feast, his own garment that he had produced.

But one day he was invited to the wedding feast and he was offered the garment of Jesus Christ. I read in verse 7:

But whatever was to my profit I now consider loss for the sake of Christ.

Have you got the formula there? "Not I, but Christ." Whether it is imputed or imparted, it has to be Christ who must be seen in us. "I counted it all loss for Christ." Verses 8-9:

What is more, I consider everything a loss compared to the surpassing greatness of knowing Christ Jesus my Lord, for whose sake I have lost all things. I consider them rubbish [literally, "dung"], that I may gain Christ and be found in him, not having a righteousness of my own that comes from the law, but that which is through faith in Christ — the righteousness that comes from God and is by faith.

He was willing to give up his beautiful suit that he had woven himself and he was willing to "count them but dung, that I may win

Christ."

Are you wearing that garment? That's the question. Are you wearing that garment or are you depending on some things that you have successfully done for your ticket towards heaven? We are living at the end of this parable. We are living in those days when the king is inspecting the guests. He is scrutinizing each one of us and He's looking only for one thing — not how good you are but how much of His Son He sees in you. Christ in us, says Paul, is the hope of glory.

Jesus came because our garment is filthy rags. Isaiah 64:6 tells us that our righteousness is filthy rags:

All of us have become like one who is unclean, and all our righteous acts are like filthy rags; we all shrivel up like a leaf, and like the wind our sins sweep us away.

In Zechariah 3:3-4 we read about Joshua, the high priest, standing before God representing the people and he was clothed in filthy rags:

Now Joshua was dressed in filthy clothes as he stood before the angel. The angel said to those who were standing before him, "Take off his filthy clothes."

Then he said to Joshua, "See, I have taken away your sin, and I will put rich garments on you."

The Lord says: "Remove those filthy rags and give him new clothes, clean clothes, which is the righteousness of Christ."

When we accept that righteousness, it is not to cover up our filthy rags because Jesus doesn't use His robe to cover our filthy rags. He takes away those filthy rags and replaces it with His righteousness. That's why it is "Not I, but Christ. I am crucified with Christ but I am still living. It is not I, but Christ must live in me." And the greatest evidence that we can give to the world that we are wearing the wedding garment is that Christ will reflect through us. Daily we must say, "Not I, but Christ," because, when we stand before the king, if we do not have the wedding garment, look at what happens in Matthew 22:13:

Then the king told the attendants, "Tie him hand and foot, and throw him outside, into the darkness, where there will be weeping and gnashing of teeth."

These are people who accepted the invitation but who were not willing to go all the way and accept the garment, too.

Now I want to close with verse 14 because that verse is confusing to many:

"For many are invited, but few are chosen."

If you read the statement at face value, it gives the impression that God calls a whole lot of people and then He says, "Well, I think I will choose you and I will choose you." The Bible, the New Testament especially, does not teach that God has chosen some to be saved and some to be lost. That's Calvinism; that's not scripture.

How many people did God choose to be saved? He loved the whole world. The three groups that are mentioned in this parable were all chosen by God for the wedding feast. Then what does it mean, "Many are invited, but few are chosen"? Well, the word "chosen" is in the passive tense, so it is the people who have been called who do the choosing. It is not God who does the choosing; it is the people who do the choosing. God has sent the invitation to how many? To all — Jews and Gentiles. What was the commission that Jesus gave to the disciples? "Go into all the world and preach the gospel." [See Matthew 28:19-20.]

What is the commission that God has given us? What did Jesus prophesy in Matthew 24:14?

And this gospel of the kingdom will be preached in the whole world as a testimony to all nations, and then the end will come.

What does the Three Angels' Message say? Revelation 14:6:

Then I saw another angel flying in midair, and he had the eternal gospel to proclaim to those who live on the earth — to every nation, tribe, language, and people.

The angel that has the gospel in his hand is to preach it to every nation, kindred, tongue and people. God has called all people to be saved but whether you will be in the group that will enjoy the wedding feast is whether you have chosen to accept the invitation on His condition. His condition is that when you come to the wedding feast you are to wear the gown that He has given you.

In some weddings you have to bring your invitation card as proof that you have been invited. I don't know if they do it here but in parts of Europe you have to bring your invitation card. When you come to the wedding feast that which God is looking for is His Son Jesus Christ. Are you wearing Jesus Christ? Have you put on Jesus Christ? Galatians 3:27 says we who are baptized into Christ have put on Christ:

...For all of you who were baptized into Christ have clothed yourselves with Christ.

Have you put on Christ? I don't mean put on to cover your sins because Christ was never given to cover our sins; He was given to take away sin and replace it with His righteousness.

It is my prayer that when you accept the invitation you will come, not to God with your righteousness, but with His. You will say to God, "I come; thank you for the invitation to the wedding feast but I have also chosen to wear the garment that You have prepared for me through Your Son Jesus Christ." It is my prayer that each one of us will be found wearing that garment when our lives are scrutinized. And God will say to us, "Come, inherit My kingdom prepared for you from the foundation of the world." I want to see each one of you there.

That wedding feast is very special. There are many wedding feasts that you have been to but most wedding feasts have punch and cake. This one will have more than that. It will be a permanent feast and it will be a feast that will have room for every one of us. But if we are found without that wedding garment, we will not make it. It is my prayer that the only thing that matters in our lives is the righteousness of Christ. I want His righteousness both imputed and imparted. I want the world to see only Christ in me because, even at my very best, I am filthy rags. It is my prayer that will be your desire, too. This is my prayer in Jesus name. Amen.

The Parable of the Pharisee and the Publican

Luke 18:9-14:

To some who were confident of their own righteousness and looked down on everybody else, Jesus told this parable: "Two men went up to the temple to pray, one a Parisee and the other a tax collector. The Pharisee stood up and prayed about himself: 'God, I thank you that I am not like other men — robbers, evildoers, adulterers — or even like this tax collector. I fast twice a week and give a tenth of all I get.'

"But the tax collector stood at a distance. He would not even look up to heaven, but beat his breast and said, 'God, have mercy on me, a sinner.'

"I tell you that this man, rather than the other, went home justified before God. For everyone who exalts himself will be humbled, and he who humbles himself will be exalted."

In Luke 18:9-14, the parable of the two worshipers, is one of those daring parables that Jesus told. It is one of those parables that got Him into trouble. What is this parable doing? Well, as we look at this parable — this is what we are going to analyze — we will discover that this parable brings out before us three very sharp contrasts. The first sharp contrast is between the two men who came to pray, the Pharisee and the publican, or tax collector. Remember, they were both members of the same church. They both worshipped the same God, but there was a sharp contrast between those two. The second thing that we notice is a sharp contrast between the two prayers that they offered. Finally, we have a sharp contrast between the answers they received from God.

Let's look at each one of these. First of all the contrast between the two men. That's found in verse 10:

Two men went up to the temple to pray, one a Pharisee and the other a tax collector

What is a Pharisee? The word Pharisee sometimes is given a very negative definition in our day today but the word Pharisee really means, "the separated ones."

What did this mean? From what were they separated? Well, over the years the rabbis of the Jewish religion had added rule after rule to the laws and instructions given by Moses so that, by the time of Christ, we had actually tens of thousands of rules of dos and don'ts. Some of them were major, some of them minor. For example, you remember one day the Pharisees accused Jesus' disciples of eating food without washing their hands? This had become a requirement for salvation, and all kinds of rules.

If you were to obey all those rules, if you were to follow those blueprints made by these rabbis, it would take you a full-time job. It would take you from morning to evening. The Pharisees separated themselves to do this very thing. They were very meticulous; they were very zealous about obeying those rules, the dos and don'ts. Because of this, they refused to mingle with the other believers whom they looked down upon because they were not obeying all the rules. If they were living today they would be the "holy Joes." They belonged to the holiness club; they were the ones who followed the blueprint to every detail. There was nothing wrong with that. It was the attitude of the Pharisees that was the problem. This was the Pharisee.

What about the publican? He was the tax gatherer. He was what we would call the IRS [Internal Revenue Service] man today and very few of us like the IRS people. But may I make it clear that tax collecting in the days of Christ was very different from the IRS collecting our tax today because they did not have a fixed rule for collecting tax.

I'll tell you what Rome did. Rome divided her country that she was dominating into provinces and then each province was subdivided into areas and in each area they were allowed to make bids as to how much tax they would collect for the Roman government. So each one gave their bids and the highest bidder would normally get the job of collecting tax for that area.

So the Roman government did not set a fixed amount of tax. It's the tax collector who gave his bid and he was required within a year to collect the amount that he had signed the contract for. Any money he collected above that amount was his. Now he never told the people how much he bid the Roman government for, so they did not know how much he owed the Roman government. But he would tell them that what he was charging them was the tax. Very often he would keep a big chunk of that because he would charge a very high tax so that he could make a lot of money.

So, normally, these tax collectors were quite rich people, but here is their problem. Number one, they were Jews collecting tax for the Romans and, therefore, they were despised by the Jews because they were traitors to their own people. I remember during a problem time in Kenya, the policemen and the soldiers who worked for the British government and who killed a lot of the Kikiu were looked upon as traitors to their own country. These tax collectors were looked upon in the same way. They were considered extortioners, exploiters; they were looked upon as traitors to God and to their own people.

But, more than this, they were looked upon as sinners who could not be saved. The Jewish priests and the religious leaders looked upon the publicans and gave them no hope of salvation. They had reached the point of no return. So here are two individuals who come to church, one who is very religious and has a very high opinion of himself, the other one who recognizes that he is a downright sinner and comes to God placing himself in the hands of his loving Savior.

Then we go to the contrast of the prayers. Look at Luke 18:11-12. Listen to the Pharisee praying:

The Pharisee stood up and prayed about himself....

May I, first of all, explain something here. It was quite common for the people of Christ's day to pray standing, so when you hear of this Pharisee standing up and the publican does the same thing, this is not unusual; it was quite common for the Pharisees, for the believers of Christ, to stand up praying. In fact, they didn't even close their eyes. They looked up into heaven; they raised their hands, and they talked to God.

This Pharisee was praying, not to God, but telling God about himself. He said to God:

God, I thank you that I am not like other men — robbers, evildoers, adulterers — or even like this tax collector. I fast twice a week and give a tenth of all I get.

"I thank thee that I am not as other men are, extortioners, unjust, adulterers, or even as this publican (at the back, wretched sinner that he is). I fast twice in the week." Remember, the Old Testament required fasting only one day a year, on the Day of Atonement, but, by the time of Christ, these rabbis had added and added until they were told that if you want to be a real good believer, a real good Jew, you had to fast twice a week, Mondays and Thursdays. This Pharisee was fasting twice a week. He was very particular about paying his tithe on everything he possessed.

But in Luke 18:13, in contrast, we have the publican standing far off. He was afraid to come and mix with the worshipers. He didn't feel that he was one of them. He felt that they were good people but he was a wretched sinner and he struck his breast. He doesn't even look up into heaven and he says:

God, have mercy on me, a sinner.

Let's pause a moment and look at these two men praying. First of all, turn to Psalms 24 because I believe that when the Pharisee was praying he probably may have had these two verses in mind. Psalms 24:3-4. The question is asked by David in verse 3:

Who may ascend the hill of the Lord? Who may stand in his holy place?

Who has the right to come before the Lord? The answer is in verse 4:

He who has clean hands and a pure heart, who does not lift up his soul to an idol or swear by what is false.

And the Pharisee may have said to himself, "That is me. I have never exploited anybody," even though, in the temple, they were overcharging for the temple offering. The Pharisee may have had this in mind. He had a tremendous eye for himself. He had a terrible eye for his fellow believer. He was a man who could present himself before God and say, "God, I thank You I am not a sinner like the man behind me." The publican was the very opposite. We do not know how old this publican was, but obviously he was not a young person. He had been a tax collector for a long time. We do not know how long he was exploiting the people but there is a text that the chief priests and the scribes were using all the time against these tax collectors. I want to give you the text. They were putting them on to guilt trips all the time and maybe even Zacchaeus had this text in mind when he was redeemed by Christ.

The text is found in Leviticus 6. It was the favorite text that the Pharisees used against the publicans. They were always hammering them with this text. Leviticus 6:2-5:

If anyone sins and is unfaithful to the Lord by deceiving his neighbor about something entrusted to him or left in his care or stolen, or if he cheats him, or if he finds lost property and lies about it, or if he swears falsely, or if he commits any such sin that people may do — when he thus sins and becomes guilty, he must return what he has stolen or taken by extortion, or what was entrusted to him, or the lost property he found [and kept, of course, for himself], or whatever it was he swore falsely about. He must make restitution in full, add a fifth of the value to it and give it all to the owner on the day he presents his guilt offering.

In other words, the law of Moses said that if you had been exploiting people, if you had been stealing, it is your duty when you are found guilty to return back and even give them an interest of one fifth because that's what verse 5 says: you have to pay interest.

Remember when Zacchaeus found Christ and Christ accepted him even though he was a sinner? What did Zacchaeus say? Luke 19:8:

But Zacchaeus stood up and said to the Lord, "Look, Lord! Here and now I give half of my possessions to the poor, and if I have cheated anybody out of anything, I will pay back four times the amount."

Well, Zacchaeus could do this but this publican obviously could not do it. He was full of guilt. He had no way — I don't know how many years he was exploiting, he may not even remember who he was exploiting — and, of course, he was really concerned.

One day I was holding a worker's meeting among the pastors out there in Africa. One of them suddenly got turned on by the gospel. He realized that there was still hope for him and he came to me. He said, "You know, pastor, I've been a minister for 30 years. I am about to retire and the tragedy is that I have no hope of salvation." And I said, "Why?" He said, "Well, I have been doing something for 30 years that I have told nobody — not even my wife — and I do not know what to do about it." I said, "What's the problem?" He said, "For 30 years, I've been keeping some of the tithe and putting it into my own pocket."

You see, out there we don't have banks in the country and so the pastors who have five, six, eight, 10, 15 churches normally go around collecting the tithes of the churches and they are the ones who bring it to the conference or to the field. And he said, "I felt that I was underpaid and I read the text in the Bible which said that the workman is worthy of his labor. I felt it was all right if I kept some, but now, after 30 years, I am feeling guilty. There is no way I can pay it back. Even if they were to deduct my salary, the total amount, for the next 10 years, I could never pay back what I have stolen. Is there hope for me?" he said.

I turned to this parable and I said, "Look, that publican felt the same way. He had exploited people and he felt that he had no right to come to the church so he stands in the back and he says, "Lord, I am a sinner. There is no way I can cleanse my guilt. I am in Your hands. I am at Your disposal." He says, "God, forgive me, a sinner." He may have tried to restore all he could but he could never pay back all that he has done. He comes to God as a sinner putting His hope in a loving merciful God.

This parable says that this publican never claimed to fast twice a week, he never claimed to pay tithe. He simply came to God and he says, "God be merciful to me, a sinner." And Jesus said,

I tell you that this man, rather than the other, went home justified before God.

Did Christ condone sin? No. But Christ knew that man cannot save himself.

To which group do you belong? All of us are sinners, I think all of you will agree with that. But somehow we have gotten the idea that we are not all the same kind of sinners, that I may be a better person than you. The reason for that is because the Bible defines sin in two ways. Sin is an act and, as far as the sinful acts are concerned, we may not be guilty of sins that somebody else commits. But sin is also what we are by nature and, by nature, we all stand on the same platform. We are all 100 percent sinful. Paul says in Romans 7:18 there is in me nothing good:

I know that nothing good lives in me, that is, in my sinful nature. For I have the desire to do what is good, but I cannot carry it out.

The fact that you have not committed gross sins does not mean that you are better than the other person.

But here was this Pharisee who was very meticulous about following the blueprint and he followed it to the very detail. But in his own eyes he thought that he was better than the others. He looked down upon this publican. So we need to look at the answer, the third contrast. Here was a Pharisee who read his Bible, who prayed four times daily (because the Pharisees were known to pray four times a day: 9 o'clock, 12 o'clock, 3 o'clock, and 6 o'clock. He fasted twice a week. He paid tithe. He was very faithful in tithe paying; these are all good things. In fact, Jesus said, "These you ought to have done."

But what was wrong with his performance? He was depending on that performance for his acceptance before God. That was where he went wrong. He was not looking at his performance as the fruits of the gospel; he was looking at his performance as that which would qualify him for heaven. He was telling God, "God, look what a good Christian, what a good believer I am." He reminds me of those who will stand in the judgment seat in Matthew 7 and say to God, "I have prophesied in Your name, I have cast out devils in Your name, I have done many wonderful works in Your name." And do you know what Christ will say? "I never knew you."

This publican looked at himself as chief of sinners. In 1 Timothy 1:15 we read these words:

Here is a trustworthy saying that deserves full acceptance: Christ Jesus came into the world to save sinners — of whom I am the worst.

Remember what Jesus said to the Pharisees? He said the sick are the ones who need a physician. The ones that are healthy do not need a physician and then he concludes, "I have come not to save the righteous, but to save the sinners." That is why in the Sermon on the Mount, Jesus begins by those words [Matthew 5:3]:

Blessed are the poor in spirit, for theirs is the kingdom of heaven.

In contrast to this, I would like you to look at a group of people that the true witness rebukes. Revelation 3. Here are a group of people. You know who they are. This is the message to the Laodicean church and what do these people say about themselves in verse 17? The very same thing that the Pharisee is saying. Revelation 3:17:

You say, "I am rich; I have acquired wealth and do not need a thing." But you do not realize that you are wretched, pitiful, poor, blind and naked.

We say to ourselves, "I thank you, God, that I am rich and increased with goods; I thank you God that I don't need anything. I keep the Sabbath; I pay my tithe." We do not know that we are wretched, miserable, poor, blind, and naked.

What do we do? How do we solve this problem?

[If you have a copy of Christ's Object Lessons by Ellen G. White, I wish you would read the chapter "The Two Worshipers," pp. 150-163, because it is dealing with this parable.] But I want you to notice what is brought out here, because you may look at yourself and you may say, "I am not self-righteous."

The sin of self-righteousness is a very subtle one. You know what Jeremiah 17:9 says?

The heart is deceitful above all things and beyond cure. Who can understand it?

But here is a clue that will help us to understand whether we are suffering from the sin of self-righteousness that may be so deep down in our subconscious that we may not be aware of it. Ellen G. White says, "Whoever trusts in himself that he is righteous, will despise others." How do you look at others who are not following the blueprint? What do you do when you see a lady walk in who may be all decked up? You may say, "I wonder why she is here. She doesn't belong here." No, she may belong here more than you do.

"As the Pharisee judges himself by other men, so he judges other men by himself" (Christ's Object Lessons, p. 151). The Pharisee makes his righteousness the measuring stick of righteousness and, when he compares his righteousness with the other person, what does he do? He gives them the idea that he is a very fine Christian. But there is only one measuring stick of righteousness — Jesus Christ — and when you and I stand before Jesus Christ, the more we recognize His righteousness, the more sinful we will realize that we are. There is no way that we could ever reach the righteousness of Christ. In word, in action, He is absolutely perfect.

When we compare our righteousness with each other, then we have the tendency to look down. There was a time (I'm glad it's dying away) when we, as a people, looked down upon other Christians. We called them Philistines; we looked down upon them. We may be shocked in heaven to discover there'll be more Philistines there than Adventists.

Several years ago the General Conference received a letter from a very fine, godly Christian. When the Communists took over in China the missionaries who were running the show for the denomination had to leave. They could not stay there. They had to come back to this country and the church fell into the hands of the nationals. We had the same thing in Uganda when Idi Amin drove away all the missionaries. These nationals had to go underground. They had to try and keep the church alive under tremendous pressures, persecution. One of them, who was a graduate of Pacific Union College and the MV leader of the China Division, was a national. He could not run away because he was Chinese. They put him in prison for several years, mistreated him, and gave him a hard time, but he remained faithful. He was one of the few who remained faithful.

About 15 years after he was in prison he wrote a letter. He had become friendly with the jailer and the jailer had promised him to post this letter. I happened to read the letter some years ago — a very interesting letter with many pages — and in this letter he said, "Brethren, we made a great mistake in our work in China" and he gave about 15 points.

In one of the areas, he said, "The trouble is that the missionaries looked upon the Chinese who said, 'Yes, yes' and who followed the blueprint and who looked very holy as the pillars of the church. But I want you to know that these are the ones who turned against the church. These were the ones who denied Christ. It's the ones who you had no confidence in, the ones who were looked down upon as sinners, who are the ones who are rallying together and holding up your church in spite of persecution."

It is hard to judge people by the outward appearance. We do not know what people are going through. But I'll tell you one thing, the moment you feel that you are better, the moment you cherish a thought that you are better than your brother, you belong to the Pharisee. That is the method of finding out. Please do not look at someone else and say, "Yes, this is what he needs or what she needs." Each one of us must examine ourselves. We must ask ourselves whether we look down upon our fellow believers. They may not be following the blueprint; they may not be living up to the standards but I'll tell you, you do not know what is going on in their hearts and minds. They may be struggling; they may be seeking God; they may be like this publican saying, "Lord, I don't have a right even to come to church. Can you please forgive me? There is no way I can make up for all the damage I have done, for all the money that I have stolen."

But look at the second half of the second quotation by Ellen White. "The prayer of the publican was heard because it showed dependence reaching forth to lay hold upon Omnipotence. Self to the publican appeared nothing but shame. Thus it must be seen by all who seek God. By faith [and what is faith?] — faith that renounces all self-trust— the needy suppliant is to lay hold upon infinite power. No outward performance can take the place of simple faith and entire renunciation of self." (Ibid., page 159). Please, don't substitute your performance for the righteousness of Christ. Christ's righteousness is the only cloak that will stand before the judgment seat of God. "We can only consent for Christ to accomplish the work" (Ibid., p. 159).

I look at one Pharisee in the Bible who was exactly like this Pharisee in this parable. Let me give you his example. Turn to Philippians 3. Look at this Pharisee, but thank God this is a converted Pharisee. In Philippians 3:3 he makes a statement. He says,

For it is we [that is, we Christians] who are the circumcision [are the ones who are truly circumcised], we who worship by the Spirit of God, who glory in Christ Jesus, and who put no confidence in the flesh...

The Jews boasted — the Pharisee boasted — that because he was physically circumcised he was a child of God, but Paul says, "No.

The physical circumcision does not make me righteous." We are the true circumcision, "which worship God in the Spirit (from the heart) and rejoice in Christ Jesus, and have no confidence in the flesh."

Now I suppose if somebody read this text to Peter and John after Stephen was just stoned and said this is the statement made by the man who was responsible for Stephen's stoning, they would say, "Impossible, impossible for this man to say this." But in Philippians 3:4-6, the apostle Paul describes what he was like before his conversion (notice it's very much like the Pharisee that we read about in Luke 18):

...though I myself have reasons for such confidence. If anyone else thinks he has reasons to put confidence in the flesh, I have more: circumcised on the eighth day, of the people of Israel, of the tribe of Benjamin, a Hebrew of Hebrews; in regard to the law, a Pharisee; as for zeal, persecuting the church; as for legalistic righteousness, faultless.

"If anyone attained to the self-righteousness [that is what it means, righteousness of the flesh], it was I." And I'll give you the facts, he says:

"Number 1, I was circumcised the eighth day. Number 2, I'm not a mixture; I'm a pure-blooded Israelite, of the tribe of Benjamin, a Hebrew of the Hebrews and, touching the law, I am a Pharisee. I have been among those who were meticulous about every one of those rules. And concerning zeal, zeal for God, I persecuted the church." Remember, Paul did not persecute the church because he thought he was doing wrong. He thought he was serving God.

...as for legalistic righteousness, faultless.

Can you imagine him praying, "God, I thank you I am not like those miserable Christians. I am a good fellow." Philippians 3:7-8:

But [there's a "but" there] whatever was to my profit I now consider loss for the sake of Christ. What is more, I consider everything a loss compared to the surpassing greatness of knowing Christ Jesus my Lord, for whose sake I have lost all things [and by that he means self-righteousness]. I consider them rubbish [literally, "dung"], that I may gain Christ....

Now look at verse 9:

...and be found in him, not having a arighteousness of my own that comes from the law, but that which is through faith in Christ — the righteousness that comes from God and is by faith.

This same man who talks about what he was as a Pharisee at the end of his life, do you know what he calls himself? "The chief of sinners." But remember, God did use him mightily. As long as you have trust in yourself, God cannot use you. Look at Peter. He had tremendous confidence in himself. "Oh Jesus," he said, "I can guarantee you that while these other disciples will forsake you, I will not. I will die for you." Did he die for Christ? He denied Him three times. And Jesus said, "Peter, when you are converted, then I can use you to feed my flock."

I want to close with how Jesus ends the parable. Go back to Luke and please apply this to yourself just like I'm going to apply it to myself. Luke 18:14 (last part):

For everyone who exalts himself will be humbled, and he who humbles himself will be exalted.

This is not the only time Christ made this statement. Go a few pages back to Luke 14 where Jesus talks about the parable of the wedding feast. One man comes to the feast and sits right in front and the other man sits at the back and when the host comes he says to the man in front, "What are you doing in front? You don't belong in the front, go back." And to the man in the back he says, "You belong here in front." Then in Luke 14:11 Jesus makes the very same statement:

For everyone who exalts himself will be humbled, and he who humbles himself will be exalted.

One of the hardest things for God to do to us is to humble His people. Humility is a very difficult thing. That is why, throughout the lives of His saints, He had to use methods. If you read 2 Corinthians 12:7, Paul says that God allowed him to have a thorn in the flesh lest he be exalted above measure:

To keep me from becoming conceited because of these surpassingly great revelations, there was given me a thorn in my flesh, a messenger of Satan, to torment me.

If you read the life of Ellen G. White, she was told by the angel that God would strike her with sickness to keep her humble.

But I want to close with 1 Corinthians 10 because there the apostle Paul gives us a warning. 1 Corinthians 10:11:

These things happened to them as examples and were written down as warnings for us, on whom the fulfillment of the ages has come.

Who is Paul talking about? Who is our example? It is the history of the Jewish nation. Paul is saying that the history of the Jewish nation has been recorded for our admonition upon whom the ends of the world is come.

With that in mind, we read verse 12:

So, if you think you are standing firm, be careful that you don't fall!

We must apply that both individually and corporately. My prayer is the closing part of the quotation on page 159 of Christ's Object Lessons: "Lord, take my heart; for I cannot give it. [She's talking about the fact that we cannot deny self in our own power.] It is Thy property. Keep it pure, for I cannot keep it for Thee. Mold me, fashion me, raise me into a pure and holy atmosphere, where the rich current of Thy love can flow through my soul."

My dear people, if all of us would have the attitude of the publican, we would no longer point our fingers at each other and condemn each other. We would not do that. Why? Because all of us would recognize that we are 100 percent sinful, saved by grace. But when people begin pointing fingers and saying that your theology is wrong and you are wrong, as long as we do that, we will have two kinds of worshipers in this church. But it is my prayer that we will all move to the platform of the publican. We will recognize that we are 100 percent sinners saved by grace alone.

When we see others go wrong, we will have the attitude that John Wesley had, "There go I but for the grace of God." We will try to help them instead of condemning them and, together, we will grow. It is my prayer that this church will be filled with publicans who can go home justified.

CHAPTER FIVE

THE PARABLE OF THE UNMERCIFUL SERVANT

Matthew 18:21-35:

"Then Peter came to Jesus and asked, "Lord, how many times shall I forgive my brother when he sins against me? Up to seven times?"

Jesus answered, "I tell you, not seven times, but seventy-seven times.

"Therefore, the kingdom of heaven is like a king who wanted to settle accounts with his servants. As he began the settlement, a man who owed him ten thousand talents was brought to him. Since he was not able to pay, the master ordered that he and his wife and his children and all that he had be sold to repay the debt.

"The servant fell on his knees before him. 'Be patient with me,' he begged, 'and I will pay back everything.' The sevant's master took pity on him, canceled the debt and let him go.

"But when that servant went out, he found one of his fellow servants who owed him a hundred denarii. He grabbed

him and began to choke him. 'Pay back what you owe me!'
he demanded.

"His fellow servant fell to his knees and begged him, 'Be
patient with me, and I will pay you back.'

"But he refused. Instead, he went off and had the man
thrown into prison until he could pay the debt. When the
other servants saw what had happened, they were greatly
distressed and went and told their master everything that
had happened.

"Then the master called the servant in. 'You wicked
servant,' he said, 'I canceled all that debt of yours because
you begged me to. Shouldn't you have had mercy on your
fellow servant just as I had on you?' In anger his master
turned him over to the jailers to be tortured, until he should
pay back all he owed.

"This is how my heavenly Father will treat each of you
unless you forgive your brother from your heart.""

One of the greatest, most wonderful blessings that we have
through Jesus Christ and through His gospel is the forgiveness of
sins. I don't know how much you are aware of it but the forgiveness
of sin was at the heart of New Testament preaching.

We read in Acts 13 where the Christian church sent out Paul
and Barnabas as the first missionaries to the Gentile world. After
exposing these Gentiles to Jesus Christ as their hope, as their
Saviour, he concluded in verse 38 and 39 by these words:

Therefore, my brothers, I want you to know that through
Jesus the forgiveness of sins is proclaimed to you. Through
him everyone who believes is justified from everything you
could not be justified from by the law of Moses.

Forgiveness of sins was one of the key messages of the gospel
preached by the early Christians. Let me give you another text
in Ephesians. Paul, writing to these Ephesian Christians says in
Ephesians 1:7 7:

In him we have redemption through his blood, the forgiveness of sins, in accordance with the riches of God's grace....

You will find the same thing in Colossians 1:14 and several other passages. Yet, when it comes time for we sinful human beings to forgive those that have wronged us, we find it very, very hard.

Not too long ago, Tammy Baker appeared in the Phil Donahue television show and he asked her a question, "How do you feel about all those people [some of whom had worked for her husband] witnessing against your husband?" And she said, "I forgave them all." Then she paused, "Except," she said, "Jerry." She meant Jerry Falwell. She could not get to the point where she could forgive Jerry Falwell and many of us face similar problems. There are some people we just do not know how to forgive. It is just so difficult.

That is why I would like, in the next two studies on the parables of Jesus, to look at two parables where Jesus dealt with the issue of forgiveness. I hope, as we finish these two studies, it will do something to us in terms of our relationship to God and in terms of our relationship to each other.

With this in mind, let's go to our scripture reading, Matthew 18. Keep in mind some things that Jesus had already taught His disciples. For example, in Matthew 5:20 Jesus had already told the disciples that their righteousness must exceed the righteousness of the scribes and Pharisees:

"For I tell you that unless your righteousness surpasses that of the Pharisees and the teachers of the law, you will certainly not enter the kingdom of heaven."

He had already told them a little earlier (Luke 12:1):

..."Be on your guard against the yeast of the Pharisees..." [that is, the doctrines of the Pharisees].

What did the Pharisees teach about forgiveness? Well, they based their teaching on forgiveness from the rabbinical teaching which said the limit is three times. I can imagine Peter thinking, "Now if our forgiveness must be exceeding that of the Pharisees, I suppose Jesus meant seven times (which is a complete figure)." So Peter, with his wonderful mind for jumping to conclusions, turns to Jesus in Matthew 18:21 and says to Jesus,

> *"Lord, how many times shall I forgive my brother when he sins against me? Up to seven times?"*

"Seven? Is seven what you meant when you said the righteousness of us disciples must exceed that of the Pharisees?"
He was in for a shock for,

> *Jesus answered, "I tell you, not seven times, but seventy-seven times."*

Remember, they had no computers in those days and writing material was a luxury so they could not keep a record of seventy times seven. They did not have diaries so, to Peter, that meant unlimited. We should forgive those that offend us how often? There must be no stop to it.

Having said this, Jesus turned around to His disciples and told them and us about this parable. First of all we will look at this parable and then we will ask ourselves, "What was Jesus trying to get tell them? Verse 23:

> *Therefore, the kingdom of heaven is like a king who wanted to settle accounts with his servants.*

Whenever Christ said "the kingdom of heaven," He was dealing with His kingdom, His system, which includes the gospel.

Here is a king who is taking a record of all those who owe him money. In verse 24 they bring him a man, one of his servants, who owed him ten thousand talents:

> *As he began the settlement, a man who owed him ten thousand talents was brought to him.*

Now what does that mean to you — ten thousand talents? We don't use talents these days so I did some research and I made quite a surprising discovery. I discovered, from the historical records that we have today, that the total amount of the tax revenue that Rome collected from her empire, including the 17 countries that she ruled, was 8,000 talents a year.

I discovered that the 8,000 talents was equivalent to approximately eight million dollars, which of course, in the days of Christ was a tremendous amount. Remember, in those days they did not have inflation. This means that when Jesus said this man owed him ten thousand talents, it was equivalent to ten million dollars. I think you will admit that is a very sizable amount even for a millionaire. That was a lot of money he owed.

Now notice what happened. Verse 25:

Since he was not able to pay, the master ordered that he and his wife and his children and all that he had be sold to repay the debt.

In other words, this man who owed ten million dollars filed bankruptcy, which means he would lose house, property, bank account, everything. But in the days of Christ it meant more than that because, remember, they were living in a slave society. If you filed bankruptcy, not only did you lose all your possessions and all your assets, but the one who accused you could take you, your wife, your children and sell you as slaves. That's terrible.

So what did this man do? The Bible tells us that he fell down. Verse 26:

The servant fell on his knees before him. "Be patient with me," he begged, "and I will pay back everything."

Notice he did not ask for forgiveness. He only asked for time. "Please give me a little bit more time and I will pay you back." Now the lord knew that he couldn't pay him back. Have you ever tried to pay back what Christ has done for you? It's a problem that faces us even today. Verse 27:

> *The sevant's master took pity on him, canceled the debt and
> let him go.*

The king canceled the debt and liberated this man from all
obligation — set him free — and this man goes on his way rejoicing,
"Praise the Lord, Alleluia," until he meets another servant who
owes him how much? Verse 28:

> *"But when that servant went out, he found one of his fellow
> servants who owed him a hundred denarii."*

He owes him 100 denarii which is equivalent to twenty dollars.
No comparison — 10 million dollars versus 20 dollars — and what
does he do?

> *He grabbed him and began to choke him. "Pay back what
> you owe me!" he demanded.*

He takes him by the throat saying, "Pay back what you owe
me!" Now the word "me" does not appear in the original but it is
understood. In other words, what he was saying was, "Pay me every
cent that you owe me."

> *His fellow servant fell to his knees and begged him, "Be
> patient with me, and I will pay you back."*

Notice that his request is identical to his own to the king but we
read in verse 30:

> *But he refused. Instead, he went off and had the man thrown
> into prison until he could pay the debt.*

It so happened that some of the other servants of the king heard
this, saw it and reported it because they were quite disgusted at
the way this man was treating his fellow servant after just being
forgiven of a tremendous debt.

In verse 31 we are told that they reported him to the king:

When the other servants saw what had happened, they were greatly distressed and went and told their master everything that had happened.

Then verse 32:

""Then the master called the servant in. 'You wicked servant,' he said, 'I canceled all that debt of yours because you begged me to. Shouldn't you have had mercy on your fellow servant just as I had on you?' In anger his master turned him over to the jailers to be tortured, until he should pay back all he owed.

"This is how my heavenly Father will treat each of you unless you forgive your brother from your heart.""

This is quite a parable. First of all, let us go to Peter's question, which tells us that he was still thinking with a legalistic mentality. The scribes and Pharisees were saying three times so he was saying, "Let me add a few because Jesus said we must exceed the righteousness of the Pharisees." So he said seven.

The gospel does not know any limit when it comes to forgiveness. It's the legalistic mentality that calculates. It calculates, "How much I shall give? How much shall I forgive?" Very often the legalistic mind thinks like this. "What is the very least I can do and still have my ticket to heaven?"

When we were teaching about tithe paying in Africa, we discovered something that is different from here. The basic record is that the average church in the North American division is about 40 percent tithe payers. It is a terrible tragedy but it is only about 40 percent. There are some areas where it has gone to up to 60 percent. But in Africa, everyone pays tithe but this is how they do it. They go down on their knees and they say, "Lord, I am sorry I am not rich like these missionaries or like these foreigners (the foreigners are always rich). You have blessed me with ten children which I am responsible to look after. I would like to pay ten percent, which is what you ask, but Lord, You understand. You are love and I am poor and You can understand my problem. Please accept ten cents." So, instead of paying ten dollars which is what he owes, he pays ten cents. He is bargaining with God and then he says, "God, thank you for still giving me the ticket for heaven."

What is Jesus trying to tell us in this parable? First of all, let us be very clear that forgiveness is treating others better than they deserve. Forgiveness is part of the word "grace," which is doing something good for somebody who deserves the very opposite. Remember that grace and forgiveness are partners, because to forgive somebody takes grace because you are doing something they do not deserve. Otherwise it is not forgiveness. True forgiveness is always doing something that the person does not deserve.

But we must remember that there was something wrong with this first servant who was forgiven ten million dollars. What was wrong with him? Why was he so hard on his fellow servant? The reason is that he did not appreciate the forgiveness he received from the king. That was the heart of his problem. I can imagine him thinking like this: "Well, I do owe a lot of money to this king. But, after all, the king is rich; he is the richest man in this country, so ten million dollars is a drop in the ocean for him." A lot of people think that way. A lot of people treat God's forgiveness that way.

Having traveled quite a bit in the world, I have discovered that here is no country in the world that dishes out foreign aid more than the United States. Almost every country you go to there is some sort of foreign aid, even sometimes to the point of where our own elderly people are suffering because their Medicare is cut down.

The thing that surprised me most is that very few of these countries really appreciate it. I remember on one occasion when we were having a drought and a famine in Kenya, the United States government came to the aid of the young people because when the young people do not eat a proper diet for a long time it involves brain damage. To help solve that problem, all the schools that had boarding students were supplied with corn and wheat and oil.

These kids did not starve even though the faculty was struggling. We did not know where to get oil; maybe that was a good thing. We did not need the advice that you don't need any oil because we could not get it and there were no desserts; things were pretty hard.

But one day those young people in the cafeteria took that corn which had been cooked for them and began making balls out of it and throwing it at each other like a snowball fight. One of the missionaries who came from Modesto, California [U.S.A.], was furious and he stood up and he said to those young people in anger, "Don't you appreciate what my country is doing for you?" One student who had the courage stood up and said, "What is your country doing for us? This corn came from your surplus which you could not even eat because it was rotting and you are giving it to us for political propaganda. Why should we appreciate it?" I know how you feel. You say, "Don't send it to them." But that's human nature.

Did it cost anything to the king to forgive that debt? I don't know how rich that king was. But, remember, the king represents God. The servant represents you and me and we have a debt to God for God said, "The soul that sins, it must die." We do not owe God money. We owe God our lives. We have no legal right to live, not one of us. We belong six feet under the ground. That's where we belong.

Two things. Number one, **God's forgiveness is limitless and unconditional.** Turn to Colossians 2. I often ask the young people a question: What comes first: confession or forgiveness? Because, as we look at this parable and as we look at several statements in the New Testament — the words of Jesus Christ — it sounds like God's forgiveness is conditional. But it isn't.

Colossians 2:13. This verse is not talking about your subjective experience. It's talking about what took place at the cross two thousand years ago:

> *When you were dead in your sins and in the uncircumcision of your sinful nature, God made you alive with Christ. He forgave us all our sins....*

What Paul is saying here is that, on the cross, God forgave the whole human race for sin. All their sins were forgiven at the cross. Notice the word "all."

Turn to 2 Corinthians 5:19. You need to read verse 17 onwards but verse 19 is what I want you to look at:

> *Therefore, if anyone is in Christ, he is a new creation; the old has gone, the new has come! All this is from God, who reconciled us to himself through Christ and gave us the ministry of reconciliation:* [19] *that God was reconciling the world to himself in Christ, not counting men's sins against them. And he has committed to us the message of reconciliation.*

Paul is saying that Jesus, through His death, forgave all human beings for their sins and has asked us to go and tell them the good news. So, number one, God's forgiveness is unconditional and it is limitless. Do you know that every sin that you committed, that you will commit to your dying day, has already been forgiven in Christ because the basis of forgiveness is the blood of Christ? That brings me to the next point.

How much did it cost God to forgive us? Was it something cheap? When a policeman catches me over speeding and out of compassion says, "I will let you go this time but the next time I catch you over speeding I will give you a citation." And you say, "Thank you." But I tell you, it cost him nothing. He doesn't take a decrease in his salary. He doesn't pay the fine.

Was it the same with Jesus Christ? How much did it cost God for Him to say, "Neither do I condemn you"? How much did it cost Jesus to tell Mary, "Neither do I condemn you"? Well, turn to Matthew 26, because Jesus was telling them how much it cost Him. At the Lord's Supper, Jesus took the cup, the juice of the grape, and in verse 28 He makes this statement:

> *This is my blood of the covenant, which is poured out for many for the forgiveness of sins.*

What did Jesus mean? Remember, Hebrews 9:22 says that, according to the law of God, there can be no remission without the shedding of blood:

> *In fact, the law requires that nearly everything be cleansed with blood, and without the shedding of blood there is no forgiveness.*

Now this may not mean anything to you. I once had a very interesting experience. I was trying to work out my income tax and I was having difficulty finding out how much I paid for my insurance for the house because there were two figures in my folder. So I called the insurance lady and she gave me the right figure. Then she said, "By the way, I have a daughter who has just gone out to Kenya as a Peace Corps volunteer." She did not know I was born there so I told her and she got excited.

She kept talking and talking and when she sent me the records which I needed, she sent me two of the letters that her daughter wrote to her. One of the first experiences her daughter had was to go to a roast feast. In America they call it a barbecue, but in Africa they kill a goat and they roast it over the fire. But what horrified her was that the children would take that meat and dip it in blood just like you would dip it in tomato sauce and they would eat the meat. She was horrified and it was revolting to her.

The word "blood" may not mean anything to you so I want to give you a text so you may understand what it meant to the disciples when Jesus said, "This is my blood." Turn to Leviticus 17:11 (there are many texts that say this, Deuteronomy 12:23 and others). This is what it meant to the disciples when Jesus said, "This is my blood":

> *For the life of a creature is in the blood, and I have given it to you to make atonement for yourselves on the altar; it is the blood that makes atonement for one's life.*

It is the blood of Christ that brings forgiveness for your sins. The blood of Christ cleanses us from all sins.

What is this blood? It is life laid down in death because that is what it means by shed blood. When you shed blood, you are taking life and, in Hebrews 2:9, we read that Jesus tasted death for every man:

> *But we see Jesus, who was made a little lower than the angels, now crowned with glory and honor because he suffered death, so that by the grace of God he might taste death for everyone.*

Then why are Christians dying? It is because Jesus did not taste the first death for all men and women. Jesus tasted the second death — the God-abandoned death — for all people. He did it not because we deserve it, but out of love for us. He did it that He may forgive us.

That is why I want to correct a statement that is misinterpreted. It says in 1 John 1:9:

> *If we confess our sins, he is faithful and just and will forgive us our sins and purify us from all unrighteousness.*

"His blood will cleanse you from all sins." Please read that statement in its context, otherwise you will go wrong. John is dealing with people who were saying, "I am not a sinner." John says, "He who says that there is no sin in him is a liar and the truth does not abide in him." But the moment you confess that you are a sinner, the moment you admit you are a sinner, remember there is blood that will cleanse you, the blood of Christ. He is faithful and He is just because He paid the price. But don't you ever treat that blood lightly.

That is why, in 1 John 2:1, John says:

> *My dear children, I write this to you so that you will not sin. But if anybody does sin, we have one who speaks to the Father in our defense — Jesus Christ, the Righteous One.*

Remember how much it cost God to forgive you: infinite cost. If you don't appreciate that forgiveness, it will be revealed by your attitude towards your fellow Christians.

That is why all through the teachings of Christ, as in the Lord's prayer in Matthew 6:12, Jesus says:

Forgive us our debts, as we also have forgiven our debtors.

Let me give you another text. Turn to Mark 11:25-26. Very often as we read this text it gives us the impression that God's forgiveness is conditional. No, God forgives us unconditionally but receiving that forgiveness is conditional. In other words, God wants us to appreciate that forgiveness because, in the New Testament, faith is a heart appreciation for Jesus Christ. Jesus is talking here.

And when you stand praying [remember, that was the custom, to stand], if you hold anything against anyone, forgive him, so that your Father in heaven may forgive you your sins.

Notice, if you are praying and asking God, "Thank You for Your forgiveness, forgive me," remember that forgiveness is asked because you appreciate that forgiveness. Because of that you have forgiven somebody who has wronged you.

In other words, as 1 John 4:19 says:

We love because he first loved us.

But if you read all of your New Testament, you will notice that forgiveness is unconditional. Let me ask you about Jesus Christ. When He was on the cross what did He say to His Father? Luke 23:34a:

Jesus said, "Father, forgive them, for they do not know what they are doing."

Were they asking for forgiveness? No. He asked God to forgive them. Maybe they did not know what they were doing when they crucified Him but they did know what they had done after the resurrection and they still did not repent. Repentance is a heart appreciation for what God has already done for me and when we have really appreciated God's forgiveness, when we realize how much it cost God to forgive us, something will take place here in our hearts so that we will treat others exactly as God has treated us. That is what Christ is trying to get across.

I want to give you several texts that bring this out. Turn first of all to Colossians and, as we turn to this text, I want to remind you of how Jesus concluded that parable. Our forgiveness must be from the heart, that means a heart appreciation. We looked at Colossians 2, now let's look at Colossians 3:12-14. This is counsel given to the Christians there which applies to us:

> *Therefore, as God's chosen people [as Christians], holy and dearly loved [that's what we are in Christ], clothe yourselves with compassion, kindness, humility, gentleness and patience. Bear with each other and forgive whatever grievances you may have against one another. Forgive as the Lord forgave you. And over all these virtues put on love [agape, God's unconditional love], which binds them all together in perfect unity.*

In other words, when you appreciate God's forgiveness, when you accept God's forgiveness from the heart, God puts into you, through the Holy Spirit, His love, which makes you forgive others just as God forgave you. When I was studying this passage I said to myself, "Wouldn't it be wonderful if all of us in this church forgave each other like Christ forgave us?" Can you imagine? I would receive a telephone call from my Conference President saying, "What's happened to your church? There's no more fighting, no more accusation. When you forgive somebody from the heart you will never say anything bad against that person. Do you know that? You will never criticize him. You will never condemn him. You will only speak good. That is the kind of church God wants. That is the kind of Christian He wants. He wants men and women who will forgive.

But it is not possible for you to forgive by your own power. You can excuse. Most of the time we forgive we are really excusing.

Genuine forgiveness is always costly. It may cost your pride; it may cost money; it may cost many things. It may cost your reputation, but it is always expensive to forgive. It was very expensive for God to forgive men. God was in Christ reconciling man to Himself. God was willing not to spare His own Son so that we may be forgiven. This forgiveness must do something to us.

In conclusion, I want to go back to Matthew 18. Look at the whole setting. Verse 33:

> *"Shouldn't you have had mercy on your fellow servant just as*
> *I had on you?"*

Genuine righteousness by faith is doing to others what God has done to you. The best example I can give you is the first Christian martyr. Here was Stephen stoned to death and before he died (you'll find this in Acts 7:59-60) he lifted up his head to God and said:

> *"Lord, do not hold this sin against them."*

"Please God, do not bring this charge upon them. Please don't condemn them for what they are doing; they are simply acting as human beings. Please forgive them."

What made Stephen do such a thing? It is because his heart was filled with appreciation and whether we appreciate Christ or not is revealed in our relationship with one another. That is why in Matthew 18:35 it says:

> *"This is how my heavenly Father will treat each of you unless*
> *you forgive your brother from your heart."*

God is looking for only one thing: how have you related yourself with your fellow man? Jesus said that what you are doing to the least of your brethren you are doing to Him. Matthew 25:40:

> *The King will reply, "I tell you the truth, whatever you did for*
> *one of the least of these brothers of mine, you did for me."*

When Christ came to this world, in order to forgive us He had to die for us. But in order to forgive us and die for us, He had to identify Himself with the human race. He became one of us. He doesn't say "the least of My created beings." He says "least of these brothers [and sisters] of mine." He became one of us. His name is Immanuel, therefore, every human being is a child of God by grace. Every human being is forgiven by God by grace and if you don't forgive your brother or sister, then you are denying God's forgiveness to that person. You are showing no appreciation for the forgiveness that you have need of in Christ.

It is my prayer that our appreciation for Christ will be manifested by our relationship to each other. If our hearts are filled with appreciation; if we really appreciate how much God has forgiven us we will treat our fellow Christians the same way that God has treated us. You will not say, "Well, I don't have the heart; that doesn't deserve forgiveness." Remember, forgiveness is doing something that a person doesn't deserve. It is grace and it is my prayer that by the grace of God we will reveal His grace to others so that the people around us will see a church that is loving, caring, and forgiving because they have appreciated the supreme sacrifice of our Lord Jesus Christ.

That is my prayer that we will become a loving, caring church because we have appreciated what Christ has done for us. May God bless us that the cross of Christ will transform us and produce in us a people that know how to forgive because the grace of God has transformed us.

CHAPTER SIX

THE PARABLE OF THE TWO DEBTORS

Luke 7:36-50:

Now one of the Pharisees invited Jesus to have dinner with him, so he went to the Pharisee's house and reclined at the table. When a woman who had lived a sinful life in that town learned that Jesus was eating at the Pharisee's house, she brought an alabaster jar of perfume, and as she stood behind him at his feet weeping, she began to wet his feet with her tears. Then she wiped them with her hair, kissed them and poured perfume on them.

When the Pharisee who had invited him saw this, he said to himself, "If this man were a prophet, he would know who is touching him and what kind of woman she is — that she is a sinner."

Jesus answered him, "Simon, I have something to tell you."

"Tell me, teacher," he said.

"Two men owed money to a certain moneylender. One owed him five hundred denarii, and the other fifty. Neither of them had the money to pay him back, so he canceled the debts of both. Now which of them will love him more?"

Simon replied, "I suppose the one who had the bigger debt canceled."

"You have judged correctly," Jesus said.

Then he turned toward the woman and said to Simon, "Do you see this woman? I came into your house. You did not give me any water for my feet, but she wet my feet with her tears and wiped them with her hair." You did not give me a kiss, but this woman, from the time I entered, has not stopped kissing my feet. You did not put oil on my head, but she has poured perfume on my feet. Therefore, I tell you, her many sins have been forgiven — for she loved much. But he who has been forgiven little loves little."

Then Jesus said to her, "Your sins are forgiven."

The other guests began to say among themselves, "Who is this who even forgives sins?"

Jesus said to the woman, "Your faith has saved you; go in peace."

On the cross, when Jesus died, the whole world — the whole human race — was forgiven and was reconciled to God. That is the clear teaching of the New Testament. That is what makes the gospel unconditional good news. However, since this glorious truth is a part of God's gift in Christ it demands a human response. That human response can be one of two things: we can either wholeheartedly accept that gift or we can willfully reject it.

These two responses are described in the New Testament by two words: belief (or faith, because in the Greek it is the same word) and unbelief. As we saw in our last study, faith or belief is more than simply a mental assent to truth. It is a heart appreciation for God's gift to mankind. John 3:16 says:

For God so loved the world that he gave his one and only Son, that whoever believes in him shall not perish but have eternal life.

God did the loving; God did the giving. We do the believing and belief is a heart appreciation for what God has done for us. When we have this response of gratitude, it does something for us. It completely transforms us in terms of our attitude towards our fellow men as well as our attitude towards God.

In other words, when we understand and when we appreciate what it cost God to save us, what it cost God to forgive us and how much He has forgiven us for, we will treat others the same way that God has treated us. That is the evidence that we have appreciated the gift of God. Likewise, our relationship to God will be very different.

Now we are going to turn to the second parable concerning forgiveness. Remember last study we looked at the unforgiving servant; the servant who did not appreciate the forgiveness that the king offered towards him. I would like to consider the parable of the two debtors. Both these parables are dealing with forgiveness. Both are expressing the same concern of God. Do we really appreciate God's forgiving grace? If we do, we will forgive others just as God has forgiven us and by our conduct — by our thoughts, words, and deeds — we will show our appreciation towards God.

With this in mind, let's go to our parable. Our study begins at verse 36. We need to know the background. Now according to verse 36 we read,

Now one of the Pharisees invited Jesus to have dinner with him, so he went to the Pharisee's house and reclined at the table.

Why would a Pharisee want Christ for lunch when we know that the Pharisees were against Christ? Well, there is a reason which is not clear in this passage but the reason is clear in a similar record in Matthew 26 where we learn two things.

The name of this Pharisee was Simon and he was a leper. We don't have much leprosy in this part of the world today but, in the days of Christ, leprosy was synonymous with sin. Here was a Pharisee and I want you to remember that a Pharisee was a "holy Joe." He was the one who was very meticulous about every little detail in terms of God's rules and laws. Here he is struck with leprosy and I can imagine him saying, "Why me? What have I done? I've been good." But Jesus healed him and it cost Simon nothing because he healed him by a miracle.

I don't know if you have noticed this, but when somebody does you a very special favor you have no peace until you do something in return for that person. It's called the principle of reciprocity. It's one of the evidences of our sinful natures because we don't like to be in debt to somebody. We have this problem all over the world. We say to ourselves, "How can I return this favor?" If we don't, we are in debt to that person and we don't like that. It hurts our pride.

So if any of you ever happen to travel into the Third World where the U.S. has given tremendous aid and the people don't appreciate you, you'll know that it is because they cannot pay you back for what your country has done for them. You are a thorn in their flesh. You have hurt their pride and it is human nature. We are the same; it has nothing to do with them; all human beings are the same.

So this Pharisee says to himself, "This man healed me. The least I can do for Him is invite Him for a meal." It wasn't out of gratitude; it was out of paying back. It was reciprocal. He tells his wife, "Cook him a meal" and Jesus and the disciples, who were a unit, all come to this meal and they all sat down to eat. They ate in the courtyard. The houses were very different from our houses. They didn't have a living room. The houses were built in a rectangle with little rooms. Obviously this Pharisee was quite wealthy and he had a courtyard in the middle which is where they ate. It was a hot day; it was dry and they would have a tray of pita bread and sauce or whatever they ate. Then they would recline; they would lie all facing that tray with their feet all stretched out. They would eat a good meal (only the men, by the way).

While they were eating, verse 37 says:

When a woman who had lived a sinful life in that town....

Now what did they mean by "that town"? Remember, Matthew also tells us in Matthew 26 that this incident took place in Bethany, the home of Mary, Martha, and Lazarus. John 12:3 identifies the woman as Mary, the same one who was caught in adultery, the same one from whom the devil was cast out seven times. So she was a reputed sinner. She was one of those persons to whom the Pharisees gave no hope of salvation.

When she came there you can imagine that it was very embarrassing. Remember that the Pharisees lived public lives so it was quite common for people to walk into the courtyard and listen to what was being discussed or what was being taught but normally it was men. Women were not taught. Their place was at home in those days. They were all reclining, all facing each other and Mary goes to the back of Jesus Christ and she falls down and she begins to weep and with her tears she washes the feet of Jesus. We find that in verse 38. She brings an alabaster box of ointment; she stoops at his feet, begins weeping, washing His feet with her tears and wiping them with her hair. She applies ointment to His feet and to His head.

Now look at verse 39:

When the Pharisee who had invited him saw this, he said to himself, "If this man were a prophet, he would know who is touching him and what kind of woman she is — that she is a sinner."

Remember, she is "unclean." He forgot that he was unclean when he had leprosy. In the Old Testament, if you touch a leper you become unclean. The wonderful thing about Christ is that when Christ touches a leper, He doesn't become unclean but the leper becomes clean. This man had forgotten that he was made clean by Jesus Christ. This man had forgotten that he, too, was a sinner.

The Spirit of Prophecy [by Ellen G. White] tells us that it was this Pharisee who had led Mary into the line of prostitution. Here is a man who had not appreciated Jesus Christ. He began to think. Notice, he doesn't say a word, he spoke to himself, which means he thought in his mind and the wonderful thing is that Jesus is a mind reader. By the way, He still is, so if you think you can hide your thoughts from him, forget it.

Jesus answered him, "Simon, I have something to tell you." "Tell me, teacher," he said.

The moment he says the word "Teacher," it tells me something. There were two ways you could address Jesus Christ. You could either call Him "Lord" or "Son of David," both expressions meant He was the Messiah, or you could call Him "Rabbi" — Rabboni — which simply means "Master" or "Teacher." The ones who rejected Christ would call Him "Master," so this gives me a clue that, even though he was healed by a miracle, this Pharisee did not believe that Jesus was the Messiah.

But this Pharisee was a victim to Judaism and what did Judaism teach? So you may understand what was going on in the mind of this

Pharisee, turn to John 9:31. These are words spoken by the scribes and Pharisees. This is their theology:

We know that God does not listen to sinners. He listens to the godly man who does his will.

The trouble is, they did not "know," but that's what they thought. So according to this Pharisee, this man could not be a prophet; he could not be a Messiah because he was touching sinners. Poor fellow, his theology was all wrong. Jesus came to save sinners. He came to touch us; He came to heal us. So he misinterprets Jesus Christ because his theology was wrong. So theology is important so that we understand truth.

Then Jesus gives Simon the parable. Let's look at the parable.

Two men owed money to a certain moneylender. One owed him five hundred denarii, and the other fifty.

That means nothing to you so I sat down and calculated. We had a study on the parable of the laborers. Do you remember how much they agreed for a salary for the whole day? One denaris — a penny. So we can take that as the wage scale for the days of Christ: a penny a day.

I took about the lowest figure (I'm not talking to students now; I'm talking to working people because the students are paid basically the minimum wage) but if you go out and work I would take the lowest wage which is about five dollars an hour. If you work for eight hours that is $40.00 and since there are 25 working days in a month I multiply 40 by 25 to get one month's salary because 500 pennies a day is equivalent to twenty month's wages. Twenty month's wages at $40 a day at 25 days a month comes to $20,000. That is how much this one debtor owed the creditor. The other 50 pennies, two month's salary, is $2,000.

The difference is between $20,000 and $2,000 and you will agree, for both debtors, middle class or poor people, they both owe, but the amount they owe is tremendously different: one $20,000 the other $2,000. We're talking in terms of dollars so it becomes meaningful.

Going to the parable, I read in verse 42:

Neither of them had the money to pay him back, so he canceled the debts of both.

They received something they did not actually deserve. That's where we get the word "grace." He unconditionally forgave them the debt — canceled the debt — and told them, "You don't owe me a cent."

Now, I'm not sure whether Simon the leper was aware what Christ was getting at, but now comes the question:

Now which of them will love him more?

And Simon answered cautiously, hedging his answer with "I suppose," because now he's beginning to suspect he's being trapped.

Simon replied, "I suppose the one who had the bigger debt canceled."

And Jesus responds:

"You have judged correctly."

"You are absolutely right."

Here the text refers to the Pharisee as "Simon," so we know it's the same Simon of Matthew 26.

Then he turned toward the woman and said to Simon, "Do you see this woman? I came into your house. You did not give me any water for my feet..."

Now this may mean nothing to you because we don't give people water for their feet when they come to our house. But, remember, in the Middle East it is dry; it is hot; it is dusty. In the days of Christ they did not wear shoes; they wore sandals, what we would call thongs. Then the custom, the common courtesy, was that when a visitor came to your house, out of courtesy, you wash his feet or you have your servant wash his feet.

Can you imagine? This man did not even wash the feet of Jesus, which means he was inviting Jesus purely out of obligation and did not even give Him the common courtesy of the Middle East.

"...but she wet my feet with her tears and wiped them with her hair."

I want to ask you a question. Why did she weep? What kind of picture do you have of this Mary? Is she at the feet of Jesus pouring out her tears and saying, "Dear Jesus, forgive me, I'm a sinner"? No, she was not asking for forgiveness; she had it already, unconditionally. She was simply a Jew who understood what that forgiveness would cost Jesus Christ. She was weeping tears of gratitude and appreciation because she, being a Jew, knew what the law said. What did the law say? You can read it in the New Testament also, Hebrews 9:22:

In fact, the law requires that nearly everything be cleansed with blood, and without the shedding of blood there is no forgiveness.

Without shedding of blood there is no, there cannot be, remission or forgiveness of sins.

Here was one person — gentlemen, this woman put us to shame — who did understand. Not one of the disciples, not one of the men who followed Jesus Christ during His earthly ministry ever understood the cross before the event, even though Jesus predicted it many times. Mary who was the only one who understood His mission. The reason she did is because, when He came to her house, she sat at His feet and learned of Him. That is only way we can learn the truth: by sitting at the feet of Jesus.

Remember, Martha complained and asked Jesus to rebuke her [Luke 10:38-42] and Jesus said, "Don't you ever ask Me to do that. She is doing the right thing. Martha, Martha, you are cumbered with many concerns about serving Me but I am telling you that she has done a good thing. She has served Me but now she is sitting at My feet and learning of Me." That is where she learned and now she comes with this expensive ointment. If you read John 12 you will discover that ointment cost 300 denarii. I have given you the figures. Three hundred denarii is 300 days' salary. You work out how much that is equivalent to today's income: 300 days' working.

Here is a woman whose heart was filled with appreciation. She was willing to come and do something that was not normally done by women in front of men. She was weeping; she was wiping His feet with her tears; she was anointing Him. Jesus says to Simon in verses 45-47, not only did you not wash My feet:

You did not give me a kiss, but this woman, from the time I entered, has not stopped kissing my feet. You did not put oil on my head, but she has poured perfume on my feet. Therefore, I tell you, her many sins have been forgiven — for she loved much. But he who has been forgiven little loves little."

Here we have two sinners; both were forgiven. Now, answer one question. Was Mary really a greater sinner than Simon? In God's eyes, no. Why not? Because, according to scripture, all of us are 100 percent sinners. The problem is, in the eyes of human beings, we are not all 100 percent sinners. "You are a worse sinner than myself" — that's human attitude. But in God's eyes, we are all 100 percent sinners.

Simon did not put himself on the same level as Mary but Mary recognized that she was a sinner saved by grace. She recognized that her sins were not small. Humans create degrees of sin. When I was a Roman Catholic we had venial sin and we had mortal sin. If you committed venial sin there was still hope through purgatory but if you committed mortal sin you'd had it unless you went to confession. God doesn't have venial sins and mortal sins. Even the smallest sin in God's eyes is terrible, like eating a forbidden fruit.

What is the problem? Before we go into that let's go to the end of the parable. Having rebuked Simon through this parable, verse 48:

Then Jesus said to her, "Your sins are forgiven."

Now she knew that, because I read on, in verse 49:

The other guests began to say among themselves, "Who is this who even forgives sins?"

So the reason He said, "Your sins are forgiven" was for the benefit of the others. What was Jesus claiming when He said to her, "Your sins are forgiven"? He was claiming to be the Messiah. He was claiming to be the Son of God who is able to forgive sins. Then in verse 50 He says to Mary,

"Your faith has saved you; go in peace."

Do you really appreciate what Christ has done for you? What is it that produced such deep, heartfelt appreciation from the heart of

Mary? Two things. Number one, she recognized there was nothing good in her. She recognized that she was a sinner. She recognized that she was wretched, miserable, poor, blind, and naked and the day we do that, praise the Lord. Revelation 3:17:

You say, "I am rich; I have acquired wealth and do not need a thing." But you do not relaize that you are wretched, pitiful, poor, blind and naked.

Why do we not know that? Because we think of ourselves as rich and increased with goods and in need of nothing. Our sin is a subconscious sin and it is my prayer that somehow that will come out in the open and that we will recognize what may be recognized.

Number two. Mary recognized that it was not cheap forgiveness. Mary recognized, knowing the law, knowing the Old Testament, coming from the home of Lazarus where they read their Bibles daily, that in order for Christ to forgive her He had to shed blood, which to the Jew meant giving up your life. In Hebrews 2:9 I read that He tasted death for how many people?

But we see Jesus, who was made a little lower than the angels, now crowned with glory and honor because he suffered death, so that by the grace of God he might taste death for everyone.

For everyone. But Mary realized that the death Jesus tasted for her was no ordinary death.

We will go to the New Testament and I will show you something. I want you to put yourself in the shoes of Mary. She probably was barefooted but I'm using a good old modern expression. Think like a Jew. In Galatians 3:10 we read (this is something that is taught in the Old Testament, Paul is simply reminding them):

All who rely on observing the law are under a curse, for it is written: "Cursed is everyone who does not continue to do everything written in the Book of the Law."

If you fail to keep the law you are under the curse. What is the curse? Ezekiel 18:4b:

The soul who sins is the one who will die.

This is the curse, and by "death" it means good-bye to life forever.

Now look at Galatians 3:13:

Christ redeemed us from the curse of the law by becoming a curse for us, for it is written: "Cursed is everyone who is hung on a tree."

Here Paul is quoting from Deuteronomy 21:22-23a. What does that text say? Well, let's go to it. The devil has obscured this passage from us. Today the Christian church, including our own, looks at the cross with Roman spectacles. It may be true that Christ died on a Roman cross but that Roman cross meant something else to the Jews and here it is:

If a man guilty of a capital offense [that means an unpardonable sin] is put to death and his body is hung on a tree [which is what the cross was equated to in the New Testament times], you must not leave his body on the tree overnight. Be sure to bury him that same day, because anyone who is hung on a tree is under God's curse.

Do you know what that means? Do you know what the curse of God is? It is the irrevocable curse of God. It means that when Jesus hung on the cross, the hope of the resurrection was taken away from Him because the Father disconnected Himself with His Son. There, as Jesus hung on the cross, He was willing to say good-bye to life forever, not just three days, but forever, that Mary may take His place.

That is what Mary understood. She was a Jew; she understood the curse of God and she realized that if Christ is the Messiah then He is a righteous God; He is a just God and a holy God and He cannot forgive Mary simply by excusing her sins. He could not say to Mary, "I am the One that gave the law. I am above the law. I don't have to keep it Myself. I made it for you creatures; therefore, I love you, Mary and I will simply forgive you." God cannot do that. He is a holy God; He is a righteous God.

If He did that, Satan would say, "What about me? You're practicing discrimination. If you can excuse her sin, you can excuse mine." But Christ did not excuse Mary's sin; He paid the price for it. Neither does He excuse your sin or mine; He paid the price for it and that price was the curse of God. Jesus was willing to say good-bye to heaven forever, not just for three days. Can that ever sink into your head or mine? He could not see through the portals of the tomb. Hope did not present to Him a resurrection. He felt that sin was so offensive that the separation was forever. Can you see why Mary's heart was so filled with appreciation that she couldn't stop crying? Can you see why she paid three hundred denarii, three hundred days' worth of wages without any deductions? You multiply that by forty (that's forty dollars a day) by 300. It's unbelievable how much money she spent on that ointment.

Mary was not only the one who anointed Him, she was also the first to go and visit the tomb. Mary was the first to be there. For her it was no longer serving self. Philippians 1:21:

For to me, to live is Christ and to die is gain.

The disciples were the same but only after the event. Before the cross they had failed to understand the significance of Christ's mission even though He told them many times that He was going to die. It was only after the cross they recognized what that meant to them.

In concluding, I am going to turn to 2 Corinthians 5:14 because this is what it should do to you and me. May I say something. Any Christian church, anybody, who legislates standards has not understood the gospel. It is the love of God that must constrain us. Here I read the famous words of Paul:

For Christ's love compels us, because we are convinced that one died for all, and therefore all died.

He tasted the death that belongs to all of us.

Do you know that you and I will never have to experience the second death? Not because Christ has bypassed it, but because you can die the second death only once and all of us have died the second death in Christ. We get the benefit; He gets the suffering. He does the dirty work but we can't remain the same. It has to constrain us and, when it constrains us, what does it do? Look at the next verse, 2 Corinthians 5:15:

And he died for all, that those who live should no longer live for themselves but for him who died for them and was raised again.

I want to pause here. Do you know what Christ meant when He said, "those who live"? Do you realize that legally you and I had no right to be born in this world? Do you know that when Adam sinned, legally he had no right to spend one more month or one more day on this earth? When we in this country sentence someone to death, to execution, we leave him there in prison for months and sometimes even for years and we have to pay our taxes to feed him while he enjoys that good food because I ate in the prisons. It's pretty good in America. But when God said to Adam and Eve (Genesis 2:17):

"You must not eat from the tree of the knowledge of good and evil, for when you eat of it you will surely die."

He meant that very day. You have no right.

Why did God allow Adam and Eve to live? Why did God allow you and me to be born? He allowed it because there was One, who is the Lamb of God, slain from the foundation of the world. We are alive not because we have a right to be but because of One who paid the price. I like those words that I find in The Desire of Ages [by Ellen G. White], p. 660: "The cross of Calvary is stamped on every loaf. It is reflected in every water-spring."

Every breath you breathe is because Jesus died for you. That is a truth. The question is not the truth. The question is how has it touched you? Verse 15 again:

And he died for all, that those who live should no longer live for themselves but for him who died for them and was raised again.

Can you imagine what kind of a church this would be if we had people who appreciated the love of God, the supreme Sacrifice? Mary understood it because God opened her eyes. She saw the truth of the cross; her heart was filled with appreciation; she didn't care what people thought of her. She didn't care how much it cost. She wanted to show Christ her gratitude and appreciation because she believed that when He died He would not rise again. It could be possible because she knew He was dying the curse of death. But she wanted to say, "Jesus, I want to show you my gratitude and appreciation before You die, not after You die."

Before you and I go to sleep, are we going to show our appreciation for Christ? I have told you this story before. I'm going to close with it because it is something that is very dear to my heart. One of the greatest missionaries that ever walked on the soil of Africa was David Livingstone. You have read his books; you have heard about him, a great man of God. In fact, I visited his birthplace in Blantyre, Scotland. He was a medical doctor, but he gave up his lucrative profession and went to Africa when it was really a dark continent, when there was sickness, hostile tribes, wild animals that were dangerous.

To make it worse, the British government gave him a hard time because he was a stubborn old fellow, very stubborn, did not believe in committees and when you do not believe in committees you get a hard time from the brethren. When he died on his knees praying to God, he was 400 miles from the coast. The British government decided to give him a royal burial in Westminister Abbey where they have all the great men of England buried.

The problem was, how could they bring his body to England? In Africa there were no trains; there were no cars. Horses could not survive there because of the tse tse fly. The Africans were willing, out of appreciation, to carry his body four hundred miles. The Africans did a wonderful thing. They said you can have his body; you cannot have his heart. So they cut open his chest, pulled out his heart and buried it in Africa, because he gave his heart to Africa. Then they carried him those four hundred miles to the coast. Now that is appreciation.

When I was deported from Uganda, there were soldiers in the airport, and they said to my wife Jean and the children, "You can go on the plane, but he remains here." That meant concentration camp and probably execution for me. I said to Jean, "Go ahead." She said, "No, I will die with you." She refused to go and the soldiers were mad so they said, "All right, you give us 700 shillings," which is $150 and that's all the government allowed me to take out in travelers checks.

So I took that $150 in traveler's checks and said, "Take it." He said, "No. I want it in cash." He knew if he used traveler's checks he would be caught. So I said, "I don't have the cash." "Too bad," he said, "then you won't go." Then one of the African members came up to the counter, risking his life and he said, "Here is the cash," and he paid it for me. That was appreciation.

God is not asking you to do things — dos and don'ts — simply because that will take you to heaven. He has given us salvation as a free gift. He wants a people whose hearts are so filled with appreciation that they will do two things. The will say to God, "As long as I live from henceforth, I shall live for You." He wants us to look at our neighbors and say, "If God so loved me when I was a wretched, miserable sinner, I must also love my neighbor." That is keeping the commandments. Love for God — appreciation for God and loving your neighbor — on these two rest all the law and the prophets.

God will produce a people like that and how will He produce them? Not by hammering them with commandments but lifting up Christ and Him crucified. It is my prayer that the Christ crucified will transform you. May God bless you that the truth will set you free.

THE PARABLE OF THE HIDDEN TREASURE

We are going to turn to one of the shortest parables that Jesus ever spoke, Matthew 13:44. It is just one verse, but it is loaded with meaning:

The kingdom of heaven is like treasure hidden in a field. When a man found it, he hid it again, and then in his joy went and sold all he had and bought that field.

It is a short parable. This parable, along with the next one, which is verses 45 and 46, are extremely important for us, especially for those of us who are living in this materialistic world. In these two parables, the parable of the hidden treasure and the parable of the pearl of great price, Jesus is trying to show His disciples — and through them, to show us — how God estimates the gift of salvation in Jesus Christ. This is something we need to ponder, because our response to that gift is in proportion to our estimate of it.

First of all, may I make it clear that this is not a far-fetched story. Jesus was not making up this story because the Jewish folklore is full of such stories. In the Bible days there were no banks; there were no security places where you could keep your money. The house was the worst place to keep your money because there were always invasions and these invaders would come into the house, ransack it, and take everything they could get hold of.

I remember when the house of one of our missionaries was ransacked in Ethiopia, they turned everything upside down. They tore even the mattresses to see if any money was hidden in the mattresses. They took their big flowerpot — they had a white carpet; can you imagine a white carpet in Africa! — and they emptied it on the carpet thinking there might be some jewelry at the bottom of the flowerpot. They emptied everything. It was quite common in the days of Christ for that to happen.

There is a Rabbinical saying and it reads like this, "There is only one safe repository for money — the earth." So it was quite common for people to sometimes put their valuables and their gold coins in a metal or wood chest and they would hide it in the middle of the garden so that it would be safe there.

I remember some years ago there was a couple who bought a house. They were just married and they couldn't afford a very big house so this was a small little house. It was run down, old, in great need of repair. It was selling for almost nothing so they bought it. The husband was a carpenter and they were planning to fix the house. One of the first things they discovered was that the septic tank was blocked. They had to break a hole, dig up the casing and the pipes and when they broke the pipes they were full of coins, American coins, silver coins that were dated way back. They were extremely valuable so they discovered that this simple, run-down house had in its grounds a treasure that was worth more than the value of what they paid for the house.

This is how it was in the days of Christ. This man obviously was a peasant farmer. The land was owned by rich land owners and they would parcel out their land to these peasant farmers. These peasant farmers would pay a rent and they would use the land for farming. Apparently this man was plowing this land which he had rented and his plow hit this chest in the ground. It was probably metal and he realized that it was something that was obstructing the plow. He dug it out and he found this chest full of coins and probably jewelry.

The first thing was that he realized the value of that treasure chest. He recognized that the chest containing coins and jewels was so expensive, so fabulous that it was worth more than all that he possessed. Now you may ask, why didn't he hide it back in the earth and come there at night and get it and he would have had the chest plus all his belongings?

It wasn't as simple as that because what would he do with those coins? The moment he tried to get rid of them he would have been found out. "Where did you get it from?" He was a poor peasant farmer. Or if his wife tried to wear the jewels, immediately there would be a question. So the best, safest, the most legal thing for him to do was to sell everything that he had, buy the land, and that would be legally his. Nobody could touch it.

Now it took some time selling the things. Can you imagine the people say, "What's wrong with this fellow? Why is he selling everything he possessed?" Well, they may not have understood, but he knew what he was doing. He knew that what he was doing was the best thing because that chest was far more valuable than his personal belongings.

This is the story that Jesus told. Remember, a parable is an earthly story that has a spiritual meaning. What was Jesus trying to get across? First of all, we must ask the question, What does the field represent and what does the treasure that this man discovered represent? I have a quotation which sums up in a nutshell what this is all about. It says, "In the parable the field containing the treasure represents the Holy Scriptures. And the gospel [the truth as it is in Christ] is the treasure." (Christ's Object Lessons, page 104.) "Those who desire to find the treasures of truth must dig for them as the miner digs for the treasure hidden in the earth." (Christ's Object Lessons, page 111.)

The truth as it is in Christ is hidden treasure. It does involve spade digging. "No half-hearted, indifferent work will avail. It is essential for old and young, not only to read God's word, but to study it with wholehearted earnestness, praying and searching for truth as for hidden treasure. Those who do this will be rewarded, for Christ will quicken the understanding." (Ibid., p. 111.) It is for this very reason that I am a very strong believer in expository preaching because in expository preaching you are required to dig. Topical preaching you can just take a group of texts and put them together but in expository preaching, I'm dealing with one verse. How can I spend 35 to 40 minutes on one verse? It involves digging.

Let's look at the treasure first. As we saw, it is the truth as it is in Christ. Turn to Ephesians 2, because it is not enough for us to find the treasure, it is important that we realize the value of the treasure. Ephesians 2:2-7 puts in a nutshell what the treasure means to each one of us. Verse 5 says,

[God] made us alive with Christ even when we were dead in transgressions — it is by grace you have been saved.

I like that God did not wait until I became good, but saved me even when I was a wretched sinner incapable of doing anything good.

Now let me explain what Paul meant here by the words "dead in transgressions" or "dead in sins." The life that you and I were born with is a life that legally has no right to exist; it has to die. We inherited from Adam a condemned life, a life that stands legally condemned to death. Therefore, we are, in a sense, born in death row, every one of us. There is no escape from that. Christ did not come to change the death sentence. If He did, He would be breaking His own law. He came to give us His life in exchange for our life. That is the treasure. The treasure is the life of Christ.

You are familiar with John 3:16. What does it say?

For God so loved the world that he gave his one and only Son, that whoever believes in him shall not perish but have eternal life.

Now what exactly did He give us? If you turn to 1 John 5:11-12, you will discover what that gift involves:

And this is the testimony [these are the facts]: God has given us eternal life, and this life is in his Son. He who has the Son has life; he who does not have the Son of God does not have life.

We are born dead in trespasses and sin but, while we were dead, God made us alive in Christ. That is the gift; that's why in brackets in Ephesians 2:5 it says "by grace you have been saved." Not only has He given us life but He (verse 6):

And God raised us up with Christ and seated us with him in the heavenly realms in Christ Jesus....

Do you know what that means? Do you know how valuable the treasure is that, in Christ, He has made us to sit together with Christ?

Now you say, "No, I am not sitting with Christ. I am sitting here on Earth." But do you know what it means to sit in Christ or sit together with Christ? Who is Christ? He is the King of kings and, if we sit with Him, then we are the kings of whom He is the King. What a privilege we have. But you say, "We are not sitting with Him right now." No, but you are sitting in Him right now.

Look at Ephesians 2:7:

...in order that in the coming ages [and that is around the corner] he might show the incomparable riches of his grace, expressed in his kindness to us in Christ Jesus.

When this man found this treasure chest, he recognized that it was exceedingly rich but he had to buy that land. He had no money for it so what did he have to do? He had to sell everything he possessed. Have you ever tried selling everything in your garage, not everything you possess but everything in your garage? You have to have more than one garage sale. Obviously, if he was a poor peasant farmer, his things were not very desirable so I can imagine it took him a long time to sell all that he had.

I can imagine that he was patiently waiting until the last thing was sold so that he had enough money to buy the land. So we have to wait patiently before that gift becomes a tangible reality. In the meantime, we patiently wait for it, says Paul.

But the question is, have you realized that, in Christ, we have received the riches of God's grace? The truth of this is hidden treasure. Why is it hidden treasure? Because people, when they read this parable that we just heard about, think that God doesn't want us to know the truth. Why is it described as hidden treasure? If you look at 1 Corinthians 2:9-14 you will discover that it is hidden, not because God has hidden it so we can't see it but because the natural mind cannot understand the truth of the Bible:

However, as it is written: "No eye has seen, no ear has heard, no mind has conceived what God has prepared for those who love him" — but God has revealed it to us by his Spirit. The Spirit searches all things, even the deep things of God. For who among men knows the thoughts of a man except the man's spirit within him? In the same way no one knows the thoughts of God except the Spirit of God. We have not received the spirit of the world but the Spirit who is from God, that we may understand what God has freely given us. This is what we speak, not in words taught us by human wisdom but in words taught by the Spirit, expressing spiritual truths in spiritual words. The man without the Spirit does not accept the things that come from the Spirit of God, for they are foolishness to him, and he cannot understand them, because they are spiritually discerned.

That is why we need to dig prayerfully; we need to dig earnestly with the help of the Holy Spirit so that we may find it.

I'm going to give you a statement that was made by Jesus Christ to the Jews. Turn to John 5:39, because this statement is important for us, too. Jesus is talking to the Pharisees and to the Jews and Gentiles:

You diligently study the Scriptures because you think that by them you possess eternal life. These are the Scriptures that testify about me....

Why does He say that you think that you have eternal life? The Jews did read the scriptures but they misread them. They did not dig deeply enough and, because they were shallow readers, they went the wrong direction. Because they were superficial readers, they thought that eternal life comes to you by doing something good.

How do I know? Because in Matthew 19:16 a young lawyer — and the word "lawyer" means somebody who reads and knows the scriptures — says to Jesus,

"Teacher, what good thing must I do to get eternal life?"

He had misread the scriptures, a problem that many of us face. So Jesus is saying, "Search the scriptures. You think that you have eternal life. You are right." But here's the answer:

These are the Scriptures that testify about me....

"The scriptures point to Me as the Way of life. You have misread the scriptures."

The result is in John 5:40:

...Yet you refuse to come to me to have life.

Did they find the treasure? No. They were superficial readers. They read the law on the surface. They forgot to read that the law points to Christ. They forgot to realize, they forgot to see, they did not discover that the law is our schoolmaster to lead us to Christ that we may be justified by faith.

But now we go back to this man. He has found the treasure. He recognizes that it is very valuable, but he also realizes he can't have the treasure and his possessions at the same time. He has to give up one for the other. That is what the parable tells us. As he went out selling these things that he owned, that were his, was he reluctant or was he happy? Well, if you go back to the parable in Matthew 13:44, we read these words:

...And then in his joy went and sold all he had and bought that field.

We have the Ministerial Association and every month we have it in a different place. Ones time we had it at a place where they had a new manager. He was trying to sell the pastors of the city that this was the place where the retirees should come. But he said when he tried to sell it to the retired people in the city, he came across a problem. He said, "We offer excellent service; we offer wonderful treatment, good surroundings; everything is good; the rooms are wonderful but there is one problem. The people that we encourage to come to our retirement home have in their garages, in their rooms, piles and piles of 30 or 40 years collection of treasure that they will not part with. We have to tell them that they have to move from a three-bedroom house to a one-room apartment and they cannot bring these valuable things that they have collected." I have a word for it but I don't dare say it because ... well, let me say it. I call it junk. But to some people it is very valuable.

When we were deported from Uganda, we lost everything. We had to say good-bye and one of the things we could not take with us were all our possessions. My wife said, "What shall I take?" We could only take one suitcase.

I'll tell you what I took. I took all my old manuscripts that I could not replace and my wife took all her family photos when the children were little tiny tots that could not be replaced. That's all we could take. Our furniture, our bank account was frozen, we could take nothing but we could take our lives with us. Those people, the nationals could take nothing out; they could not even live and many of them died. Three of those folks lived in our home and one of them was a driver. I said to him, "Would you like to see what they are discovering?"

I gave him a pile of photographs of skeletons, skulls, bones of children, women, men that they are finding everywhere. Are you willing to give up everything you possess — even your life — for the gift of Jesus Christ? Let me put it this way. Salvation is free; there is no problem there. Salvation is a gift but what is the gift? It isn't a toy; it isn't some gadget you like; it isn't a train set; it isn't one of those airplanes that you fly. It is the life of Christ; that's the gift. But the problem is you can't cling to your life and receive the life of Christ. You have to give up your life in exchange for the life of Christ.

Is it a sacrifice? Was it a sacrifice for that man to sell everything he possessed? If you said, "Yes," then you have not understood what he understood. He went with joy. Why? Because what he had was "junk." What he discovered was valuable. So our lives are "junk." It can last only 70, 80, if you are lucky maybe 100 years. We do have a member who is 102. But every time I go to a nursing home I say to myself, "Lord, don't you ever let me get to that stage. I have given my life up long ago. Please bring it to an end when I finish my job here. I don't want to end up in a place like this." I have another life that will be given to me that is the most wonderful life. It never dies and it makes me sit with Christ Jesus.

But here is the problem. These people were not willing to give up their righteousness. The Jews were not willing to give up their life. That is why I want to take you to the next passage. I would like to encourage you to go to the bookstore or go to the library and get Deitrich Bonhoefer's book Cost of Discipleship. He was one theologian who was willing to stand alone for the truth during the Second World War. There were other famous theologians — Walhauser, Kittle — who were anti-Semitic; they took sides with Hitler. But Bonhoefer said, "I am willing to die for the truth of the gospel." He did die, at the age of 39.

Here it is, Romans 6:8, the cost of discipleship:

Now if we died wiwth Christ, we believe that we will also live with him.

You can't hold on to both lives because not only is the life we were born with sinful but it is a life that belongs to the camp of Satan. It belongs to the kingdom of this world which will one day be destroyed. The life that Christ gives you is not only eternal life, it is a life that belongs to the kingdom of heaven.

These two kingdoms are at war. There is a great controversy between Satan, the prince of this world, and Christ, the Lord of heaven. These two kingdoms can never be reconciled. You cannot have dual citizenship. You have to give up one for the other. Anyone who does not see the value of the gift of Christ is a fool. But the moment you realize how valuable Christ is to you, you will be willing to give up everything.

What does it mean, giving up this life? We have seen Romans 6:8; let us turn now to Matthew 10 to show what giving up your life might include, because, in the future, you may face it. These Ugandans have faced it already and many of them were willing to give up everything for Christ. Read the whole of Matthew 10 some time but I would like to read verses 37-39. It's a very costly price:

Anyone who loves his father or mother more than me is not worthy of me; anyone who loves his son or daughter more than me is not worthy of me [I think you will have to admit this is tough]; and anyone who does not take his cross and follow me is not worthy of me. Whoever finds his life will lose it, and whoever loses his life for my sake will find it.

When the gospel is preached in its clarity, when men and women discover the hidden treasure, you and I will have to make a choice. In that choice, you and I may have to give up some loved ones. Christ spoke these words to the Jews. Do you know even to this day what it means for a Jew to become a Christian? It means that he loses his citizenship. A Jew who becomes a Christian in Israel is deprived of his citizenship. The family of a Jew who becomes a Christian have a funeral service because to them their child has died. That is what it costs to be a Christian in Israel today. Can you imagine what it was in Christ's day? Today only about four percent are genuine Orthodox Jews but in the days of Christ almost everyone went to the synagogue.

Can you imagine what it meant for the disciples to become Christians? They had to give up everything and the time will come when you and your parents will disagree with the truth and you will have to part company. Are you willing to give up everything? Are you willing to give up your relationship to those who hate the gospel? Are you willing to give up your life? Are you willing to give up your righteousness?

Let me give you an example here. There was a Jew who had great value for his righteousness. His name was Saul, and this is how he described himself before he discovered the treasure. Philippians 3:4b-7:

If anyone else thinks he has reasons to put confidence in the flesh, I have more: circumcised on the eighth day, of the people of Israel, of the tribue of Benjamin, a Hebrew of Hebrews; in regard to the law, a Pharisee; as for zeal, persecuting the church; as for legalistic righteousness, faultless. But whatever was to my profit I now consider loss for the sake of Christ.

Paul was willing to give up his self-righteousness for Christ because he discovered that the righteousness of Christ is the only righteousness which will stand the test in the judgment and that his righteousness was filthy rags. He says in verse 8:

What is more, I consider everything a loss compared to the surpassing greatness of knowing Christ Jesus my Lord, for whose sake I have lost all things. I consider them rubbish, that I may gain Christ....

The moment he discovered the treasure, he was willing to give up his righteousness. Verse 9:

...and be found in him, not having a righteousness of my own that comes from the law, but that which is through faith in Christ — the righteousness that comes from God and is by faith.

Let me give you another example. Turn to Geneses 21. God promised Abraham a son and, after waiting for a long period of 25 years, He gave him that son. Unfortunately, 13 years earlier, Abraham had already produced a son called Ishmael. One day Ishmael was mocking his half-brother, Isaac. The word "mocking" is much stronger than our English word. He was actually poking his finger into him and saying, "You rascal; why were you born? Don't you realize I have lost my birthright through you?"

Sarah saw this so she came to Abraham. Genesis 21:8-10:

The child grew and was weaned, and on the day Isaac was weaned Abraham held a great feast. But Sarah saw that the son whom Hagar the Egyptian had borne to Abraham was mocking, and she said to Abraham, "Get rid of that slave woman and her son, for that slave woman's son will never share in the inheritance with my son Isaac."

Imagine how Abraham felt about this. Genesis 21:11:

The matter distressed Abraham greatly because it concerned his son.

"Yes, Sarah, he is not your son. It is easy for you to say, 'Get rid of him,' but he happens to be my son."

Here is a husband and wife disagreement. Do you know how they solved the problem? They took it to God. I wish Sarah had taken it to God when she advised him to go to Hagar. That was her opinion.

Now Genesis 21:12, they go to God:

But God said to him, "Do not be so distressed about the boy and your maidservant. Listen to whatever Sarah tells you, because it is through Isaac that your offspring will be reckoned.

Did Abraham obey or did he disobey? Was it easy; was it hard? It was hard, but he obeyed.

Paul takes this story and he gives us the spiritual meaning of it in Galatians 4:21-23:

Tell me, you who want to be under the law [you who want to cling to your self-righteousness], are you not aware of what the law [the Book of Moses] says? For it is written that Abraham had two sons, one by the lsave woman and the other by the free woman. His son by the slave woman was born in the ordinary way [human effort, human righteousness]; but his son by the free woman was born as the result of a promise [the gift of God].

Then in verse 24 he says that these two represent the two covenants: the Old Covenant, which is salvation by works, and the New Covenant, which is salvation by faith in the promise of God — Jesus Christ. Galatians 4:24-26:

These things may be taken figuratively, for the women represent two covenants. One covenant is from Mount Sinai and bears children who are to be slaves: This is Hagar. Now Hagar stands for Mount Sinai in Arabia and corresponds to the present city of Jerusalem, because she is in slavery with her children. But the Jerusalem that is above is free, and she is our mother.

Now look at verse 28. Addressing the believers, Paul says,

Now you, brothers, like Isaac, are children of promise.

But it doesn't stop there. Galatians 4:30-31:

But what does the Scripture say? "Get rid of the slave woman and her son, for the slave woman's son will never share in the inheritance with the free woman's son." Therefore, brothers, we are not children of the slave woman, but of the free woman.

You can't have both. You have to give up one for the other. This man was willing to crucify the flesh and all that it possesses for Jesus Christ. That's the parable.

I want to close by turning to two passages. One is John 12:25:

The man who loves his life [the life that you were born with] will lose it [it's condemned already], while the man who hates his life in this world will keep it for eternal life.

There are two lives that are before you. There is your earthly possession, your righteousness, all your ambitions that you have in this world, or you have Christ.

When you accept Christ, you are to give up everything in your heart. Between this world and between the kingdom of God stands the cross of Christ and the cross of Christ will not allow anything of the world to pass into the kingdom of God. It is a tragedy today that the Christian church, including our own, is borrowing ideas from the world. We are depending on worldly resources. It is a terrible thing that we have to depend on human philosophy even to search the scriptures. Nothing can go over. We must give up all.

This brings me to a very sensitive point. The North American division reports today that 30 percent of Seventh-day Adventists in this division pay no tithe whatsoever, neither to the local church nor to the Conference nor to Independent Ministries. They do not pay tithe, period. Now God doesn't want your money but He wants you and this tells me that 30 percent of my members are not willing to give up what they have for Christ.

Today it is 10 percent, tomorrow it may be 50 percent, and the day after tomorrow it may be 100 percent. Remember the words of Jesus (Luke 17:32):

Remember Lot's wife.

What did He mean by that? You see, Lot and his wife had become rich in cattle, in gold, in silver and they used their wealth to rise up in the country where they were living, in Sodom. He was sitting at the gate, which in Hebrew means that he had reached a high position. He was an official in the city of Sodom and God comes to him through Abraham and says to him, "This city is going to be destroyed. I'm sending two angels to help you out."

They could take nothing with them, just flee for their lives. But Lot's wife could not bear the thought of saying good-bye to her beautiful home in Sodom and she turned around and turned into a pillar of salt. She was not willing to give up all. Cling to nothing; it's not worth it because if you cling, if you say, "I want to pay tithe but I can't afford it; I have bills to pay," please read Matthew 6:33:

But seek first his kingdom and his righteousness, and all these things [clothing, food, a roof, protection] will be given to you as well.

Do you believe that? It's a part of the gift. Do you believe that God is able to supply all your needs?

The next text is Matthew 6. The man who hid the treasure never enjoyed it because he died. He clung to his life which didn't last very long and obviously he never told his family that he had hidden this treasure there because this peasant farmer found it. Matthew 6:19-21. Here is Jesus talking in the Sermon on the Mount:

Do not store up for yourselves treasures on earth, where moth and rust destroy, and where thieves break in and steal [a common problem in those days and today]. But store up for yourselves treasures in heaven, where moth and rust do not destroy, and where thieves do not break in and steal. For where your treasure is, there your heart will be also.

The moment this man found this treasure, no longer was his heart in his possessions. The moment you discover Christ, the things of this world become meaningless. When I look back, I hear my friends telling me, "You're a fool." When I was entering the ministry, some of my own Adventist friends said, "You're a fool" because I was an architect earning at that time — 25, maybe 30 years ago now — more than I'm earning today as a minister. Ten percent of the cost of building was in the pockets of the architect. My friends today have houses, cars. One of them has a car that talks to him: "You have forgotten to put your seat belt on." "You are speeding." Wonderful car! "Your oil is running low, please check." Same monotone voice but it talks to him.

I have a Saviour that I talk to and, I'll tell you, that car of my friend will disintegrate. My Saviour will come some day and give me everything that the world can never give me. So please do not think that it is a sacrifice to give up all for Christ. It isn't. I am much happier now than I ever was in architecture with all the money I had.

Jesus Christ is the most valuable thing you have. Where is He? In heaven. So I close with these words. I will repeat this and I will keep repeating it: The righteousness that qualifies you for heaven now and in the judgment and when Christ comes is never in you. It is always in Christ. We have this treasure in Christ. The value is in Christ. The faith that makes that righteousness yours is not in heaven; it is in you.

Satan can destroy your faith. In our Sabbath School study one day, there were two groups of people: those who were not willing to wait for the Second Coming of Christ, who said His coming is delayed, but there were others who said, "We are going to wait until the treasure comes." They held on to their faith. Jesus said (Matthew 10:22):

All men will hate you because of me, but he who stands firm to the end will be saved.

Please, don't let the trinkets of this world keep you from Christ. I realize America is a wonderful place; there's an answer for everything; there is a hope for everything but all the blessings of this country cannot be compared to the wealth of Jesus Christ. Be willing to give up everything because if you don't, you may find that you have given up everything indeed for nothing.

So may God bless you that you will not only discover the treasure but you will be willing to sell all and follow Jesus Christ is my prayer. Amen.

CHAPTER EIGHT

THE PARABLE OF THE PRICELESS PEARL

Matthew 13:45-46:

Again, the kingdom of heaven is like a merchant looking for fine pearls. When he found one of great value, he went away and sold everything he had and bought it.

In this study we are going to turn to the second of the twin parables that we began in our last study. Both parables — The Hidden Treasure and The Pearl of Great Price — reveal Christ's evaluation of the kingdom of God. While the two parables are identical in many respects, there is a major difference. The man who found the hidden treasure did it by chance. He was plowing his land; he was a peasant farmer and accidentally he came across this great chest of wealth. He recognized its value and was willing to sell all for it.

But in this second parable, we discover that this merchant actually sought for this pearl of great price and, after much searching, found it. These two parables revealed two classes of people. One of them is those who come across the gospel by chance. My wife, Jean, was coming home one day from work in London, England, and it was pouring cats and dogs which is typical English weather. She had forgotten her umbrella so she decided to find shelter. She ducked into a building which was called The New Gallery Center, an evangelistic center for the Seventh-day Adventist Church. Waiting for the rain to stop, she heard a man by the name of George Vandeman preach, just by chance. She was taking shelter from the rain. That was the first time she ever heard of this church and that was the beginning of her conversion.

But there are many people who are seeking and searching for the pearl of great price. This was true in the days of Jesus. Many in the days of Christ were tired of the formal, legalistic religion that was being taught by the scribes and Pharisees. It gave them no peace, it gave them no assurance, and, to make matters worse, these people at the temple were charging tremendous prices for the sacrifices. They couldn't afford it. They were seeking for that which their hearts were longing and Jesus said (Matthew 11:28):

Come to me, all you who are weary and burdened, and I will give you rest.

Now, of course, pearls were highly valued during the whole of the ancient times. They were fished by divers. These divers did not have oxygen tanks. They were fished especially in the Red Sea, in the Persian Gulf, and in the Indian Ocean. These pearls were used for adornment so we are discussing jewelry here. They were used for adornment especially as a necklace. Some of these necklaces and some of these pearls were worth millions.

I want to give you two examples. Before his assassination by Brutus, Caesar presented the mother of Brutus with a pearl worth $200,000. That's a lot of money. The story is told that Cleopatra owned a pearl worth $3,000,000. Pearls were something very valuable and, obviously, this merchant was a gem collector and a jeweler. Like many of the Middle Eastern gem collectors, he was looking; he was searching for this flawless pearl and, when he found it, he was willing to give up all, sell everything that he possessed for this one pearl.

Now a business man would call him a fool because you "don't put all your eggs in one basket." It's unwise but this merchant knew the value of this pearl. He was willing to give up all for this one pearl. Now what is this one pearl? Well, let me read you from *Christ's Object Lessons*, p. 115. It puts it in a nutshell very beautifully what this pearl is. I want you to listen to it:

"Christ Himself is the pearl of great price.... The righteousness of Christ, as a pure, white pearl, has no defect, no stain. No work of men can improve the great and precious gift of God."

"No work of men can improve the great and precious gift of God." I am repeating this because this was the Galatian problem. The Galatians were trying to improve that pearl by their good works, by circumcision, and other things. To continue:

"It is without a flaw. In Christ are 'hid all the treasures of wisdom and knowledge.' (Colossians 2:3.) He is 'made unto us wisdom, and righteousness, and sanctification, and redemption.' (1 Corinthians 1:30.) All that can satisfy the needs and longings of the human soul, for this world and for the world to come, is found in Christ. Our Redeemer is the pearl so precious that in comparison all things else may be accounted loss." Ibid.

When Luther was getting rid of all the idols and all the relics from his church after he discovered this great pearl, his superior said to him, "When you get rid of all these things, what are you going to put in their place?" Luther replied, "Jesus Christ. Man only needs Jesus Christ." And I say the same today, "Men only need Jesus Christ."

But here's the problem. In order for that merchant to have that pearl as his own, he had to sell everything he had. He had to give up everything he possessed. What's the problem with that? Doesn't scripture present Jesus Christ as a gift? "God so loved the world that He gave...." Then why is Jesus presenting in this parable the idea that we have to give up all for Christ?

Let me put it this way. In order for us to receive that pearl of great price, it is like changing your citizenship. When I became an American citizen in 1975, I had to raise my right arm and I had to swear before the court that I would give up all allegiance to every foreign potentate. There are thousands who would like to become

American citizens and are more than willing to give that up because they see the value of this country in a material sense.

You cannot be a citizen of heaven — which is under Christ — and a citizen of this world — which is under Satan — at the same time. You have to give up one for the other. What Christ is trying to show here is that there can be no mixture between the world which is under the evil one and the kingdom of God which is under Christ. There is a cross and that cross will allow nothing of the world to cross over.

Turn to Matthew 19. I am going to use several references from Matthew and I would like to encourage you when you study your Bibles, please dig deep. Don't read the surface. In Matthew 19, Jesus is talking to this young man who was a victim to Judaism, who thought he could go to heaven by doing good. Jesus said to him in Matthew 19:21:

If you want to be perfect [which no man can be of his own], go, sell your possessions and give to the poor, and you will have treasure in heaven. Then come, follow me.

In other words, Jesus was telling this young man, "Give up your wealth in exchange for my wealth." Now if this young man really realized that the One who was speaking to him was the King of the universe, he would be a fool to reject it, but he did not recognize in Christ the pearl of great price. So the next verse tells me that he went away sorrowfully. He was not willing to give up. Verse 22:

When the young man heard this, he went away sad, because he had great wealth.

But going down to verse 27 we come across what Peter says to Jesus.

Peter answered him, "We have left everything to follow you! What then will there be for us?"

"Jesus, that young man did not do it, but we did. We gave up our fishing rights; we gave up our boats; we gave up our profession and followed You. What then will there be for us?" as if he was making a great sacrifice. In other words, "What is there in it for me?"

Jesus realized that Peter still had not fully understood the gospel and He did not rebuke him. Listen to what Jesus says in Matthew 19:28:

Jesus said to them, "I tell you the truth, at the renewal of all things, when the Son of Man sits on his glorious throne, you who have followed me will also sit on twelve thrones, judging the twelve tribes of Israel...."

Can you imagine? Jesus is appealing to their egocentric nature and then He goes on in verse 29:

"...And everyone who has left houses or brothers or sisters or father or mother or children or fields for my sake will receive a hundred times as much and will inherit eternal life."

Was that merchant really sacrificing when he sold all for the pearl of great price? The answer is "No." There are people today everywhere who are searching for the pearl of great price.

Several years ago I found a statement in Gospel Workers (by Ellen G. White), p. 301, and I put it in the back of my Bible to remind myself every time I stand behind this pulpit:

"But this I do know that our churches [not the Baptist, not the Methodist, our churches] are dying for the want of teaching on the subject of righteousness by faith in Christ, and on kindred truths."

Our churches are dying.

The question is, when you have found the pearl of great price, what are you going to do with it? Are you willing to give up all? First of all, may I make it clear that it is not a sacrifice. Turn to Philippians 3, because here we read about a Pharisee who did find the pearl of great price on the Damascus road. Before that he had a very high opinion of himself. He was a Pharisee and, regarding the law, he was blameless. Notice how he responded when he found the pearl of great price. Listen to what the apostle Paul says about his great exchange.

In verses 4-6 he describes what he was, what he had, what he had accomplished as a Pharisee, but in verse 7-9 he says:

But whatever was to my profit I now consider loss for the sake of Christ. What is more, I consider everything a loss compared to the surpassing greatness of knowing Christ Jesus my Lord, for whose sake I have lost all things. I consider them rubbish, that I may gain Christ and be found in him, not having a righteousness of my own that comes from the law, but that which is through faith in Christ — the righteousness that comes from God and is by faith.

You see, Paul could not cling to his righteousness and at the same time receive the righteousness of Christ. The two cannot be mixed. That is why I plead with you to study Galatians because the Galatians were trying to mix the two. You cannot have both. It is all of Christ and none of you. "Not I, but Christ." Yes, it is painful to our ego; it is painful to our pride when our glory is cast to the dust. But I'll tell you, I'd rather have that than to be found naked in the day of judgment.

Now you say, "Does it apply to us?" Let the Bible speak. Turn to Revelation 3. Here is Jesus, the True Witness, speaking to the last generation of Christians. He is speaking to Laodicea in verse 17. I want you to look at verse 17 carefully because here we have two opinions.

"You say [That's the first opinion. Who does the "you" stand for? Us.], 'I am rich; I have acquired wealth and do no need a thing.' But [the True Witness says] you do not realize that you are wretched, pitiful, poor, blind, and naked."

Now which of these two are correct? Peter discovered the hard way that Christ was correct and he was wrong. Remember Jesus said, "All of you will betray Me, deny Me." And they all said, "Is it I?" Peter later on stood up and said, "Jesus, You may be right about these other fellows. You are wrong about me. I will die for You." Did he? He couldn't stand up for Christ before a young maid who came up to him. But he discovered that he is right only in Christ.

There is a problem in verse 17. There are two opinions that disagree, but I want you to look at the solution. Verse 18:

"I counsel you to buy from me gold refined in the fire, so you can become rich; and white clothes to wear, so you can cover your shameful nakedness; and salve to put on your eyes, so you can see."

I know one thing, we will not take this counsel as long as we are not convinced that Christ is right, but the moment we are convinced that He is right, then we will take the counsel. What is the counsel? "Buy from me gold..., white clothes..., and salve...." So it is not our egocentric faith that makes us rich; it is the faith of Jesus Christ that makes us rich. So it isn't our righteousness that clothes, but it is the righteousness of Christ that will be able to stand the scrutiny of the judgment. And, of course, it is not our viewpoint that we see, but what God sees.

I want you to look at the word "buy." The fundamental principle of the word "buy" means you give up something you have and something you may even cherish for something you want. This merchant found the pearl of great price but he could not have it until he sold everything he had. You and I may find the pearl of great price. Are you willing to give up your righteousness? Are you willing to give up your pride and, I say, even our own denominational pride? Are we willing to give up everything?

Several years ago when I was wrestling with the message of Christ our righteousness, I came across a statement in the book Testimonies to Ministers (by Ellen G. White), p. 65. When I read it I thought, "Well, maybe this is an overstatement." But the longer I live, the more I become convinced that this is a truth that needs to be hammered out:

"And because the Spirit is to come, not to praise men or to build up their erroneous theories, but to reprove the world of sin, and of righteousness, and of judgment, many turn away from it. [Now this is the statement.] They are not willing to be deprived of the garments of their own self-righteousness. They are not willing to exchange [some theologians call this the great exchange] their own righteousness, which is unrighteousness [or, in other words, filthy rags], for the righteousness of Christ, which is pure unadulterated truth."

The hardest part of the formula of "Not I, but Christ" is the first part. It is hard for us to come to God like beggars with nothing in our hands. It is hard, but the pearl of great price is the only thing that will take us through. Now what do we give up? What really is involved in selling all? I would like to suggest three things.

Number One. We must give up our life in exchange for His life. The life that you and I were born with originated in Adam. The life God created in Adam was a perfect life. It was a life created in the image of God. It was controlled by love. But the life that Adam passed on to us was not the same life. It was a ruined life. It was a life that sinned. It is a life that is bent towards self. It is a life that is condemned. It is a life that must die.

Now Jesus did not come to change the death sentence. He came to fulfill it. On the cross, the corporate life of the human race came to an end. In 1 Corinthians 15:45-49 Paul uses two statements about Christ that are very interesting. We need to study those two statements:

So it is written: "The first man Adam became a living being"; the last Adam, a life-giving spirit. The spiritual did not come first, but the natural, and after that the spiritual. The first man was of the dust of the earth, the second man from heaven. As was the earthly man, so are those who are of the earth, and as is the man from heaven, so also are those who are of heaen. And just as we have borne the likeness of the earthly man, so shall we bear the likeness of the man from heaven.

He calls Christ "the last Adam" and he calls Christ "the second man." Have you ever asked yourself to what those two statements refer?

As "the last Adam," Christ was the sum total of the first Adam. Remember, in Hebrews, the word "Adam" means "mankind," the concept of corporate oneness. So Christ, as the last Adam, was the sum total of the first Adam. In other words, in the incarnation He gathered to Himself all who belonged to the first Adam, which includes every one of us. Then, on the cross, He did away with the Adamic race. He did away with us. He did away with the life that stood condemned. And then, in the resurrection, He raised us up with a new life: His life, of which He is the Head. So as the second Man, He is the Head of a new, redeemed humanity.

For you and me to pass from the old life to the new life, you and I have to surrender to the cross of Christ. Let me give you a couple of texts, because the word of God is what speaks. Romans 6:8. The context is baptism and you will notice as you read from verse 3 onwards, that baptism is our participation, our identification with Jesus Christ crucified, buried, and resurrected. That's why it is always in immersion. There is no value in the immersion; it's what it points to that has value.

Romans 6:8 tells us two things that baptism points to. Maybe we should read Romans 6:7 also but let's read Romans 6:8 first:

Now if we died with Christ, we believe that we will also live with him.

You have to give up your life in exchange for His life. Is that a sacrifice? Well, I'll tell you, it's like giving up one dollar for a million dollars. What sacrifice is that? In fact, many in this country are trying it by giving that one dollar or whatever it is to the lottery, hoping that they will be the one to win.

We don't have to do it. It's available to all of us: the life of Christ in exchange for your life. I wish I had time. I would tell you what that life implicates, not only eternal life because eternal life in a world of sin is terrible. It is an eternal life in a world of happiness, in a world where there is no suffering, there is no pain, and there is nothing but joy and peace and love.

The same thing is said in 2 Timothy 2:11. Young Timothy needed to know this and all you young people need to know this.

Here is a trustworthy saying: If we died with him, we will also live with him....

Let me repeat an illustration, because it is one that has left a deep impression in my mind. When I first went to Ethiopia, I took the week of prayer at our college there. There was an Egyptian called Darwit. This is a true story. This was in 1973 and apparently there was an argument in their classroom at the college.

The disagreement was with the professor who told them that it is not right for Christians to carry arms and shoot people. This Egyptian who was taking mechanized agriculture said, "No. When

I go back to my country, I shall fight against those Zionists" (which was, of course, the Jews). During the week of prayer when I gave them time for questions, this young man stood up and asked, "Is it a sin to carry arms and fight for my country?" I said to Him, "Darwit, any Egyptian who does not fight for his country should be ashamed of himself." He liked that answer.

Then I asked him, "Could I ask you a question?" He said, "Sure." I said, "Have you ever seen a dead Egyptian fight for his country?" He said, "No. Once you die, you can't fight for your country." I said, "Thank you. Are you a Christian?" He said, "Yes." "Then may I remind you," I responded, "that you are dead and your life is hid in Christ. And, by the way, Christ was a Jew." Telling an Arab that he's a Jew is an unpardonable sin. He said, "I am not dead." I said, "Please turn to Colossians 3:3." I gave him some other texts, but Colossians 3:3 says:

For you died, and your life is now hidden with Christ in God.

"You have given up your life in exchange for Christ's life," I told him. "That is what baptism is all about."

He refused to accept it. I said, "All right, Darwit. It's not my problem; it's your problem." Two weeks later I went back to Addis Ababa to one of the colleges 200 kilometers away. Later Darwit was testing this tractor with his instructor and they were coming down this hill. Most of our colleges in Africa are on the top of hills, which is good in America because you have cars but there you have to walk (which is good, too). He was coming down this hill, sitting on the fender. His instructor was testing a John Deere tractor and he discovered the brakes had failed; there were no brakes on the tractor. The speed was increasing and, in his panic, he tried to get into lower gear to slow it down but that tractor didn't have synchronized gears so it went into neutral and it stayed there.

The instructor was wise; he jumped off and called to Darwit, "Save yourself." Darwit froze on the fender and the tractor hit a tree, capsized, and pinned him under. He was crushed; it took the college 20 minutes to bring another tractor, lift up the crashed one, and pull him out. His chest was crushed. We had a missionary's wife there who was a nurse; she examined him and discovered that he was dead. Hoping there might be some life there, they rushed him to the nearby Sudan Interior Mission hospital three miles away. Two doctors — one was a Swedish doctor, the other was an Ethiopian, trained in America — both examined him; they both pronounced him dead.

Meantime, the students were in the chapel praying furiously and, as the nurse was covering his body, his eyes blinked and the nurse shouted, "He's alive!" One of the doctors re-examined him and discovered a faint sign of life. We took him in our mission plane to our hospital for intensive care. He was unconscious for two weeks and, when he regained consciousness, I went to visit him. He was all bandaged up; the only space that was open were his eyes and his mouth. He was in bad shape.

I bent right down to his ears and I said, "Darwit, how are you?" I shall never forget what he said. He said, "Pastor, Darwit is dead. You are talking to a Christian." Well, I hope, young people, God won't have to use such a drastic method to convince you of truth. We have to give up our life in exchange for Christ's life. I am crucified with Christ. It is no longer I, but Christ must live in me and the life I now live I live by faith. The fruits of that is holiness of living.

Number Two. We must give up our wealth for His wealth. That's a bargain. I don't know how much money you have, but all the money in the world is nothing compared to the wealth of Jesus Christ. Jesus said (Matthew 16:26):

What good will it be for a man if he gains the whole world, yet forfeits his soul? Or what can a man give in exchange for his soul?

I want to give you some texts. We won't have time to read them except to look at one of them. Matthew 6:20, 21, 33:

But store up for yourselves treasures in heaven, where moth and rust do not destroy, and where thieves do not break in and steal. For where your treasure is, there your heart will be also. ...But seek first his kingcom and his righteousness, and all these things will be given to you as well.

You are familiar with Matthew 19:21; we covered that [above]. But I would like to look for a moment — I won't go into detail, because we will cover it in another parable — at Luke 12:16-21, the parable of the Rich Fool. Let's turn to it. Here was this fool; who was making money left, right, and center and he did not have enough room in his barn so he built bigger barns and so on. After he got all that money we see in Luke 12 what happened. Verses 20-21:

But God said to him, "You fool! This very night your life will be demanded from you. Then who will get what you have prepared for yourself?" This is how it will be with anyone who stores up things for himself but is not rich toward God.

Notice the two words. Then he goes on, verses 22-23:

Then Jesus said to his disciples: "Therefore I tell you, do not worry about your life, what you will eat; or about your body, what you will wear. Life is more than food, and the body more than clothes."

Then he talks about considering the lilies of the valley. God is able to supply all your needs but, even if He doesn't, if He allows you to dwell in poverty in this world, we are rich in Christ. That is the pearl of great price.

Number Three. This is a hard one. We must give up our righteousness for His righteousness. It is not "I plus Christ" righteousness. We must give up our righteousness for His righteousness. Why is this hard? Because we are proud people. For me to give up my righteousness is to admit that in me there is nothing good. If you think that is hard, I want you to try an experiment. Please don't blame me for the results. Next time you go to the shopping mall, find somebody smaller and weaker than you (maybe someone in a wheelchair). Go up to that person and say, "I have discovered something about you."

That person will say, "What have you discovered?" And you say, "From head to foot you are rotten; there is nothing good in you." That person may sue you, so you had better not give him or her your name because you have insulted that person. Yet the Bible says there is in earth nothing good. There is none righteous, not even one. Even this bush preacher is a sinner — 100 percent — saved by grace. Are you willing to give up your righteousness?

Let me turn to one text only. I've given you Philippians 3 and Revelation 3 but turn to Galatians 5:4. I want you to be very alert to this statement. It's all of Christ or nothing of Him:

You who are trying to be justified by law [another term for self-righteousness] have been alienated from Christ; you have fallen away from grace.

You can't have it both ways. It is either all of Christ and none of you or it's all of you and none of Christ. There can be no mixture.

Remember that here Paul is not discussing the law as a standard of Christian living. Here he is discussing the law as a method of salvation. There is no merit in our law-keeping no matter how wonderful it is. The only righteousness that qualifies you and me for heaven here and in the judgment is the righteousness of Christ. The fruit of that is Galatians 5:13-14:

You, my brothers, were called to be free. But do not use your freedom to indulge the sinful nature; rather, serve one another in love. The entire law is summed up in a single command: "Love your neighbor as yourself."

In other words, the fruit of accepting the pearl is very simple. If somebody gave you a new Porsche car with all the gas you need, what good is it if you left it in your garage? What will you do with it? When I was a teenager, I had the fastest motorcycle in Kenya. In those days, the Japanese didn't know how to make motorcycles. It was a British Vincent, had above speed of 140 miles an hour. I could wheelspeed that thing at 90 miles an hour. Powerful thing. This was before I was converted. I used to go to the cinema, park my Vincent there, and go in. When I came back, there were crowds of young people admiring and I would watch and say, "That's mine." I wanted everybody to see that I had the fastest bike in the country.

When you receive the pearl of great price you don't want to hide it. You want to show it to everybody. "See what I have found." Jesus said (Matthew 5:14a):

You are the light of the world.

Do you know that, in the original, the word "you" is in the plural form and the word "light" is in the singular? We are many but we are only one. All that the world needs to see in this church is Jesus Christ. Christ in you the hope of glory and you cannot do that unless you are willing to give up your righteousness for His.

Here's something that I think you all need to know. Mary, the only person among all the followers of Christ who understood the cross before the event, comes to Jesus with an alabaster box. I don't know how many of you have seen a Middle Eastern alabaster box. They are beautiful; they are carved; they are ornate, beautiful caskets. In those days it was not a screw-type of cover; in those days the cover was sealed. In that alabaster box was a very precious ointment.

According to Mark, that ointment was worth 300 pence plus which today is equivalent — if you worked it out — to $9,000. In those days the wage scale was a penny a day (Matthew 2) and 300 pence, if you took the minimum wage, is $4 an hour, eight hours a day, an average of $30 a day, and we multiplied by 300 days you got $9,000 of ointment in that box. But nobody knew until she broke that box and then the fragrance of that ointment filled the whole room. Are you willing to be broken that Christ in you may come out of you and be seen? That is the question.

The world desperately needs to see the Pearl of Great Price. Where is He? He is in you — that is, if you are a converted Christian — but the world cannot see it as long as you glory in the treasure box, in the earthen vessel. Remember 2 Corinthians 4:7:

But we have this treasure in jars of clay to show that this all-surpassing power is from God and not from us.

It is my prayer that you will be willing to give up your life, your wealth. When I say "give up your wealth," I don't mean that you have to literally give it up now. God has no problem with you being rich and having lots of material things, but God does have a problem if you cling to those things. Are you willing to give up, when the time comes, your homes, your bank accounts, your plastic cards, your racing cars, your motor boats, or are they clinging to you and you clinging to them? That is the question.

One of the evidences is that you are still clinging to your tithes. It is an outward sign that you have not given up everything because if you have in your heart said good-bye to all your wealth, there would be no problem giving one-tenth plus offerings. Am I correct? It is as simple as that. It is my prayer that you will give up all to God.

I want to close by saying something here that I hope will help you. I have discovered since coming to America that we have a problem here that I did not face in Africa. Africa is poor. Most of the African countries that I worked in were poor. Ethiopia was the third poorest country in Africa. Uganda under Idi Amin economically became bankrupt. They would be shocked if I went back to Africa and told them that a large percentage of Americans are unhappy in spite of their wealth. One of the biggest problems I found here is that people have very low self-esteem. I have discovered that, in a competitive world and in a capitalistic system where everyone is trying to grab, this is quite common.

When Adam sinned and we became nothing, God looked down from heaven. He saw this clay to which we all belong and He said, "I am going to redeem that clay and I'm going to make it more precious than anything." Do you know that God has raised the human race in Christ to be above every other created being? Do you know that in Christ we are above the angels? Then stop drooping your hands and your heads. Remember that, in Christ, you are the child of God. In Christ, we have become the pearl of great price and, when the universe is cleansed, the whole universe will come and look at the human race that was redeemed and say, "What a privileged group this is."

I want you to know that we are not dirt any more. In Christ, God has raised us up and made us sit in heavenly places in Christ Jesus. The wonderful thing is not only is Christ the Pearl of great price but He wants us to be part of that Pearl. He wants us to remind ourselves who we are in Christ.

It is my prayer that when you realize who you are you will then no longer have any poor self-esteem. Anyone who has poor self-esteem or poor self-worth has not discovered the Pearl of great price. Jesus who was rich, 2 Corinthians 8:9, became poor that we who are poor may become rich. We were redeemed, says Peter in 1 Peter 1:18-19, not by silver and gold but by the precious blood of Jesus Christ. In 1 John 3:1a we are told:

How great is the love the Father has lavished on us, that we should be called children of God! And that is what we are!

It doesn't matter what you look like. It doesn't matter whether you are uneducated. It doesn't matter if you don't have too many clothes in the wardrobe. The poorer you are, the more you will appreciate the Pearl of great price. It is my prayer that not only will you be willing to give up all for Christ, but that you may recognize that, in accepting Christ, you yourself have become the pearl. May God bless you.

CHAPTER NINE

THE PARABLE OF THE GROWING SEED

Turn to Mark 4:26-29. This is a wonderful parable that has to do with Spring, at least it has to do with the seasons. This is Jesus speaking.

He also said, "This is what the kingdom of God is like. A man scatters seed on the ground. Night and day, whether he sleeps or gets up, the seed sprouts and grows, though he does not know how. All by itself the soil produces grain — first the stalk, then the head, then the full kernel in the head. As soon as the grain is ripe, he puts the sickle to it, because the harvest has come."

In 1970, Jean and I drove to Benton Harbor in Michigan to pick up an African pastor who was sent by his Union, the East African Union, to study at Andrews University for a further degree. This was in December and you know we have no winter in Kenya. As we were driving on the way to Andrews he looked out in horror and he said to us in amazement, "What has happened?" he said. "Has America been hit by a pestilence?"

We said, "What do you mean?" He said, "Can't you see, all the trees are dead?" We had to explain to him that in America we have four seasons. I had often wondered why the missionaries who came from this part of the world to Africa missed the seasons but now, having lived here for so many years, I realize that the seasons are wonderful. I realize that winter is the worst month, at least you may not agree with me but it is a time when everything is dead and cold. You young fellows who like skiing will disagree with me but, when you get my age, skiing is not a pleasure.

One of my churches took me out skiing. It was terrible. I must have fallen down at least fifty times. First of all, the shoes you have to put on are terrible because you can't bend. Then the next thing you do is put your ski on and the first ski I put on took off before I gave it permission. The most embarrassing part was after having fallen for about the fortieth time a girl — she must have been at least four or five years old, couldn't be any older than that, one of those girls who come up here — comes sliding down and came to a screeching halt and here I was flat on my back and she said, "Can I help you?"

I thank God for Spring when the snow melts and everything comes back to life. In Spring, the dogwood and all the other flowering trees really make any place worth living in just for the Spring. It's a wonderful time. It is a time when the farmers sow their seeds. It's the time when the home gardener plants his seedlings. Then the Summer comes with long daylight hours when everything grows and begins to bear fruit. Then of course, we have the Fall, which is harvest time.

In the Middle East they also have the four seasons, not as strong, not as drastic as here but they still have the four seasons. For a spiritual illustration, Jesus used the work of a farmer planting the seeds, the seeds germinating and producing grain, and the harvesting.

I want us to analyze this parable, so let's begin with Mark 4:26. There is a job the farmer has to do and there is a job that he cannot do. His job is sowing the seed or casting seed into the ground. Remember, when we witness the gospel we are sowing the seed, but the farmer could not germinate that seed. You can do whatever you like but you cannot germinate it.

Some of us who are not expert gardeners are impatient. One day I had a seed that I had planted; I brought it all the way from England because it is a vegetable that doesn't grow here and after five days

I saw nothing so I pulled it out to see whether it had germinated. I must have done some damage because it never germinated after that.

So the farmer, as it says in the text, goes to sleep. If it was in America, he wouldn't go to sleep, he would go fishing. But in those days there was no fishing unless it was your trade. The farmer went to sleep and he rested night and day. In England and in this country you would say day and night but the Jews began the day with night. He would wait until the seed germinated, sprouted, came up, grew, and produced the seed.

I want to emphasize all this because very often we try to do what is not our work. Notice in Mark 4:28 it is the earth that brings forth fruit. It is not the farmer who produces the fruit. Our job is witnessing. I have looked and looked in the Bible for the word "soul-winning" and I cannot find it because soul-winning is the work of God. Our job is witnessing. When Jesus told the disciples to go into all the world He didn't say to go and win souls. He said to go and preach the gospel. That's in Mark 16:15:

He said to them, "Go into all the world and preach the good news to all creation."

In Acts 1:8 the disciples were told:

But you will receive power when the Holy Spirit comes on you; and you will be my witnesses in Jerusalem, and in all Judea and Samaria, and to the ends of the earth.

They will be His witnesses. Our job is witnessing.

We do not pressure people to come into the church because that seed that you have sown has to germinate and it cannot germinate until something very important happens. I want to give you a couple of texts to show you what has to happen when a seed germinates. Because if it doesn't happen, if people come into this church with the seed not germinating, there is a problem and the pastor loses his hair. Last week we heard some very sad news. Two of our young pastors of this Conference gave up the ministry. It was too much to handle the pressures.

What is required for a seed to germinate? Well, let Jesus speak first. Turn to John 12:24 and notice that something has to take place for that seed that we may have sown to germinate. We cannot germinate the seed. The farmer could not do it; he really had to rest and wait.

I tell you the truth, unless a kernel of wheat falls to the ground [this is what the farmer does] and [besides falling into the ground] dies, it remains only a single seed. But if it dies, it produces many seeds.

When you travel through these parts and you see the wheat fields you will notice there are some patches of ground where there is no wheat growing. It isn't because the seed wasn't sown. It is because either the birds took it or the seeds did not germinate. In the previous parable in Mark 4:3, Christ gives us the parable of the sower and, remember, some seeds fell on hard ground, they could not germinate. Some seeds fell on the wayside and were taken by the birds. Some seeds fell on thorny bushes and others fell on good ground.

But the seed has to germinate. That's the first step and, in order to germinate, it has to die. "But," says Christ,

But if it dies, it produces many seeds.

Notice this is the principle of the gospel. You do not produce fruit by hammering the members on the head. In my suggestion box, I've had notes without any signatures which say, "You need to tell the people what they must do." If the life of Christ is germinated in you, it will spontaneously produce fruit because the text says so.

I want to come back to John 12 later. Turn to 1 Corinthians where Paul is correcting an error that was created or raised up in the Corinthian church. Some of them were teaching that there is no resurrection. Paul makes this statement in 1 Corinthians 15:36:

How foolish! What you sow does not come to life unless it dies.

Verses 37-38:

When you sow, you do not plant the body that will be, but just a seed, perhaps of wheat or of something else. But God gives it a body as he has determined, and to each kind of seed he gives its own body.

Let's go back now to John 12; let's get the next verse, verse 25, where John applies this principle of nature, this example from nature, to the Christian life.

The man who loves his life will lose it, while the man who hates his life in this world will keep it for eternal life.

"If you refuse to die," says Jesus, "you will end up dying forever. But whoever surrenders his life to death, to the death of the cross in this world shall keep it for eternal life."

Two things happened at the cross. When we celebrate the greatest event in history, the crucifixion of our Lord Jesus Christ, we realize that two things happened there. The life that Christ assumed, which is the corporate life of the human race that needs redeeming, died on the cross, not for just three days. It died the wages of sin and the death of the wages of sin is good-bye to life forever.

But God did not want us to be in the grave forever because He "so loved the world that He gave [us] His one and only Son" (John 3:16). Have you ever asked yourself what He did? We are told in 1 John 5:11b what He gave:

God has given us eternal life, and this life is in his Son.

He gave us the life of His Son, which is eternal life, in exchange for our death. Now that is the gospel. Not I, but Christ. When you accept the gospel, you are surrendering your life to the cross of Christ in exchange for the life of Christ. You surrender your life, which already stands condemned, which has to die — I don't know why we cling to it — in exchange for the life of Christ, which can never die.

In Christ we don't have conditional immortality, which is what Adam had at creation. We have eternal life but remember that seed, which is the gospel witnessed to you, has to first bring your life to an end. In other words, the gospel demands that you die in order that you may live. Now that sounds like a paradox, but let me give you the words of scripture then I'm going to my favorite author. I know some of you don't like him. That's because you don't understand him.

Let's go to 2 Timothy 2:11:

Here is a trustworthy saying: If we died with him, we will also live with him....

There are some who want to live with Christ without dying with Him. The power of salvation is not in the resurrection; it is in the cross. The cross saves you because it was at the cross that the exchange took place, where we died and, in exchange, God gave us His life. The resurrection was only the evidence of that gift.

But, remember, Paul is saying to Timothy that if you die with Christ, your life with Christ is guaranteed, but if you don't die with Christ, you shall not live with Him. Turn back to my favorite book. I gave you my favorite author now I will give you my favorite book, Romans. We covered this already but let me remind you. Romans 6:8. The context is baptism:

Now if we died with Christ, we believe that we will also live with him.

Please don't try to germinate the seeds you have sown. That's not your job. It is the work of the Holy Spirit. It is the Holy Spirit who pricks the conscience of the individual and says, "Look, unless you die, there is no life." My job, your job is simply to expound to the people we meet the truth as it is in Christ. Lift up Jesus Christ and Him crucified. The Holy Sprit will do the rest.

It is not the farmer who does the germinating; it is not the farmer who does the sprouting; it is not the farmer who produces the fruit. So please stop trying to depend on your pastor to produce fruit out of you. He cannot do it. Turn to the book of Galatians. Galatians 6:12:

Those who want to make a good impression outwardly are trying to compel you to be circumcised. The only reason they do this is to avoid being persecuted for the cross of Christ.

We give out these little sheets of paper at Sabbath School — and I have no problem with that — but one of the papers came back with no name, just a text. Someone asked, "What does this text mean?" I didn't say anything. It was from the Sermon on the Mount, Matthew

6:1. The text was used out of context; it was not set correctly but I knew what the thought that the person had behind the text. The text says:

Be careful not to do your "acts of righteousness" before men, to be seen by them. If you do, you will have no reward from your Father in heaven.

Give it secretly? It is not wrong to report. Paul reported when he came back. It is wrong to report so that you may have a star in your crown. It is wrong to report so that people may see what a wonderful Christian you are.

Paul is saying that those who insist on legalism — that's what he is dealing with here — will insist that you do this and that. In contrast, Paul says in Galatians 6:14 (listen to the contrast):

May I never boast except in the cross of our Lord Jesus Christ, through which the world has been crucified to me, and I to the world.

But let us witness, and witnessing does not mean giving Bible studies. It's simply telling people what Christ means to you. If Christ means nothing to you, then you will have nothing to witness. But let me pray that you will witness, every one of you. Let the Holy Spirit do the germinating because, without that germinating, there is no fruit.

Going back to this parable, the farmer does his job and he does a good job. He plants the seed but notice what happens. He sleeps and he waits and sometimes we may have to wait a long time. When we were in Ethiopia and I was teaching the Bible in our college there, some of the students — there were three of them, it was just after the Marxist Revolution — had become Marxists. They felt that the Christian church had failed. They felt that the solution to the world's problems was not in the gospel of Jesus Christ, it was in Marxism.

They gave up Christ and they gave me a hard time. They tried to undermine the scripture. They tried to undermine Christ and they were downing everything that belonged to the church and lifted up Marxism. They were all bright students. They received scholarships to Leningrad University after they graduated. There they went to an atheistic country where they saw atheism in practice and their eyes were opened. Thank God for a Christian mother. One of the boy's mother sneaked a Bible into his suitcase. It was not an English Bible. It was an Amharic Bible and they began to study the Bible now privately in their room in an atheistic country.

They tried to remember what that Pastor Sequeira taught them. One remembered this and one remembered that and they put their minds together. They discovered the truth through their own personal study and they all gave their hearts to Christ. This was in 1978. In 1985 I was at the General Conference in New Orleans and this gentleman comes running to me and hugs me. I looked at him and he looked very much like one of those three boys. He said, "Don't you know who I am?" And I said, "I'm not sure because who you resemble cannot be here because you were anti-capitalist and you were anti-Christian when I last saw you." He said, "Yes, but the Lord opened our eyes." The seed was shown in 1978. It was germinated years later.

I read a text in Isaiah 55:11 which says that:

...So is my word that goes out from my mouth: It will not return to me empty, but will accomplish what I desire and achieve the purpose for which I sent it.

The seed is sown; we leave it to God to work out the germination. It germinates; it begins to produce fruit. I want now to go to a statement that you need to know. I have already mentioned the truth, now I want to give you scripture. You are very familiar with it. John 15:5:

I am the vine; you are the branches. If a man remains in me and I in him, he will bear much fruit; apart from me you can do nothing.

How much can you do without Christ? Nothing.

When that seed germinates what does it mean? It means that you have said good-bye to the old life and you have accepted that new life of Christ. You confess it in your baptism and Paul says in Romans 6 you rise out of the water in newness of life. That new life, believe it or not, can produce fruit in a sinful body. Don't ask me to explain that. It is a truth of the Bible.

There are some of our scholars who are saying today that it is impossible for Christians to overcome sin completely. Then you are undermining the life of Christ. In Christ, the law of sin and the law of the Spirit, two forces, met in one Person, Jesus Christ. Romans 8:2:

...Because through Christ Jesus the law of the Spirit of life set me free from the law of sin and death.

Verse 3 says:

For what the law was powerless to do in that it was weakened by the sinful nature, God did by sending his own Son in the likeness of sinful man to be a sin offering. And so he condemned sin in sinful man....

Jesus condemned sin in the flesh and that same life wants to live in you today. But Christ doesn't live in you to save you. He saved you on the cross but He lives in you because you have accepted that life in exchange for your life. You have accepted His life in exchange for your life.

Every Christian who has experienced germination will say with Paul (Galatians 2:20):

I have been crucified with Christ and I no longer live, but Christ lives in me. The life I live in the body, I live by faith in the Son of God, who loved me and gave himself for me.

I believe that if we have understood the true gospel, and if we have surrendered to the cross and have really experienced germination, we will not need promotional programs to produce fruit.

This is Ellen G. White's commentary on Romans 6. It is found in Bible Commentary, Volume 6, page 1075:

"The new birth is a rare experience in this age of the world. This is the reason why there are so many perplexities in the churches. So many [not some, so many] who assume the name of Christ are unsanctified and unholy. They have been baptized [they went through the act; they went through the water] but they were buried alive. Self [that is, the old life] did not die, and therefore they did not rise to newness of life in Christ."

For a pastor, the hardest thing to do is to pastor a church full of seeds that have not germinated. You lose your hair or you give up in anguish.

You cannot produce fruits in a church by promotional programs. That is the fair showing of the flesh. Fruit is the by-product of a faith relationship with Jesus Christ. Jesus is telling this parable to the Jews. The Jews were trying to produce fruit by promotional programs, by incentives, by hammering their people on the head so that the young man came to Jesus and said, "What good thing must I do to go to heaven?" Do you remember what Jesus said to Nicodemus, one of the religious leaders of Judaism? He said, "Nicodemus, you have failed to understand the very foundation of true religion. Don't you realize that which is born of the flesh will always remain flesh? You need to born again. You need to be born from above." [See John 3.]

There are too many Christians who belong to the family of Ishmael because Ishmael was a by-product of human effort. But it is not Ishmael who belongs to God. It is Isaac and Isaac was born from above. So it is my desire that we understand this.

Now I want to look at what happens. Going back to Mark 4, the farmer let the earth or God through nature (which was created by God) bring forth fruit of herself. Notice it is the earth that does it. Then, there is progress, there is a growth: first the blade appears, then the ear, after that the full corn in the ear. There is the blade first, then the ear, then the fruit. The grain ripens and (verse 29) when the fruit is brought forth, immediately he puts in the sickle because the harvest is come. Now how do we apply this?

I want to close by turning to a passage that is very relevant to us today, Revelation 14, and I want to show you the similarity of this parable with what Revelation 14:6-11 is saying:

Then I saw another angel flying in midair, and he had the eternal gospel to proclaim to those who live on the earth — to every nation, tribe, language and people. He said in a loud voice, "Fear God and give him glory, because the hour of his judgment has come.

Worship him who made the heavens, the earth, the sea and the springs of water."

A second angel followed and said, "Fallen! Fallen is Babylon the Great, which made all the nations drink the maddening wine of her adulteries."

A third angel followed them and said in a loud voice: "If anyone worships the beast and his image and receives his mark on the forehead or on the hand, he, too, will drink of the wine of God's fury, which has been poured full strength into the cup of his wrath. He will be tormented with burning sulfur in the presence of the holy angels and of the Lamb. And the smoke of their torment rises for ever and ever. There is no rest day or night for those who worship the beast and his image, or for anyone who receives the mark of his name."

Revelation 14:6-11 is sowing the seed. What is the seed? It is the everlasting gospel. How do we sow the seed? There are three steps:

Step number one is the first angel which has the everlasting gospel to preach to every nation, kindred, tongue, and people.

Step number two is to warn the people that if they reject the seed, if they do not separate themselves from Babylon, they will fall. Why? What does Babylon stand for? Daniel 4:30:

...He said, "Is not this the great Babylon I have built as the royal residence, by my mighty power and for the glory of my majesty?"

Babylon represents the religion of self. It represents Judaism; it represents legalism; it represents paganism; and Babylon committing fornication represents Galatianism. Galatianism was a mixture of "I plus Christ." That's why I am glad we are studying the book.

Revelation 14:10-11 is dealing with the third step:

"...He, too, will drink of the wine of God's fury, which has been poured full strength into the cup of his wrath. He will be tormented with burning sulfur in the presence of the holy angels and of the Lamb. And the smoke of their torment rises for ever and ever. There is no rest day or night for those who worship the beast and his image, or for anyone who receives the mark of his name."

If you deliberately, willfully, persistently, and ultimately refuse to die with Christ so that you may come alive with Him; if you deliberately reject the gospel, then you will face the wrath of God which is poured out without mixture. You will die forever.

Then in verse 12 and onwards he deals with those that have germinated, the believers:

This calls for patient endurance on the part of the saints who obey God's commandments and remain faithful to Jesus.

They are witnessing the love of Christ shed abroad in their hearts through the Holy Spirit. Remember the ingredient that keeps the commandments is love and Christ gives this love through the Holy Spirit.

Verse 13:

Then I heard a voice from heaven say, "Write: Blessed are the dead who die in the Lord from now on."

"Yes," says the Spirit, "they will rest from their labor, for their deeds will follow them."

Remember the farmer sowed the seed and he rested. We sow the seed and we rest, so if you die in the process of witnessing, don't worry; you are only sleeping. And our works will grow up. Young people, we need new farmers. The old ones are retiring. "And their deeds will follow them."

Verses 14-15:

I looked, and there before me was a white cloud, and seated on the cloud was one "like a son of man" with a crown of gold on his head and a sharp sickle in his hand. Then another angel came out of the temple and called in a loud voice to him who was sitting on the cloud, "Take your sickle and reap, because the time to reap has come, for the harvest of the earth is ripe."

We can sum all this up by one text, Matthew 24:14:

And this gospel of the kingdom will be preached in the whole world as a testimony to all nations, and then the end will come.

When the gospel has been preached to all the world, there are only two choices that will be left for the human race: either I die with Christ — that's the one choice — or I cry out against Him and say, "Crucify Him."

I don't know which choice you will make, but I'll tell you one thing. If you will die with Christ, you will be raised up again and live with Him. If you refuse to die with Him, God will say to you (Matthew 25:41):

"Depart from me, you who are cursed, into the eternal fire prepared for the devil and his angels" (not for you).

It is my prayer that the seed of the gospel that you have been hearing will germinate and that we will have fruit in the church. It is my prayer that every one of us will sow seeds and leave the Holy Spirit to germinate and produce fruit. When that happens, the earth will be lightened with the glory of God. May God bless us.

CHAPTER TEN

THE PARABLE OF THE RICH FOOL

Luke 12:13-21:

Someone in the crowd said to him, "Teacher, tell my brother to divide the inheritance with me."

Jesus replied, "Man, who appointed me a judge or an arbiter between you?" Then he said to them, "Watch out! Be on your guard against all kinds of greed; a man's life does not consist in the abundance of his possessions."

And he told them this parable: "The ground of a certain rich man produced a good crop. He thought to himself, 'What shall I do? I have no place to store my crops.'

"Then he said, 'This is what I'll do, I will tear down my barns and build bigger ones, and there I will store all my grain and my goods. And I'll say to myself, "You have plenty of good things laid up for man years. Take life easy; eat, drink and be merry."'

"But God said to him, 'You fool! This very night your life will be demanded from you. Then who will get what you have prepared for yourself?'

"This is how it will be with anyone who stores up things for himself but is not rich toward God."

One of the last letters that Paul ever wrote was to young Timothy. I want to read a couple of verses as my introduction to this parable that we have just read. In 2 Timothy 3:1-3 Paul says:

But mark this: There will be terrible times in the last days. People will be lovers of themselves, lovers of money, boastful, proud, abusive, disobedient to their parents, ungrateful, unholy, without love, unforgiving, slanderous, without self-control, brutal, not lovers of the good, treacherous, rash, conceited, lovers of pleasure rather than lovers of God....

This parable from Luke 12:13-21 of the rich fool has very important lessons for us living in these last days. Number one, we are living in a capitalist country and number two, we are living in a time when materialism has become the god of mankind. It is therefore important that we understand what Christ is trying to get across in this parable.

First of all I want you to look at the background. Jesus was teaching the multitude. He was exposing to them vital truths pertaining to the kingdom of God about God's providential care; about the danger of rejecting the gospel and the promptings of the Holy Spirit; about our response to His kingdom. Then suddenly while He was talking, this young man pops up his hand and he's asking a question. That's in Luke 12:13:

Someone in the crowd said to him, "Teacher, tell my brother to divide the inheritance with me."

You will notice that the request was completely out of context. Obviously this man had not come to hear Jesus Christ; he had come to use Jesus Christ. We have people today who come to church for various reasons and this young man had done the same thing. Now what was the problem? To understand his request you will have to understand the background of this man's culture.

According to the Jewish culture, something that was quite commonly known in the times of Jesus Christ, the division of inheritance was not done like it is done today. Number one, the wealth went only to the men — to the sons — because the daughter got it from her husband's side. Number two, if there were two sons, which seems to be the case because there were two brothers, they did not get the equal share of inheritance. According to Deuteronomy 21:15-17, the inheritance was divided into three parts if there were two sons and the first son — the elder son, who was known as the firstborn — always got a double portion:

If a man has two wives, and he loves one but not the other, and both bear him sons but the firstborn is the son of the wife he does not love, when he wills his property to his sons, he must not give the rights of the firstborn to the son of the wife he loves in preference to his actual firstborn, the son of the wife he does not love. He must acknowledge the son of his unloved wife as the firstborn by giving him a double share of all he has. That son is the first sign of his father's strength. The right of the firstborn belongs to him.

This young man was not happy with this policy because he happened to be the younger of the two. I think he would have agreed with it 100 percent if he was the older. But he wasn't; he was the younger and, by this time, Jesus had already made a name for Himself for being a nonconformist. He had already attacked some of the rules and traditions of the Jewish religion.

This young man, aware of the reputation of Jesus Christ, thought that he could use Jesus Christ to fight for what he felt were his rights. He felt that the inheritance should have been divided equally between him and his brother. Notice how Jesus reacted. Verse 14:

Jesus replied, "Man, who appointed me a judge or an arbiter between you?"

After answering this young man, Jesus turns to the multitude and notice what He says, because the lesson He brings out is for us too. Verse 15:

Then he said to them [that is, the multitude], "Watch out! Be on your guard against all kinds of greed; a man's life does not consist in the abundance of his possessions."

Covetousness is one of the major human problems. It is one of the reasons why this world has so many problems.

Having warned them, He gives this parable. The New English Bible puts it this way: "Beware! Be on your guard against greed of any kind" for two reasons. Number one, possession is not everything. That's the first thing Jesus says in verse 15. Possession of material things is not everything and number two, wealth does not give you life or happiness.

With this in mind, turn to Luke 12:16-21, which is the parable for our study. The parable is about a man, obviously a farmer, who had great success in farming. I read in verse 16:

And he told them this parable: "The ground of a certain rich man produced a good crop."

As we read the parable, we discover there were three problems with this young man. Number one, you will notice that he only thought of himself. No plans were made for God and no plans were made for his fellow man.

Notice verses 17-19 and count the number of times he uses the personal pronoun, the word "I" and the word "my." You will find that the word "I" is used six times and the word "my" is used at least five times in the original language:

"He thought to himself, 'What shall I do? I have no place to store my crops.'

"Then he said, 'This is what I'll do, I will tear down my barns and build bigger ones, and there I will store all my grain and my goods. And I'll say to myself, "You have plenty of good things laid up for man years. Take life easy [remember, in those days there was no Social Security, so this man felt that he now had everything he wanted to his dying day]; eat, drink and be merry."'"

Now that's an incomplete statement. He should have finished it by saying, "Eat, drink, and be merry, for tomorrow you die." God had to tell him because God responds,

"But God said to him, 'You fool! This very night your life will be demanded from you. Then who will get what you have prepared for yourself?'"

This man had an "I" problem and this is the major problem that faces the human race because we are all born egocentric. I want to give you a passage that brings out the same issue. Turn to James 4:13-16. I want to show that what James is saying here is very similar to our parable. This is discussing a group of people who have the same mentality as this young man in the parable:

Now listen, you who say, "Today or tomorrow we will go to this or that city, spend a year there, carry on business and make money."

Here is a group of people who feel that they are going to make money. Verse 14:

Why, you do not even know what will happen tomorrow. What is your life? You are a mist that appears for a little while and then vanishes.

Remember, in the Middle East it doesn't rain very much, but every morning, because of the tremendous change of temperatures between day and night, there's a kind of a mist that hovers over the ground and that's what he means by the vapor. As soon as the sun comes up, that all gets burned up and disappears. James is using that as a metaphor.

You are a mist that appears for a little while and then vanishes.

Our life is like a vapor. Once I witnessed a very tragic death and my wife had to remind me of something I had forgotten. The first time I ever came to Walla Walla, Washington, was in December 1982 to speak for the Ministerial Club at the College and the family that put me up were a very godly couple. They were both younger than I and their lives were snatched like that. Our lives are like a vapor. I thank God that they died in Christ. That is the wonderful hope that we have.

Christ is warning us against people who have allowed money, who have allowed materialism to take the place of our confidence and our wealth in Jesus Christ. So James goes on to say in this passage, James 4:13-16 in verse 15,

Instead, you ought to say, "If it is the Lord's will, we will live and do this or that."

In other words, we must always place God in our plans. We must always allow Him to be at the head of our plans. God is not against our making our plans. He has given us the privilege of making our choice but we must never make plans without God. This is what the text is saying.

Verse 16 adds:

As it is, you boast and brag. All such boasting is evil.

Anyone who does not have God in his plans cannot succeed. God has no objection to you becoming rich but He does warn you that if you are seeking for wealth without Him that eventually you will end up a pauper.

Let's go back to Luke 12. God is against anyone who is living independent of Him. This was the second problem. He thought that he could gain happiness; he could enjoy life through his own personal effort and material gain. He equated material blessings with happiness. He thought that riches could give him everything he wanted. I have news for you because wealth does not bring you happiness. In my life, I have lived in two countries that may be considered the richest countries in the world. One is the United States and the other one is Sweden. Sweden is supposed to be the richest country in Europe and probably one of the richest countries in the world.

Both these countries have a very high standard of living. About three years ago I had to speak for a publishing department seminar in Portland and the head nurse of the Portland hospital who was a missionary with us in Ethiopia took me out for a meal. She took me to a very posh restaurant. I've forgotten the name; I don't think I will ever step in there again. It was a very expensive meal. Next to us was a Swedish family who was visiting America from Sweden. They were discussing America not knowing that this African bush preacher understood Swedish.

I was listening and they were comparing Sweden with America. I remember one of the girls saying to her brother, "This country is not as great as our country." They were comparing the things you can get here and the brother said, "Well, yes, but they have things here that we don't have." They were comparing the materialism of both countries. But do you know that the highest suicide rates in the world are in these two countries? Do you realize that there are greater social problems in these two countries than in any other country in the world? Money does not bring happiness; it brings problems.

One dear lady in Africa told my wife, "When I leave the house, I don't even lock my door. Do you know why? Because I have nothing to be stolen. You overseas people have to lock your door. You have to have a dog there. You have to have a guard. You must be miserable." She was right; the more you have, the more you are concerned.

I want to give you a text which is in this light that materialism does not bring you happiness. It is given to young Timothy because it is in our youthful years that we think wealth is happiness. I want you to listen to what the apostle Paul is counseling this young man. 1 Timothy 6:9-10, the same idea that Jesus is bringing across but coming from a different angle. Verse 9:

People who want to get rich fall into temptation and a trap and into many foolish and harmful desires that plunge men into ruin and destruction.

Now these are strong words. In other words, Paul is not saying and God is not saying it is wrong to get rich but to those who want to get rich, Paul is saying "Be careful" because riches is one of the snares of Satan. Then he explains what he means in verse 10:

For the love of money is a root of all kinds of evil....

Notice Paul is not saying money is the root of all evil but the love of it, the coveting of the money is the root of all evil.

Some people, eager for money, have wandered from the faith and pierced themselves with many griefs.

The Protestant Christians can be divided into basically two camps: Armenians and Calvinists. One of the differences is that the Calvinists say that if God has chosen you to be saved, it is impossible for you to be lost. It is on this doctrine of predestination or rather double predestination that you have the idea of "once saved, always saved."

But the Armenians teach that it is possible for a believer to fall from faith. You see, there are two extremes that we must avoid. One extreme is the Calvinist extreme which says that if you have accepted Christ and you are saved you can never be lost. That is unbiblical. The other extreme is just as bad and many Armenians fall into this trap. The Calvinists fall into the trap of "once saved, always saved." The Armenians fall into the trap that every time you make a mistake you become unjustified. Nowhere in the Bible does it teach that. Both of these extremes are unbiblical.

Since we are justified by faith, it is possible for us to lose justification by unbelief. Unbelief is the deliberate, willful turning of our backs to God. Satan has many ways of doing this. Persecution is one of them. But the other two we need to be aware of. Perverting the gospel is one of them. That is how he tried it on the Galatian Christians. Notice that Paul says anyone who moves from justification by faith to justification by works of the law has fallen from grace and Christ has become of no value. Galatians 5:2-4:

Mark my words! I, Paul, tell you that if you let yourselves be circumcised, Christ will be of no value to you at all. Again I declare to every man who lets himself be circumcised that he is obligated to obey the whole law. You who are trying to be justified by law have been alienated from Christ; you have fallen away from grace.

The third way that Satan destroys our faith is by dangling the trinkets of this world before us — materialism. I tell you, it is not easy to avoid it in a materialistic country. When I was at a college one weekend, some of the young students who are very sincere asked me a question, "How can we walk in the Spirit? How can we maintain a living connection with Jesus Christ?" I had to confess to them that it is much easier to walk with Christ in a country where persecution exists. In Ethiopia, it was easy for us to walk in the Spirit. In Uganda under Idi Amin, it was easy. It is extremely hard to walk in the Spirit in a country like America where it is so easy to get everything.

I want to warn families coming from poor countries to America: please don't let the materialism of this country get you because now you are facing that danger. You never faced it in your own country; you are facing it here. But we who live here have to take this message seriously. That is why in 1 Timothy 6:12a Paul says,

Fight the good fight of the faith.

Now this young man did not realize this. He did not realize that true happiness does not come from material wealth. I would like to read a couple of statements. In Ecclesiastes 2:3-11 is a man who is talking out of experience. This is not some philosophy; this is out of experience. He says,

I tried cheering myself with wine, and embracing folly — my mind still guiding me with wisdom. [What he is saying here is, "I tried to get the best of two worlds."] I wanted to see what was worthwhile for men to do under heaven during the few days of their lives.

I undertook great projects: I built houses for myself and planted vineyards. I made gardens and parks and planted all kinds of fruit trees in them. I made reservoirs to water groves of flourishing trees. I bought male and female slaves and had other slaves who were born in my house. I also owned more herds and flocks than anyone in Jerusalem before me. I amassed silver and gold for myself, and the treasure of kings and provinces. I acquired men and women singers, and a harem as well — the delights of the heart of man. I became greater by far than anyone in Jerusalem before me. In all this my wisdom stayed with me.

I denied myself nothing my eyes desired; I refused my heart no pleasure. My heart took delight in all my work, and this was the reward for all my labor.

Here was a man who did everything for himself. Now look at verse 11:

Yet when I surveyed all that my hands had done and what I had toiled to achieve, everything was meaningless, a chasing after the wind; nothing was gained under the sun.

Do we have to repeat the same thing? Why can't we learn from this preacher (that's what Ecclesiastes means)?

When I was teaching in our college in Ethiopia, one young man stood up in the class and said, "You know, Pastor, we agree with all that you have taught us. We agree that Christ is everything but it's easy for you to say that Christ is everything because now you are an old man. We would like to enjoy this world and, when we get to your age, we'll accept Christ." Now that, by the way, is one of Satan's greatest traps for young people and that is why I would like now to turn to the third problem that this man faced.

Please go back to Luke 12. This man said to himself, "I'm going to eat, I'm going to drink, and I'm going to be merry." Luke 12:20:

"But God said to him, 'You fool! This very night your life will be demanded from you. Then who will get what you have prepared for yourself?'"

In other words, this man did not take into account — and it's a problem that all young people face — the fact of the problem of death. Death can overtake you at any time. Do you know that the young man who spoke those words is dead today? He was shot in the Marxist revolution. He did not live to my age. He never reached the age I was when I was teaching there. I don't know whether he accepted Christ because this happened after we left the college.

Young people, there are two things that you need to keep in mind. Number one, death can come any time. You don't have to live in difficult countries. We have had the experience of two people whose lives were crushed in a split second. Number two, every time you resist the Holy Spirit you are hardening your conscience further and further so that you will reach a point of no return. Many, many young people who said, "We will enjoy life until we get old." Many of them became old and never accepted Christ because they reached the point of no return.

Judas was one of them. Judas did not respond and, as he failed to respond, his conscience became harder and harder until he reached the point of no return. There in the upper room we are told that the devil entered into him and that was the end of him. So as we turn to this parable Jesus says in verse 21:

"This is how it will be with anyone who stores up things for himself but is not rich toward God."

You have to choose between God and wealth. Remember in the Sermon on the Mount where Jesus said (Matthew 6:24a):

No one can serve two masters.

You can't serve money and you can't serve God. God has no problem with you becoming rich. Abraham was rich but he always put God first.

Our scripture reading stopped here but I would like to read you the rest of the passage. Jesus takes this parable, turns to the disciples — His followers, not the multitude but His followers — and He warns them (Luke 12:22-24):

Then Jesus said to his disciples: "Therefore I tell you, do not worry about your life, what you will eat; or about your body, what you will wear. Life is more than food, and the body more than clothes. Consider the ravens: They do not sow or reap, they have no storeroom or barn; yet God feeds them. And how much more valuable you are than birds!

Then He goes on about our stature and then about the lilies. Then in verse 29 He says,

And do not set your heart on what you will eat or drink; do not worry about it.

Now comes the punch line. Verses 30-31:

For the pagan world runs after all such things, and your Father knows that you need them. But seek his kingdom, and these things will be given to you as well.

But some of you say, "We have been seeking the kingdom of God but I have problems; I have financial problems; I have house problems." Well, listen to the next verse (Luke 12:32):

Do not be afraid, little flock, for your Father has been pleased to give you the kingdom.

Sometimes God withholds things from you because He wants to give you the kingdom. Sometimes He allows you to go through problems so that your faith may be strengthened to develop patience.

It is my prayer that in all your planning, especially young people, you put God first because the material world doesn't give you happiness. Also, the material world doesn't guarantee you eternal life. Your only hope is Jesus Christ. It is my prayer that, in spite of living in the world around us, we all will learn to put God and

His kingdom first. One day we will hear these wonderful words, "Come inherit the kingdom which was prepared for you from the foundation of the world." This is my prayer in Jesus name. Amen.

141

CHAPTER ELEVEN

THE PARABLE OF THE BARREN FIG TREE

Luke 13:6-8:

Then he told this parable:

"A man had a fig tree, planted in his vineyard, and he went to look for fruit on it, but did not find any. So he said to the man who took care of the vineyard, 'For three years now I've been coming to look for fruit on this fig tree and haven't found any. Cut it down! Why should it use up the soil?'

" 'Sir,' the man replied, 'leave it alone for one more year, and I'll dig around it and fertilize it. If it bears fruit next year, fine! If not, then cut it down.' "

One Sabbath afternoon, many years ago, I received a phone call from the head deacon of a neighboring church and he said on the phone — he sounded very desperate — "I can't find my pastor; we have an emergency. Could you please come straight away?" So I said, "What's the problem?" He said, "Two of our young people from our church were looking for badgers in the Boise River. One of them went under and we can't find him. The frogmen are here. They are looking; it's almost four hours. The parents have just arrived and they need support. They need help. So could you please come?"

I rushed there and when I arrived the body had just been found. It was under water for four hours, so the boy was dead. The mother was beside herself. The father was on the shores of the river; she was about 50 yards away. As I arrived at the scene, there was a member of her church making a statement to her, scolding her, "Why on earth did you allow your boy to swim on the Sabbath? Don't you realize he is now lost forever?" I could have punched him. But at that time the mother needed help. So I took her aside, and I put my arm around her shoulder and said, "Look, sister, that is not quite true." She turned around to me and I will never forget the words she said. "My son gave his life to Jesus Christ a year ago. He was baptized and now He has allowed this to happen, and I've lost him forever. I want nothing to do with God." She wasn't my member, but I felt I had a duty and I spent almost two solid years before I could turn her around.

The reason I have told you this is because this has been one of the major problems that has faced the human race right from the very beginning of the fall. Jesus told parables for various reasons. This parable from scripture was used by Jesus Christ as an illustration. To understand what he's trying to get across, we need to understand the background. Turn to Luke 13:1. Jesus was presenting a series of studies to a multitude and there were among that multitude some who were eye witnesses to a very terrible incident. Apparently Pilate had sent his soldiers and killed, butchered, a number of Galilaeans who were offering sacrifices at the temple.

This, of course, was well known at that time and these people were telling Jesus, obviously wanting to know, "What is their eternal fate?" That is in verse 1:

Now there were some present at that time who told Jesus about the Galileans whose blood Pilate had mixed with their sacrifices.

I want you to notice how Jesus responded. Luke 13:2:

Jesus answered, "Do you think that these Galileans were worse sinners than all the other Galileans because they suffered this way?"

In other words, the report that came to the people from the Pharisees, and this was commonly known at that time, was that the reason God allowed Pilate's soldiers to murder these men and women was because they were sinners. They had no right to be offering sacrifices in the temple. So Jesus is asking the question, "Is this why they died?" Was God punishing them for what happened? I want you to look at the answer. Verse 3:

"I tell you, no! But unless you repent, you too will all perish."

These people did not die because they were sinners, but "unless you repent."

What did He mean by that? Well, let's go one step further, because Jesus repeats the whole thing again in another incident. Verses 4-5:

"Or those eighteen who died when the tower in Siloam fell on them — do you think they were more guilty than all the others living in Jerusalem? I tell you, no! But unless you repent, you too will all perish."

To understand this problem, we need to go back to the first book that was ever written in the scriptures. Do you know which was the first book that was ever written in the scriptures? It was Job, not Genesis. You are all familiar with the book of Job. Remember that Job had been stricken with some terrible calamities, and three of his friends (so called, I suppose they meant well) came to him to comfort him. Now we need to read the book of Job and see what the dialogue was all about. Two of those friends insisted that the reason Job was going through all this was because he had some secret sin that he was not confessing. In other words, God was punishing him. Job was trying to defend himself. Job said, "No, I don't have any secret sins." Then the two men were saying, "No, otherwise this would not happen to you." The argument went on and on and the third man joined them and, eventually, God spoke.

God did two things. He rebukes Job for defending his self-righteousness. Number two, He rebukes Job's friends for wrong theology. "You have no right to say that this man is suffering because he has been doing something wrong." This has been a problem all through the history of mankind. We have people today who feel that God punishes us because we are doing things that we should not be doing.

That young boy died in Christ. What he was doing was wrong, but he died in Christ. If I'm lost because I am doing something bad, then I have to teach, to be honest, to be logical, that I am saved because I am doing right. Salvation is, therefore, no longer a gift to sinners. But Jesus was correcting them. What was the problem that led Jesus to give this parable?

God came to the Jews and He planted a fig tree. The fig tree was the good news of salvation, but the Jews bore no fruit. Let me give you an example. The good news that God gave the Jews was the Messiah, Jesus Christ. But before Christ came, God sent John the Baptist to prepare the way. Read what is said in Luke 3:7:

John said to the crowds coming out to be baptized by him, "You brood of vipers! Who warned you to flee from the coming wrath?"

John did not mince his words. Now look at verse 8:

"Produce fruit in keeping with repentance. And do not begin to say to yourselves, 'We have Abraham as our father.' For I tell you that out of these stones God can raise up children for Abraham."

The Jews were depending on their nationality, they were depending on their performance, they were depending on the various things they did, such as circumcision, for their salvation. But God said, through John the Baptist, "The fact that you are a child of Abraham does not qualify you for heaven."

Jesus is dealing with the same issue. What He is trying to say in Luke 13 is, "You have rejected my gift, therefore you are bearing no fruit." What is the fruit of repentance? It is joy; it is peace; it is long-suffering; it is patience. That is the fruit of the spirit. But they did not have that because they had rejected the gospel. How do I know? Turn to the end of chapter 13. Notice that as Jesus goes on and on He concludes Luke 13 with these words. Luke 13:34:

"O Jerusalem, Jerusalem, you who kill the prophets and stone those sent to you, how often I have longed to gather your children together, as a hen gathers her chicks under wings, but you were not willing!"

God looked for fruit among Israel and found none. Luke 13:35:

"Look, your house is left to you desolate. I tell you, you will not see me again until you say, 'Blessed is he who comes in the name of the Lord.' "

Here is a man who planted a fig tree. Now we do not grow figs in the northwest. I don't know how many of you have lived in California, but at one meeting I was in the south and they had a row of fig trees planted there at the college. I said to the farmer, "Could I have a seedling because I would love to have a fig tree in my garden?" He said, "I'm sorry, you are living in the wrong place. Your fig tree will not make it there." So I want to say a few words about a fig tree, because a fig tree was the most valuable tree in Israel in the days of Christ. The reason is that a fig tree in Israel produced fruit three times a year. Isn't that wonderful? It's like our avocado trees in Africa. We had so many avocado pears that we got tired of them.

The Jews would often plant a fig tree in their vineyard, which is what this man did, in case of a drought. Figs were guaranteed, except for two months of the year, April and May. So this month they would not have any figs, but the rest of the year, ten months, they had figs. They had something to eat, so it was the most valuable tree in Israel. It took about three years for a fig tree to produce fruit and, apparently, this man, after the three years were up, went on another three years waiting. Every season, every time, month after month for ten months a year, he went there and looked for fruit, and the Bible says, "He found none."

Remember that God sent prophets, He sent people to find fruit among Israel and to find a positive response and He found none. Now when we go to the parable it says, "The vineyard owner." Look at Luke 13:7:

"So he said to the man who took care of the vineyard, 'For three years now I've been coming to look for fruit on this fig tree and haven't found any. Cut it down! Why should it use up the soil?'

This man said, "I planted this tree in my vineyard in order that it may bear fruit, but instead it's using the nutrients of the soil, it's hindering the sun from the vineyards. It has no value to me. It's bearing no fruit. The only thing to do is to cut it down." The dresser said: "Please, Lord, can you give it one more chance?" Verse 8:

"Sir," the man replied, "leave it alone for one more year, and I'll dig around it and fertilize it. If it bears fruit next year, fine! If not, then cut it down."

Of course, Jesus Christ was God's ultimate chance for Israel. God is wonderful. He allowed the Jews even to crucify His son and still did not cut them down. He waited for almost three and a half years and when they stoned Stephen to death, they were confessing publicly their rejection of God's ultimate revelation, Jesus Christ. It is at that point God said, "I leave your house desolate." That doesn't mean that the individual Jew cannot be saved. It simply means that the Jewish nation no longer represents the church of God. He took that privilege and gave it to the Gentiles, the Christian church.

Now, I suppose you will say to me, "This doesn't apply to us." Why? "Because we haven't rejected Jesus Christ." Whether you accepted or rejected Jesus Christ is not the message of this parable. The message is that, if you have accepted, you will show fruits. If you have rejected, you will show no fruits. That's the message of this parable.

So if you say, "I have accepted Christ," God will say to you, "Where is the fruit?" Matthew 7:16:

"By their fruit you will recognize them...."

Now what does He mean? What are the fruits of repentance? Number one, one of the fruits of a person who has accepted Jesus Christ, is that they are never any longer critical of other people, because they have discovered they are sinners saved by grace. But if you look at Galatians 5, the fruit of the spirit is love, joy, peace, long-suffering. Galatians 5:22-23a:

But the fruit of the Spirit is love, joy, peace, patience, kindness, goodness, faithfulness, gentleness and self-control.

But the greatest fruit that I read in the words of Jesus Christ is, "You shall be my witnesses." Jesus said to the disciples in Matthew 5, verses 14a and 16:

"You are the light of the world. ...Let your light shine before men, that they may see your good deeds and praise your Father in heaven."

Once we had a Personal Ministry Committee meeting, and the main problem that was discussed was how we can get our people to witness. I would like to tell you a story because I know people are afraid to witness. This took place in England. I do not know how many of you have heard of the famous preacher Alexander White. He was a very famous preacher. He has passed away now. He preached in London at St. George Church. There was a man who was a traveling salesman, who every Sunday would make sure he was in London to listen to Alexander White. He was so impressed by the message that it touched him. He wanted to witness, but he had a problem. He was afraid to give Bible studies. He was afraid to open his mouth and tell people what the Bible teaches.

But he got an idea. He said, "You know, one thing I can do. I can't preach, I can't give Bible studies, but I can do one thing. As I travel in my business I can invite people to go and listen to Alexander White." So he did that. One day he called one of his customers and said, "Please, could you go and listen?" This man was a non-believer. He was not a Christian and this man said, "No, I don't want to waste my time." The salesman insisted, even said to him, "I'll come and take you to the church." To please him he said, "All right, I'll come, reluctantly." He went and heard Alexander White, was so impressed by the message that he gave his heart to Jesus Christ.

The salesman felt that he should go and tell Alexander White this wonderful truth that one of his listeners had given his heart to Christ. So the next day he went to Alexander White's house, knocked on the door and introduced himself and said, "I would like to let you know that your preaching is not in vain. This man, who I invited, gave his heart to Christ last Sunday."

Alexander White looked at him and said, "You know, I've been trying to find you. I've been trying to meet you for a long time." The salesman said, "Really, do you know me?" He said, "No, I don't know you, but I know your name. Come in." He took him to his office, pulled out a file and produced twelve letters from individuals who had given their hearts to Christ because this man, the salesman, had invited them to the church. Four of those men wrote from seminaries. They had become ministers. I'm told that it was Alexander White's preaching, but it was the salesman who deserves the credit.

All that God wants you do to do is tell people what Christ means to you because Jesus wants us to bear fruit. The Bible is clear that we are saved by grace without works, but genuine justification by faith is not stagnant. It bears fruit. We may not see the result of our fruit. We human beings look at results to see whether our works are successful or not. Leave the results to God's hands. Our job is to witness Jesus Christ. It is God's job to win souls. That's not our job, it's His job. Our job is to tell the world. Acts 1:8b:

"...You will be my witnesses in Jerusalem, and in all Judea and Samaria, and to the ends of the earth."

Don't think just because you accepted Christ that this parable does not apply to you or to me.

I want you to be clear that what Christ is saying here is that every tree must bear fruit. You may not see the fruit, but there has to be fruit. In Matthew and other parables of Christ, for example, is the parable of the sower. What happened to the seed, which is the gospel, that fell on good ground? It germinated, it sprung up, and it began to produce fruit, some thirty fold, some sixty fold, some a hundred fold. And that is why, in the judgment, God will bring up our works not as the basis of salvation, but as an evidence. It is my prayer that we will realize that when we accept Christ, we become alive to bear fruits.

I want to give you a couple of examples to see this in its correct perspective. I think that we need to look at examples that will lead us to a clearer understanding. A good place to start would be John

14, where a young man, one of the disciples called Philip, comes to Jesus and says in John 14:8:

Philip said, "Lord, show us the Father and that will be enough for us."

What did Jesus reply? Verse 9b:

"Anyone who has seen me has seen the Father."

Then Jesus in verse 10 and 11, points out that the evidence that he is the Messiah is that the Father who dwells in him is doing the works:

"Don't you believe that I am in the Father, and that the Father is in me? The words I say to you are not just my own. Rather, it is the Father, living in me, who is doing his work. Believe me when I say that I am in the Father and the Father is in me; or at least believe on the evidence of the miracles themselves."

Then in verse 12 He goes on to say:

"I tell you the truth, anyone who has faith in me will do what I have been doing. He will do even greater things than these, because I am going to the Father."

Notice, "anyone who has faith in me will do what I have been doing."

Let's go to the apostle Paul and see where he puts it into a beautiful perspective. Ephesians 2:8-9 is the fig tree:

For it is by grace you have been saved, through faith — and this not from yourselves, it is the gift of God — not by works, so that no one can boast.

Salvation is by grace; it is a gift that is received by faith. But now look at verse 10. Verse 10 is the fruit:

For we are God's workmanship, created in Christ Jesus to do good works, which God prepared in advance for us to do.

Now I can go on and on and give you several examples, but the fig tree was the gospel message first given to the Jews. God wanted the Jews to lighten this earth with His glory by the message of righteousness in the Messiah. What did they do? They pushed that message aside and went into legalism. Did the Jews do many good works? Yes. They did much good works, but it was not the fruits of the gospel. We must never, ever equate works of the law with works of faith. Works of the law is man trying to be good so that he may qualify for heaven. That is why they went wrong. If you did bad, you were punished; if you did good, He would take you to heaven.

Works of faith are the fruits of the gospel. Faith without works is dead. James 2:26:

As the body without the spirit is dead, so faith without deeds is dead.

Genuine justification by faith produces works, and God is looking in every individual for fruit. But remember, the fruit doesn't save you; it is the evidence that you have already been justified in Jesus Christ. And I'll tell you, the world needs to see that fruit. The world needs to see in the church love, joy, peace, long-suffering, because the world doesn't judge us by our doctrines. They couldn't care less about our doctrines. They want to see men and women who are set free from anxiety, from insecurity, and who have peace, who have joy, who have love. Then they will know and they will say, "Yes, now we believe the gospel is the power of God unto salvation." God gave the Jews 1,500 years to fulfill their mission. They failed.

It is my prayer that we will not fail. Of all professing Christians, we must be number one in lifting up Jesus Christ. If we fail, and this tree is cut down, who is God going to go to? He has tried the Jews, He has tried the Gentiles, who else does He have to turn to? The angels to do the work? No, He wants us human beings who have experienced the joy of salvation to witness the gospel. It is my prayer that we will be His witnesses, that we will flood our neighborhoods with the good news of Jesus Christ, by our joy, by our peace, by our long suffering, by our kindness, by our sympathy and understanding. And we can say that, "I am a sinner saved by grace. I want to share with you what Jesus means to me." May God bless us that we will be a fruit bearing church in this coming year and that God may fulfill in this church his purpose. May we yield to this commission. God wants us to go and witness Him. Amen.

CHAPTER TWELVE

THE PARABLE OF THE WHEAT AND THE WEEDS

Matthew 13:24-30:

Jesus told them another parable: "The kingdom of heaven is like a man who sowed good seed in his field. But while everyone was sleeping, his enemy came and sowed weeds among the wheat, and went away. When the wheat sprouted and formed heads, then the weeds also appeared.

"The owner's servants came to him and said, 'Sir, didn't you sow good seed in your field? Where then did the weeds come from?'

" 'An enemy did this,' he replied.

"The servants asked him, 'Do you want us to go and pull them up?'

" 'No,' he answered, 'because while you are pulling the weeds, you may root up the wheat with them. Let both grow together until the harvest. At that time I will tell the harvesters: First collect the weeds and tie them in bundles to be burned; then gather the wheat and bring it into my barn.' "

This parable, along with the parable of the dragnet found in verses 47-50, go together. Both of them deal with the co-existence of good and evil until the permanent separation that will take place at the coming of Christ. This parable has very important lessons for us and I would like to share those lessons with you.

First of all, let's look at the parable. To us — living 2,000 years after Christ in America — this sounds like a far-fetched story that Jesus told, but actually what Jesus was telling was very common. It was very common, after a farmer planted his wheat — which is a very important crop in Israel — for an enemy to come at night and plant weeds ("tares" in some translations). This was commonly done out of revenge. Because of this, the Roman government passed a law that you could not do this. It was illegal. But it was common to plant weeds in the field of a farmer on whom you were trying to take revenge.

It's hard enough dealing with the weeds that grow naturally, but the "tares" weren't ordinary weeds. They were commonly known as the "bearded darnel," which belongs to the family of the rye grass. When these weeds grew, the plant in its early stage looked identical to the wheat, so you could not tell the difference. It's only when they begin to mature that darnel is shorter and the color of the grain is grayer than the wheat. But what was the problem with these weeds? As I mentioned, it was not just an ordinary weed. The grain of the darnel was poisonous. So you can see why people were planting this out of revenge. The only way to save his crop was for the farmer and his laborers to go just before the harvest and pluck or root out the darnel first and tie them in bundles to be burned and then harvest the wheat. That is what the parable Jesus told was about.

There were at least four main parables that Jesus was telling the multitude. So when it says in verse 24, "Jesus told them another parable," the "them" is the multitude. After the parables were all over, Jesus sent the multitude away and went into the house. Matthew 13:36:

Then he left the crowd and went into the house. His disciples came to him and said, "Explain to us the parable of the weeds in the field."

The disciples singled out this parable and asked Jesus for an explanation. They didn't seem to mind the other parables. This one they singled out and we have to ask ourselves, why?

But before we do, let us look at the interpretation Jesus gave this parable. He told it to the multitude; He gave no interpretation. He let them reason out for themselves. But in verse 37 up to verse 47 you have an interpretation of this parable that Jesus gave to the disciples. Number one, Verse 37:

He answered, "The one who sowed the good seed is the Son of Man."

So the good seed happens to be Christ. Remember, Christ is the life. He gave His life for the world. The word "seed" in the Bible represents life. That's why we are saved through Abraham's seed — singular — which is Christ.

The good seed is the proclamation of Christ to the world. Remember Jesus said to go into all the world and preach the gospel. Matthew 28:19:

Therefore go and make disciples of all nations, baptizing them in the name of the Father and of the Son and of the Holy Spirit....

That's the sowing of the seed. Then in Matthew 13:38a Christ tells us:

The field is the world....

That's the mission that Christ has given us: "Go and sow the seeds into the world." Matthew 13:38a:

The field is the world, and the good seed stands for the sons of the kingdom.

In other words, the believers represent the wheat here. The wheat that has germinated, the wheat that has been born again.

The wheat represents those who are born again, those who have accepted the life of Christ in exchange for their life, which stands condemned. But then, in Matthew 13:38b-39a:

The weeds are the sons of the evil one, and the enemy who sows them is the devil.

Christ tells us that the enemy that sowed the bad seeds is the devil because he tells us that the weeds represent the children of the wicked one, the enemy that sows them is the devil and the harvest is the end of the world. Verse 39b:

The harvest is the end of the age, and the harvesters are angels.

Now that, basically, is what the parable is all about.

Number one, what is the application? The answer is two-fold. There are some scholars who feel that Christ is referring to the world and that both believers and unbelievers will co-exist until the end of the world and the coming of Christ. But if you look at the parable very carefully, it is obvious that what Jesus had in mind is not the world, but the church.

Yes, the good seed is sown in the world, but please notice: the enemy takes his evil children and he sows them into the church. So what Christ is saying here is that the church, because of what the devil has done, is a mixture of converted and unconverted people and the problem is how we can distinguish between the two. Christ says we cannot. I would like to read you a statement. There is a statement in Testimonies, Vol. 5, p. 172, by Ellen G. White. I want to bring it to your attention, because we need to keep this statement in mind.

"The accession of members who have not been renewed in heart" [that means unconverted] "and reformed in life is a source of weakness to the church. This fact is often ignored. Some ministers and churches are so desirous of securing an increase of numbers that they do not bear faithful testimony against unchristian habits and practices. Hence many join the church without first being united to Christ." [That means the good seed has not germinated in their lives.] "Hence, many join the church without first becoming united to Christ. In this Satan triumphs. Such converts are his most efficient agents. They serve as decoys to other souls. They are false lights, luring the unwary to perdition."

That is one of the missions the devil employs. He fills the church with unconverted people. In Revelation 12:10-17, we have the history of the Christian church in a nutshell:

Then I heard a loud voice in heaven say:

"Now have come the salvation and the power and the kingdom of our God, and the authority of his Christ. For the accuser of our brothers, who accuses them before our God day and night, has been hurled down. They overcame him by the blood of the Lamb and by the word of their testimony; they did not love their lives so much as to shrink from death. Therefore rejoice, you heavens and you who dwell in them! But woe to the earth and the sea, because the devil has gone down to you! He is filled with fury, because he knows that his time is short."

When the dragon saw that he had been hurled to the earth, he pursued the woman who had given birth to the male child. The woman was given the two wings of a great eagle, so that she might fly to the place prepared for her in the desert, where she would be taken care of for a time, times and half a time, out of the serpent's reach. Then from his mouth the serpent spewed water like a river, to overtake the woman and sweep her away with the torrent. But the earth helped the woman by opening its mouth and swallowing the river that the dragon had spewed out of his mouth. Then the dragon was enraged at the woman and went off to make war against the rest of her offspring — those who obey God's commandments and hold to the testimony of Jesus.

It's very interesting. It begins with Christ, who redeemed the world, and with the church being persecuted. The early Christian church was persecuted. Satan tried to destroy the Christian church through persecution. But as the church father Tertillian said, "The blood of the martyrs was the seed of the church. The more you mow us down, the more we will bring people in." And persecution failed. It failed miserably.

Then Revelation 12:15 goes on to explain how the devil tried a second method of destroying the church, and, by the way, he was quite successful, not by destroying the church, but by perverting it:

Then from his mouth the serpent spewed water like a river, to overtake the woman and sweep her away with the torrent.

The second method was to fill the church with water, which in Revelation 17 represents people. After Constantine, he flooded the church with people, so that numerically the Christian church grew by leaps and bounds, but these unconverted people brought in all their heresies and the church was plunged into darkness.

But I thank God that He is not going to leave His church that way, and so, at the end of the chapter, we find God stepping in, opening the earth to trap the flood, purifying the church and, finally, He will have a remnant. The word "remnant" means "faithful ones," those who are faithful in spite of opposition, in spite of persecution. Satan is going to make war on them, but they are going to remain faithful unto the end.

But in this parable we are studying, Jesus tells us that the devil is doing this and that; this has always been his method. You know that even among the disciples one was of the devil. Now the first question I want to ask in terms of the application is, Why? Why did the disciples single out this parable from all the others? What was in their thinking when they asked Jesus, "Please, we want this parable to be explained" [Matthew 13:36]? Well, you must remember the disciples were victims to Judaism.

One of the things that the Jews believed and taught in the days of Christ is that when the Messiah comes He would not only restore the political kingdom of Israel back to the Jews from Roman bondage, but they taught and they believed and were very sincere, that the Messiah would cleanse the Jewish nation of all impure mixed blood, so that he would produce a stainless Jewish nation that was made up of pure Jewish blood.

Now it's very interesting that Hitler did the same thing, but he thought that the Jews needed to be exterminated and they got a taste of their own medicine in the Holocaust. But this is what they believed and what was bothering the disciples, because they were victims of this theology, was the fact that the people who were crowding around Jesus were not those pure, holy-looking Jews, but publicans and sinners. And they were. They represented the people — the laborers — who came to the farmer and said, "Should we get rid of these fellows?"

Remember the story of Jesus healing the daughter of the Canaanite woman? Jesus left the Galilee area, went to Tyre and Sidon, which today is Lebanon. A lady came up, a Canaanite woman, an unbeliever, and the disciples said to Him, "Please get rid of her, she is not one of us. Get rid of her!" Remember how Jesus tested her and found that her faith was very determined. She was a remnant. She refused to give in. Jesus called her a dog. Jesus ignored her. He did everything, but she would not give in.

Then Jesus turned to her and said [Matthew 15:28]:

Woman, you have great faith! Your request is granted.

She was a Canaanite woman but, to the disciples, she was a dog. She was an outcast. She did not deserve to belong to the covenant people of God but, to God's eyes, she was His child. She called Jesus, "Lord, Son of David," which is a typical Messianic term.

Unfortunately, there are too many today who have the same mentality. There are too many in our churches today who feel that we need to cleanse the church, get rid of all the sinners so that we may have a pure church. That's the work of God because the answer the farmer gave, who represents Jesus was, "No! Because, in trying to remove the weeds, you will remove the wheat."

Until the very end the two will look alike, and we human beings do not have the capacity to distinguish between the true believer and the unconverted person who is coming to church. In 1 Samuel 16:6-7, listen to what the prophet writes here:

When they arrived, Samuel saw Eliab and thought, "Surely the Lord's anointed stands here before the Lord."

But the Lord said to Samuel, "Do not consider his appearance or his height, for I have rejected him. The Lord does not look at the things man looks at. Man looks at the outward appearance, but the Lord looks at the heart."

Now we have this statement:

The Lord does not look at the things man looks at.

What's the difference?

Man looks at the outward appearance, but the Lord looks at the heart.

You and I cannot read the hearts of men and women. Let me give you another text. Proverbs 16:2. You have the same idea brought out here:

All a man's ways seem innocent to him, but motives are weighed by the Lord.

I want to tell you about an incident that took place several years ago when China had its Marxist revolution. We had to close down the China division [of the SDA Church]. The missionaries, who were many from this country, had to come back. They had to flee for their lives, but one of the division officers in the China division was a national, a graduate of P.U.C. Where could he go? He was a Chinese. Even though he could not go anywhere, he remained faithful to Christ, and so the Chinese Marxist government took him and put him in prison. I believe he was there for 20 or 21 years. How would you like, young people, to spend 20 years of your best years in a Marxist prison where they don't give you angel food cake or spaghetti or salad? This is what I ate w hen I ate with the prisoners here in America.

That young man remained very faithful even in prison. They tried to brainwash him. They tried everything. Fifteen years later he wrote a very long letter. I had the privilege of reading that letter, which was written to the General Conference. He had managed to befriend one of the jailers, even convert him, and he gave this letter to the jailer, who promised to mail it and he did mail it. In that letter he expressed some real concerns where he felt the church had failed to prepare his own people for a crisis. And one of the things that he mentioned was that the missionaries were very generous, very kind, and very helpful to the Chinese people who had learned to bow down to the missionaries and say "yes" to everything. They gave them scholarships; they gave them the praise and honor, but those who were quiet, those who did not say much, were ignored. But when the crisis came, it was these people — one of them was the principal of the college — who actually denied Christ and were the greatest enemies of the church. The ones who were ignored remained faithful to Christ.

When I read that I was impressed for the simple reason that we had a similar experience in Africa. In Uganda under Idi Amin, in Ethiopia, in the Marxist revolution — the ones who we least expected to remain strong for Christ were the ones who were willing to die for Christ, and the ones who had such wonderful blessings from this church failed. I remember a man who was sent to the Philippines by the church and given a degree through denominational money. He was the one who organized the labor union in our hospital and tried to get rid of the doctors.

We are going to be in for a surprise. You will be amazed who will remain faithful and who won't. May I make it clear that the one who thinks he will stand will fall. We do not have the capacity to distinguish who is a true Christian and who is not. We have no idea what some people are struggling with. We have no idea, but I thank God, He reads their hearts.

As the parable tells us, the great danger is that, if we try to get rid of the sinners, we will pull out the wheat. Jesus is not discussing discipline here. He is discussing judging. If you read Matthew 7:1, Jesus says never judge:

Do not judge, or you too will be judged.

Please follow that counsel when you see a brother or sister go wrong. Please don't come and report him to the church. Those are not the steps. You go to the person personally and, out of love, try to help him to correct the problem and, if he or she doesn't listen, then take two or three witnesses. If they don't listen, then you report it to the pastor and the church.

Remember, Christ is not discussing discipline; He is discussing judging and we have no right to judge. Paul says the same thing in Romans 14. We must not judge each other because that is the work of God. Now, the church will always have the weeds in it. There has never been a time when there have been no weeds. The mixed multitude were a great hindrance to the Jews in the exodus. Judas was a child of the devil, in fact the Bible says so. John 6:70:

Then Jesus replied, "Have I not chosen you, the Twelve? Yet one of you is a devil!"

We will always have weeds. The question is not whether we have weeds. The question is, which of the two are you: weeds or wheat? I can't tell. Nobody else here can tell, but there are two people who can tell: God and the Holy Spirit, because He can read your heart. He knows whether you have genuinely accepted Him or not.

The next thing I would like to bring to your attention is weed pulling. Pulling out weeds is always a negative work, and that is not the work God has given to the church. The work that God has given to the church is to sow the good seed. That's our mission. Leave God to pull out the weeds. He will do it in his own time, but our mission is to go into all the world and preach the gospel. Sow the good seed.

Those why try to produce a "pure" church will end up where the Pharisees have ended. The Pharisees tried to produce a pure church in the days of Jesus Christ. They would have nothing to do with the sinners or the publicans. They only mixed with those who belonged to their club. They called it the Holiness Club. There were two things wrong with them:

They were self-righteous.

They looked down upon others.

Luke 18:11:

The Pharisee stood up and prayed about himself: "God, I thank you that I am not like other men — robbers, evildoers, adulterers — or even like this tax collector."

All of us are one hundred percent sinners saved by grace. We have no right to judge anybody. I don't know if you realize we are all of the same stock. We share the same life. Given the right chances, given the right environment, the right circumstances, you and I, everyone of us, can do exactly as Hitler did in the Holocaust.

Don't ever say to me, "What happened in Germany can never happen here in America." May I remind you that 55 million babies are aborted every year in the world of which 1.6 million are in this country. Investigators have found that 90 percent of these abortions are not done because of necessity, but because of convenience. If life begins at conception, that is worse than the Holocaust. So don't ever believe that it can't happen here. We are all of the same stock.

Given the chance, the right environment, it will happen. We can do it. That is why God has not ordained the church to separate the wheat from the weeds. Our job is to present the truth. It is God who has ordained the angels to pull out the weeds.

Look at Matthew 13:39-42:

..And the enemy who sows them [the bad seed] is the devil. The harvest is the end of the age, and the harvesters are angels [not us]. As the weeds are pulled up and burned in the fire, so it will be at the end of the age. The Son of Man will send out his angels, and they will weed out of his kingdom [which means His church and that is why I believe this parable is referring to the church] everything that causes sin and all who do evil. They will throw them into the fiery furnace, where there will be weeping and gnashing of teeth.

Notice, Christ chooses His words. In the Hebrew language there are 12 words that go under the umbrella of "sin." The word "iniquity" is very interesting. It means doing something with a selfish motive, whether it is good or bad. In the Sermon on the Mount, in Matthew 7:21-22, Jesus said in the last days:

Not everyone who says to me, "Lord, Lord," will enter the kingdom of heaven, but only he who does the will of my Father who is in heaven. Many will say to me on that day, "Lord, Lord, did we not prophesy in your name, and in your name drive out demons and perform many miracles?"

Jesus says in response [verse 23]:

Then I will tell them plainly, "I never knew you. Away from me, you evildoers!"

What they were doing was good, but their heart was wrong. That's why we cannot judge, because we do not know the hearts of men and women. God knows and these people were doing iniquity. They may be proclaiming the name of Christ, they may be doing many good works, even casting out devils, but they were doing iniquity. Therefore, He shall cast them into the furnace of fire.

This is exactly what Matthew 7 is saying [same as Matthew 13]:

There will be weeping and gnashing of teeth.

They will be crying, "But, Lord, open the door. We have been part of your church." They will even quote, "We have been part of your remnant church." Please remember, the world "remnant" means "faithful." It does not mean "the last bit of cloth." It means those who are faithful towards the end. Elijah said to God, "All Israel have departed from you. I am the only one." And God said, "No, there are 7,000 who are still faithful." Do you know what God calls them? The remnant.

Now I want you to be clear about this. The remnant refers to those who are remaining faithful to God until the very end and, when the devil will make war, that war will separate. When the shaking comes, it will separate, but it is God who will allow the shaking, who will bring in the shaking through circumstances. The shaking is to separate the wheat and the weeds. The shaking is the beginning of the separation.

It is my prayer when the shaking comes to this church, that not one of you will be separated from the body of Christ. Because you can deceive your pastor, you can deceive your friends, you can deceive everybody around you, but there is one Person you cannot deceive and that is our Lord Jesus Christ. He knows what is in you, and it is my prayer that when the separation takes place, which is the end of the world, and we are living in those times, we will not be among those who will be collected by the angels to be burnt.

But my prayer in the meantime is that we fulfill the mission of this church: Go into all the world and sow the seeds. There are people out there who belong to God, whose hearts are in the right direction, but who have not heard the good news. Please let us go out and be witnesses for Christ. That is our job. Our job is not to clean the church. Our job is to sow the good seeds. Let God do His job. He will do it in His own time. He will cut this work short in righteousness. May God bless you that we will be the laborers who will sow seeds, plant the good seeds, and leave the harvest and the judging and the separation to our Lord Jesus Christ. Amen.

THE PARABLE OF THE TEN VIRGINS

Matthew 25:1-13:

At that time the kingdom of heaven will be like ten virgins who took their lamps and went out to meet the bridegroom. Five of them were foolish and five were wise. The foolish ones took their lamps but did not take any oil with them. The wise, whoever, took oil in jars along with their lamps. The bridegroom was a long time in coming, and they all became drowsy and fell asleep.

At midnight the cry rang out: "Here's the bridegroom! Come out to meet him!"

Then all the virgins woke up and trimmed their lamps. The foolish ones said to the wise, "Give us some of your oil; our lamps are going out."

"No," they replied, "there may not be enough for both us and you. Instead, go to those who sell oil and buy some for yourselves."

But while they were on their way to buy the oil, the bridegroom arrived. The virgins who were ready went in with him to the wedding banquet. And the door was shut.

Later the others also came. "Sir! Sir!" they said. "Open the door for us!"

But he replied, "I tell you the truth, I don't know you."

Therefore keep watch, because you do not know the day or the hour.

This parable has to do with a wedding feast. In this parable, we are told that the bridal party had to wait and, while this parable has been applied to what we call "The Midnight Cry" in the history of the Adventist church, if you look at the parable in its context, you will discover that Christ was applying this parable in reference to His second coming.

Now the Millerites were not wrong, because they linked it to the second coming. They were wrong only in the date. It is important as we look at this parable that we look at the context. Remember that in the days when the Bible was written, they did not use chapter and verse division. So this parable is really an extension, an expounding of what Christ has already touched on in chapter 24, especially from verse 26 onwards where He deals with the fact that when Christ comes the second time, even the believers will be caught off guard unless they are watching.

Let me give you the closing verses of Matthew 24 to give you an idea of the setting, because you will notice as you read these verses that this parable is dealing with these two groups within the church. I'm going to read Matthew 24:44-51:

So you also must be ready, because the Son of Man will come at an hour when you do not expect him [remember, he's talking to believers].

Who then is the faithful and wise servant, whom the amster has put in charge of the servants in his household to give them their food at the proper time? It will be good for that servant whose master finds him doing so when he returns. I tell you the truth, he will put him in charge of all his possessions. But suppose that servant is wicked and says to himself, "My master is staying away a long time," and he then begins to beat his fellow servants and to eat and drink with drunkards. The master of that servant will come on a day when he does not expect him and at an hour he is not aware of. He will cut him to pieces and assign him a place with the hypocrites, where there will be weeping and gnashing of teeth.

Then He says,

At that time the kingdom of heaven will be like ten virgins who took their lamps and went out to meet the bridegroom.

Notice, this is the context. Now I think you need to know some of the background. First of all it was quite common in the days of Christ among the common people, not among the wealthy, to have weddings at night. It is unheard of here but it was common there. There were two reasons. Number one: It was quite hot in the Middle East, especially some months of the year, so they preferred to have weddings at night when it was cool. The rich could have it in the daytime because they had people to fan the guests. But the poor could not afford the fanning. Number two: It was quite common for the bride and the bridesmaids to wait for the groom to come.

Here is the situation. There was no public transportation in those days. The wedding was held in the home of the bride. The husband or the groom may have come from a long distance. He had to travel either by foot or by horseback or by donkey or, if he was wealthy, by chariot. But this wasn't such a wedding. It was a common wedding. History tells us that sometimes the waiting of the bride and the bridesmaids would last two solid weeks. Can you ladies imagine waiting for two weeks? The groom normally gets jittery knees when the wife is late. When I got married, my wife Jean was caught up in a crowd that was just coming out of a soccer game. It was a very important soccer game which in England is a big thing. I began to wonder if she had changed her mind. Can you imagine waiting two weeks?

The reason I am mentioning this is because the bride's party, the ten virgins, were all aware of this fact. Keep this in mind. All of them were looking forward to the coming of the groom. All of them were aware of the delays that could take place. All of them had lamps because that is the way you welcome the groom. Now the Middle East lamp was very small. You could hold it in your hand. It was a clay pot with a wick and the oil in it would last only for a short period of time. So it was wise to carry some extra oil with you.

The parable tells us that all of the ten virgins went to sleep. We human beings have a very hard time waiting. Patience is not one of our virtues. Remember in the garden of Gethsemane in Matthew 26:40-41, what did the three disciples do while Jesus was praying in agony?

Then he returned to his disciples and found them sleeping. "Could you men not keep watch with me for one hour?" he asked Peter. "Watch and pray so that you will not fall into temptation...."

They went to sleep. And Jesus said,

The spirit is willing, but the body is weak.

I told the children a story about how it is easy for us to sleep. One day I was traveling in Kenya on my motorcycle. I was doing 65-75 miles per hour and, believe it or not, I went to sleep. You may think that is impossible but I was on the road for eight hours and I was drowsing. I went to sleep and when I woke up there right in front of me was a huge elephant.

Well, I'm glad it wasn't the second coming of Christ. It took all my wit and I had to be calm because this wasn't tarmac road. This was very loose sand and there were two deep ruts where the trucks had gone. I was in one rut and the elephant was covering both the ruts so I had to climb over the sandhill. You try that and the moment you slow your bike down you've had it. So I had to open up the throttle and climb that sand hill. When I passed him, I could just barely touch him. I said, "That's what happens when you go to sleep."

But all ten virgins went to sleep until the announcement was made that he was coming and this was a common part of their culture. They would have a scout waiting at a distance looking for the coming of the bridegroom's party and he would come running and announce it. That's why we link this with the midnight cry when Samuel Snow changed the date and said, "He's coming on October 22." That was the midnight cry.

So far, outwardly, there was no difference between the five wise and the five foolish virgins. They were all sleeping. They looked alike. They were dressed all in the same uniforms. You can never tell who will be able to stand from the outward appearance because they all looked alike. It's only when the announcement was made and they woke up that we see a difference and the difference is within. One group was wise enough to have extra oil with them; the other was not. Remember that both groups knew that the delay could take place.

Now the big question is, "What did the oil represent?" Most people would immediately say the oil represents the Holy Spirit and that is right, but there is the context that we must be clear on. The oil does represent the Holy Spirit but it represents the Holy Spirit dwelling in you by faith. I want to give you a couple of texts that will help you. Turn to 2 Corinthians 4:7. I want to read a statement there made by the great apostle Paul:

But we have this treasure [which is Christ in you and Christ in you is by the Holy Spirit] in jars of clay to show that this all-surpassing power is from God and not from us.

The second passage I would like to read is Ephesians 3. I want to remind you of the background that caused the apostle Paul to make this statement. Ephesians was a prison letter. Paul had witnessed — preached — at Ephesus for approximately three years. It was the longest time he had ever spent in one area. Then he was taken prisoner, not for some crime he had committed but for preaching the gospel to the Gentile world. While in prison, he wrote this letter and, in chapter 3, he shares with the Ephesian Christians his concern. What was this concern?

The Ephesians Christians came to reason this way. They said, "If God cannot protect the great apostle Paul who is now languishing in a Roman prison, what hope is there for us lay people?" So they began to lose confidence in the gospel and in Christ. Paul heard about this and he writes to them of his concern in Ephesians 3:13:

I ask you, therefore, not to be discouraged because of my sufferings for you, which are your glory.

"Please don't get discouraged; I am in prison because God wants me there."

If you read this letter, you will notice that he never calls himself a prisoner of Rome. He calls himself "a prisoner of our Lord Jesus Christ." For example, look at Ephesians 4:1:

As a prisoner for the Lord, then, I urge you to live a life worthy of the calling you have received.

He says don't faint because I am in prison for preaching Christ. Then he says in Ephesians 3:14:

For this reason [because you are discouraged] I kneel before the Father, from whom his whole family in heaven and on earth derives its name.

He is praying earnestly and this is his prayer. Verse 16:

I pray that out of his glorious riches he may strengthen you with power through his Spirit in your inner being....

That's the oil dwelling in the inner man and Paul's prayer is that we should be strengthened with might through the Spirit who dwells in us. But the very next verse he switches from the Spirit to Christ. Verse 17:

...so that Christ may dwell in your hearts through faith....

To Paul the Spirit dwelling in you and Christ dwelling in you are synonymous. You'll find it in many places, for example, Romans 8:9-10 makes it absolutely clear that Christ dwells in the believer.

You, however, are controlled not by the sinful nature but by the Spirit, if the Spirit of God lives in you. And if anyone does not have the Spirit of Christ, he does not belong to Christ. But if Christ is in you, your body is dead because of sin, yet your spirit is alive becasue of righteousness.

The oil, which is the Holy Spirit — which represents Christ also — dwells in you through the Holy Spirit and Paul is saying that his prayer is twofold. The Spirit dwelling in you may strengthen you and this is only when Christ dwells in you by faith. Now the word "dwell" — in the Greek there are two words for dwelling — is very important because Paul uses the word that means, "to dwell permanently."

The Bible never preaches "once saved, always saved," even though this bush preacher has been falsely accused of doing it. I would recommend that those who have accused this bush preacher of it to read the reformed position of what the basis of this teaching (once saved, always saved) is. It is based on predestination. It is not based on justification by faith.

The idea of "once saved, always saved" is based on the fact that God has predetermined some people to be saved and some people to be lost — they call them reprobates — and that if you have been chosen to be saved you can never be lost because God is sovereign and what He chooses will happen. This is a far cry from justification by faith. Christ dwells in us by faith. Is it possible for your faith to be destroyed? The answer is, "Yes." The moment you say good-bye to your faith, you are saying good-bye to Christ. Remember, the oil is in you by faith.

Because the groom had not come early enough, the virgins went to sleep. There is no rebuke in the parable against them sleeping. The rebuke is that they did not have oil. Their faith dwindled away while they were waiting. That is why I read to you Matthew 24:48. These foolish servants which represent the foolish virgins are saying, "My lord delays his coming. Let us go back to the world, enjoy ourselves, and, when we hear the announcement, we can come back."

In Ethiopia, one young man at college told me, "Pastor, I'm young; I really want to enjoy life. When I get your age, I'll accept Christ." I said, "What guarantee do you have that you will reach my age?" He said, "No problem. I will reach your age; don't worry." But he did not reach my age. He was killed in the Marxist revolution in Ethiopia. I hope that he had accepted Christ. I was not there when he died.

There are two things that Christ is concerned about here:

The coming of Christ will take even God's people off guard.

Only those whose faith has endured unto the end will be able to meet Him.

The plea of this is that Christ may dwell in your hearts by faith. I want to turn to two passages regarding this. Matthew 24 is in the context of the second coming. While the delay takes place, the believers may be sleeping, but the devil will not be sleeping. Because he is not sleeping, wickedness will increase and, because wickedness will increase, Jesus says in Matthew 24:12:

Because of the increase of wickedness, the love of most will grow cold....

The love of His truth, the love of His coming, will grow cold.

The other passage is also dealing with the second coming of Christ and is found in Luke 21:34-36:

"Be careful, or your hearts will be weighed down with dissipation, drunkenness and the anxieties of life, and that day will close on you unexpectedly like a trap. For it will come upon all those who live on the face of the whole earth [notice all will be taken by surprise]. Be always on the watch, and pray that you may be able to escape all that is about to happen, and that you may be able to stand before the Son of Man."

The only way you will be counted worthy is by faith alone.

Jesus is saying in this parable that even Seventh-day Adventists — remember, these ten virgins represent not only believers but believers who are waiting for the groom, so they are Adventist believers — will be taken off-guard. The devil loves to have us predict specifically that certain events will take place and for us to think it will come. Right now there is a movement that says that Christ will come in a Jubilee year. Let me tell you what happens when we do this. I'll give you my own experience.

When I first became an Adventist in 1958, there was a Suez crisis. Nasser had taken the Suez Canal from Britain and I remember the evangelists in those days saying, "This is the beginning of the war of Armageddon. The end is here." I waited and waited; the end did not come. Then came the Six-Day war and something else in between — I forget all the events — and at every crisis we say, "The end is here!" Then came Cuba during President Kennedy's time and I heard the same thing. When you keep hearing that a specific event is the end, you get tired of it. You have the "Peter and the Wolf" syndrome. That, unfortunately, is happening to a lot of our people today.

Our young people are asking, "How soon is soon? My grandfather believed in the soon coming of Christ." We have scholars today who no longer believe the coming is near. I am talking of scholars in the Adventist church and that is exactly what the devil is causing us to do. We need to be aware that we have to be flexible. He may come in a way that is least expected. Situations may take place that we least expected according to our predictions. I am very concerned with speculating regarding the prophecies of Daniel and Revelation.

I want to give you an illustration of what I mean by "unawares." In Rwanda we had a missionary from Italy. He was a young chap and, as many young fellows do, he loved to take long showers. He was in an area where there was plenty of water and he was in the shower. He thought he was Caruso because he was singing at the top of his voice, enjoying his shower. While he was doing this, some thieves came in a truck and they emptied his house, believe it or not. His bags, his furniture, his cooker, his fridge, his clothing, everything. He was totally unaware; he was singing his head off and these fellows were having a wonderful time taking his things.

When he opened the shower door, all he had was a towel around him because the towel was all he had! Nothing more. Everything was taken, even his pants. He was taken off-guard. You may think this is impossible but it actually happened. It hit him so hard that he gave up the mission field, came to this country, and took up dentistry. He's practicing as a dentist where he won't be caught off-guard because he has his people on the chair.

Be careful that you do not have specific views of how events will take place. There was a time when we would give our people charts; this would take place and this would take place. The parable tells us that all ten virgins were sleeping and all ten virgins were taken by surprise but there was a difference between five of them.

The word "midnight" here is simply a symbol that means "unexpected time." If you read the passage in Matthew 24 above you will notice that one of the examples that Christ used is the thief. The thief comes at midnight, because that's when you are fast asleep. When you read in your Bibles that Christ will come as a thief in the night, it simply means that He will come at a time when we least expect Him.

So it is wise to be flexible, but it is not the knowledge of the events and the signs that will be what will take you through. The question is, "When Christ comes, will you have oil in your lamp?" Let me put it in the words of Jesus Christ Himself. Turn to Luke 18:8. I am not saying this, Jesus is:

"I tell you, he will see that they get justice, and quickly. However, when the Son of Man comes, will he find faith on the earth?"

Will Christ find faith on earth? Can God produce a people who are willing to be patient?

The reason the delay has taken place from our human point of view is found in 2 Peter 3:9. Peter tells us that there has been a delay not because God is slack in keeping His promise; that is not the reason for the delay. The reason is:

The Lord is not slow in keeping his promise, as some understand slowness....

That's exactly what many of our people are saying today. In fact, I have had people say, "Why don't you preach the second coming more often?" When it comes, will you be ready? What I need to preach to you is justification by faith because that will make you ready for the second coming.

I want to add something here and don't misunderstand me. When we preach the second coming of Christ we are not preaching the gospel. We are preaching the hope of the gospel. We must make a distinction between the gospel which is good news to all people and the second coming of Christ, which is good news only to the believer. Do you know what the second coming is to the unbeliever? Read Revelation 6. It's the day of wrath. So how do we make the second coming good news? It is not by preaching the second coming but by preaching the gospel. Then to the believer we can say, "Your hope is in the second coming."

The message to the believer is, "Be patient. You have a hope but don't give up that hope." Here it is in 2 Peter 3:9:

The Lord is not slow in keeping his promise, as some understand slowness. He is patient with you, not wanting anyone to perish, but everyone to come to repentance.

That is why in Matthew 24:14, Jesus said:

And this gospel of the kingdom will be preached in the whole world as a testimony to all nations, and then the end will come

That is because God wants none to perish. Do you know He gave that job of preaching the gospel to us? So if anyone is to blame for the delay, it is us. Of course, God knows in His full knowledge the day He will come. But the question here is that when the sound is given, "He is coming," and it takes us off-guard, all of us, will you have oil in your lamp? Will Christ still be dwelling in you by faith? That's the big question.

We are told five of these virgins were foolish and five were wise. The word "foolish" here means "thoughtless" and the word "wise" here means "prudent" or "thoughtful." Young people, may I say this much: We are aware that there is going to be a delay, but what is the solution? Should we go into the world and enjoy ourselves until we think He is coming? The answer is, "No." I'll tell you why. It is possible for us as believers to pray for each other. It is possible for us to help each other. It is possible for us to sympathize with each other. It is possible for us to counsel each other. But there is one thing we cannot do. We cannot share with you our faith. You cannot transfer faith from one person to another. Everybody must have his own faith in Christ. You cannot transfer that.

That is the issue here. When these virgins woke up, the five foolish virgins discovered that their vessels were empty of the oil which is there by faith. They go to the five wise and the say, "Can you share with us some of your faith, some of that oil?" What is the answer? "I'm sorry, we cannot do that. You go and buy for yourselves." This brings us immediately to the last message and to the last generation of Christians, Revelation 3:18. Here Jesus, the True Witness, is saying that our works will not carry us through the crisis:

I counsel you to buy from me gold refined in the fire, so you can become rich; and white clothes to wear, so you can cover your shameful nakedness; and salve to put on your eyes, so you can see.

I would like to mention that the Roman Catholic scholars — not all of them, but many of them — identify the oil with the merits of the saints which they have obtained through their good works. That's unbiblical; that's a Roman Catholic point of view. The oil is not our merits; it is the Holy Spirit dwelling in our hearts by faith. Jesus is telling the last generation of Christians, the Laodicean church, "You think that you are rich and increased with goods but you do not know that you are empty. You are wretched, miserable, poor, blind, and naked. Therefore, my counsel to you is to buy gold tried in the fire." What is that gold tried in the fire? It is faith that has gone through the press and has come out refined. It is the faith of Jesus Christ. The rich robe is the righteousness of Christ, the white raiment.

In other words, when Christ comes to this earth, will He find a people whose faith is unshakable, whose faith has not disappeared? Because this is the issue. Jesus said in Matthew 10:22 that only those whose faith endures unto the end will be saved:

All men will hate you because of me, but he who stands firm to the end will be saved.

So I would like to remind you that one of the qualities that will be experienced by the last generation of Christians, the five wise virgins is this: "Here is the patience of the saints."

Yes, the delay is here because, to God, 150 years is nothing. To Him a thousand years is like a day, but to us human beings, 150 years is too long. But, young people, I plead with you, it doesn't matter how wrong we were in presenting that Christ's coming was soon because some of you don't believe that soon is soon. Remember, don't you ever give up your faith.

I want to close by giving you an example that took place in New Testament times. In Hebrews, Paul is writing to Jewish Christians. I want to use this text in Hebrews 10 to persuade you so that you will not make the same mistake as some have done. Paul describes this in Hebrews 10:25:

Let us not give up meeting together, as some are in the habit of doing, but let us encourage one another — and all the more as you see the Day approaching.

Don't stop coming to church because there is a delay, especially as we realize that the end is near. The tragedy is that 50 percent of the membership of our churches in our North American Division no longer attend church. There was an article in the Ministry magazine on the celebration churches, which are causing a tremendous stir. I have never been to one so I am not giving any judgment, but I have read articles on both sides. The article made a statement which, of course, gives us something to think about. At least one thing positive about the celebration churches is that a lot of backsliders are coming back. I'd rather see a backslider in a celebration church than not in church at all.

But it will take more than music to prepare our people for the crisis. We have to ground you in Christ. Now, look at Hebrews 10:35:

So do not throw away your confidence; it will be richly rewarded.

Notice the word "confidence" is synonymous with "faith." I will show it to you as we go along. Verse 36:

You need to persevere so that when you have done the will of God, you will receive what he has promised.

The Jewish Christians were becoming a little bit — to use the expression — "miffed" because they thought that Christ was delaying His coming. Paul is saying here, "You need to be patient." Verse 37:

For in just a very little while, "He who is coming will come and will not delay."

So they were saying the same thing that we are saying today. He is delaying His coming. But Paul is saying, "A very little while and He will come."

These words "little while" can mean two things. They can mean a "little while" from God's point of view, which I think is what he is saying, or, from man's point of view, the "little while" is too long. A "little while" means tomorrow. Verse 38:

"But my righteous one will live by faith. And if he shrinks back, I will not be pleased with him."

Here is a clear text that does not teach "once saved, always saved." If you draw back from your faith in Christ and in your hope in Him, God says, "I will not be pleased with you."

Then, in verse 39, he makes this prayer and I hope it is our prayer, too:

But we are not of those who shrink back and are destroyed [so it is possible to shrink back and be destroyed], but of those who believe and are saved.

Until Christ comes to fulfill that prayer, Paul spends a whole chapter in Hebrews 11 giving you incidents, historical accounts, of men and women who were burnt, fried, eaten by lions, and killed in all kinds of ways. But they had one thing in common. They had a faith that would not give up.

Then he ends Hebrews 11:39-40:

These were all commended for their faith, yet none of them received what had been promised. [They were waiting for the first coming of Christ and they died before He came.] God had planned something better for us so that only together with us would they be made perfect.

That means they would not see the coming of Christ except through the grave.

Having done this, he persuades his readers in Hebrews 12:1-2 by these words:

Therefore, since we are surrounded by such a great cloud of witnesses, let us throw off everything that hinders and the sin that so easily entangles...

Please read that text in its context. What is Paul saying here? Paul is saying, "Put aside any weight, any sin that is responsible for destroying your faith or that is pulling your faith away."

...And let us run with perseverance the race marked out for us...

What is the race?

...Let us fix our eyes on Jesus, the author and perfecter of our faith...

From beginning to end, He is my righteousness. He is the Author, the Finisher, and the Source of our salvation, of our faith.

...who for the joy set before him endured the cross, scorning its shame, and sat down at the right hand of the throne of God.

Paul is saying here that Jesus went through all this to make sure that you and I would be in heaven.

Please don't disappoint Him by throwing away your faith. Yes, He may have delayed His coming from our point of view, but I can guarantee you, He will come and He will have a people. Do you know what He will say about these people who are wise? "Here are they who have the patience of the saints and the faith of our Lord Jesus Christ" [Revelation 13:10b].

It is my prayer that no matter how discouraged you are and how tempted you are to stop going to church or to believe the message of our pioneers, you will never give up your faith in Christ. Because when you say good-bye to faith, you are saying good-bye to Christ. When you say good-bye to Christ, it doesn't matter whether your names are on the books or whether you have been a church officer in the past, you've had it.

There are some backsliders who, when we call upon them and say, "Would you like us to remove your name from the books?" say, "Please don't do that." They have the idea that, because their names are in the books, they have a ticket to heaven. I'm sorry, you may have it in gold letters in our books but that doesn't qualify you for heaven. The question is, "Will your faith endure unto the end?"

Will you, while you are sleeping — that's not physical sleeping but spiritual sleeping — turn your backs to the only hope, Jesus Christ? Will you say, "He has delayed His coming; I might as well enjoy myself and, when I get old like Pastor Sequeira or like some of these retirees, then I will join the church."

I am really happy to see so many young people in church. I appreciate the retirees; I feel they are doing a tremendous work, but I really appreciate the young people coming to church. I pray that you will never give up your faith in Christ, because that's your anchor. It is my prayer that everyone reading this will be among the five wise virgins and that, when Christ comes — even though we are caught off-guard — we will still have faith that will carry us through, is my prayer in Jesus' name. Amen.

CHAPTER FOURTEEN

The Parable of the Ten Talents

Matthew 25:14-30:

Again, it will be like a man going on a journey, who called his servants and entrusted his property to them. To one he gave five talents of money, to another two talents, and to another one talent, each according to his ability. Then he went on his journey. The man who had received the five talents went at once and put his money to work and gained five more. So also, the one with the two talents gained two more. But the man who had received the one talent went off, dug a hole in the ground and hid his master's money.

After a long time the master of those servants returned and settled accounts with them. The man who had received the five talents brought the other five. "Master," he said, "you entrusted me with five talents. See, I have gained five more."

His master replied, "Well done, good and faithful servant! You have been faithful with a few things; I will put you in charge of many things. Come and share your master's happiness!"

The man with the two talents also came. "Master," he said, "you entrusted me with two talents; see, I have gained two more."

His master replied, "Well done, good and faithful servant! You have been faithful with a few things; I will put you in charge of many things. Come and share your master's happiness!"

Then the man who had received the one talent came. "Master," he said, "I knew that you are a hard man, harvesting where you have not sown and gathering where you have not scattered seed. So I was afraid and went out and hid your talent in the ground. See, here is what belongs to you."

His master replied, "You wicked, lazy servant! So you knew that I harvest where I have not sown and gather where I have not scattered seed? Well then, you should have put my money on deposit with the bankers, so that when I returned I would have received it back with interest.

"Take the talent from him and give it to the one who has the ten talents. For everyone who has will be given more, and he will have an abundance. Whoever does not have, even what he has will be taken from him. And throw that worthless servant outside, into the darkness, where there will be weeping and gnashing of teeth."

This parable of the talents immediately follows the parable of the ten virgins and this is because the two parables complement each other and together they form a unit. The parable of the ten virgins dealt with the oil in the lamps, which represents the Holy Spirit dwelling in our hearts by faith. The parable of the talents represents working for Christ while we are waiting for the coming of the Lord. In other words, both parables are addressed to believers, to the disciples.

In the parable of the ten virgins, the bridesmaids, who represent the believers, are represented as waiting for the groom, who is Christ. In this parable of the talents, the servants or the slaves are working while they are waiting for the coming of their lord. Put together, we will discover that the best way to watch and wait and to be prepared for the coming of Christ is to be busy in the Master's business.

I am going to divide our study into two parts. First of all, we will analyze this parable and look at what its significance is as Christ presented it to His disciples. Then I would like to take the lessons we learn from this parable and apply it to our present situation. There are some very important areas that we need to cover. The parable of the talents may be divided into three scenes. The first scene is the distribution of the gifts. The second scene is the use made of the gifts. The third scene is the day of reckoning.

I would like to take each one of and look at them. Matthew 25:14-15 is dealing with the distribution of the gifts:

Again, it [the kingdom of heaven] will be like a man going on a journey, who called his servants and entrusted his property to them. To one he gave five talents of money, to another two talents, and to another one talent, each according to his ability. Then he went on his journey.

The first thing to do is explain a point that is clearly brought out in some versions of the Bible but is not quite clear in other translations. The word that Jesus used here is not "servants" but "slaves". There is a world of difference between the two. A slave is a person who has no rights, who has no freedom, who owns nothing at all. Even the shirt on his back is owned by his master.

I want you to keep this in mind because the Bible teaches us in 1 Peter 1:18-19 that we have been bought by Jesus Christ, not with silver and gold but by the precious blood of Christ:

For you know that it was not with perishable things such as silver or gold that you were redeemed from the empty way of life handed down to you from your forefathers, but with the precious blood of Christ, a lamb without blemish or defect.

In other words, the word "redeemed" is the word that was used in the days of Christ to buy a slave back and we have been bought. That is why you will notice when Paul writes his epistles that in some of them he introduces himself as "I, the apostle Paul, a slave of Jesus Christ." Keep that in mind because it has a very important concern as we look at this parable.

Look at verses 14 and 15, the distribution of the gift. The story is about a man who goes into a far country. Now obviously this man is Jesus Christ. He has redeemed us, He has bought us, we belong to Him, but now He leaves us and goes to a very far country which, of course, is heaven. But before he leaves, he does something. He calls his servants and delivers to them his goods, "entrusts his property to them"; that's in verse 14. Verse 15:

To one he gave five talents of money, to another two talents, and to another one talent, each according to his ability.

Notice why he gave them different talents. He gave the talent in proportion to how much he knew each servant was capable of using it.

Now we have already seen that the man going to a far country is Jesus Christ. What are the talents? First of all, the word "talent" was a weight measure used in the days of Christ for silver. One talent was approximately 75 pounds of silver and someone who knows a little bit more about economics than I do gave me the figures. He said that today one talent — 70 pounds — of silver would be worth $6,000. So five talents would be $30,000; two talents would be $12,000 and, of course, one talent would be $6,000. That is quite a sizable sum of money.

But, of course, that word "talent" is used only as a metaphor. The question is, "What do those talents represent?" Turn to Ephesians 4:7-8 where Paul gives us some insight as to what those talents could be. Here is what the apostle Paul says:

But to each one of us grace has been given as Christ apportioned it. This is why it says [now he is quoting from the Old Testament, Psalm 68:18]: "When he ascended on high, he led captives in his train and gave gifts [or we could use the word "talents"] to men."

Paul is saying here that every believer is given grace according to the measure of the gift of Christ.

Number one, the gifts represent the abilities that Christ gives us. These are not our abilities but they are His abilities that He gives us through the Holy Spirit. Remember, the Holy Spirit gives every believer a gift. Now I want you to notice in Matthew 25:14 that none are excluded. He gives every servant a gift. They are not all the same talents, they are all different, but everyone is given a gift. Likewise, every believer receives a spiritual gift of the Holy Spirit. Every one of us, without exception. Now if you want to add to that our natural talents, that's fine, although the talents here are those that belong to Jesus Christ. But you could add to this natural talents under the control of the Holy Spirit because natural talents can be used by the flesh. I mentioned an experience and I would like to repeat it because it brings it out very clearly. We had a young couple who came out to work as missionaries in Ethiopia. The wife was very kind, very generous by nature. There are human beings who are born that way. I had a friend in college who was an atheist. He was very generous by nature. He would give the shirt off his back; he would give his meals and everything to the poor. He was generous by nature and this sister was the same way.

It is one thing being generous and kind and soft-hearted in America where the poor are very limited and even they receive help and welfare from the government. But when she came to Ethiopia, the third poorest country in Africa, she didn't realize that her natural kindness would be a hindrance. Her friends in her local church told her she would make a wonderful missionary because she was so kind. But when she came to Ethiopia and the people — especially the young people — discovered her soft heart, they squeezed every ounce of kindness from her. She was absolutely appalled at the tremendous need that there was in that country and she gave everything she had until she could give no more. By the end of one year she was exhausted, her resources were depleted, and she was heading for a nervous breakdown. We had to ship them back home.

She called me up and she said, "You know, it's going to be very hard for me to go back." I asked, "Why?" She said, "I was coming here with great expectations from my fellow believers. They thought I would make a wonderful missionary. Now I'm going back as a failure." I said, "Sister, can I be very honest with you?" She said, "Yes." I said, "You came here with your natural kindness. God had to exhaust you. He could not do that in America. He brought you here to Ethiopia to exhaust you so that you may go back, not with your resources but with Christ's because Christ's resources never get exhausted."

Do you remember the five loaves and the three pieces of fish? How many did He feed? Five thousand. Do you remember in the story of Elijah the little bit of oil and the small amount of flour that the woman had? How long did it last under God's control? When God controls even your natural talents they will never get exhausted because God's resources are limitless. So the talents here represent the gifts of the Holy Spirit and it could include our natural talents used by the Holy Spirit.

But what I want you to notice in verse 15 is that each servant was given not the same amount but the amount each could handle. Likewise, God doesn't give us all the same gifts. I would like to emphasize there are no spectators in the Christian church. God never intended that there would be any spectators. This is not a football game where a few people are exhausting themselves trying to win the game while thousands watch and do nothing but simply shout and scream.

The second scene is the use made of these gifts. That is found in Matthew 25:16-18:

The man who had received the five talents went at once and put his money to work and gained five more. So also, the one with the two talents gained two more. But the man who had received the one talent went off, dug a hole in the ground and hid his master's money.

You will find in verses 16 and 17 that the first two slaves made good use of their talents: they doubled their amount and were able to give back twice what their master had given them before he left for this far country. But I would like you to look at the third man. First of all, I want you to notice that this third man did not hide his talent nor did he complain that the talent that the master gave him was too small. That was not the issue. He did not hide the talent because he could do nothing with it. Please notice you will not find that in the parable.

What is the issue? Look at verse 18:

But the man who had received the one talent went off, dug a hole in the ground and hid his master's money.

He doesn't tell us why in this verse. We have to go to the third scene, the reckoning, to find out why he hid the money. Let's look at the reason. Verse 25; listen to why he hid the money:

So I was afraid...

He was afraid of his master. Does that tell you anything? He had not understood his master. To him his master was not a loving, benevolent master. He was an exacting, demanding judge.

So I was afraid and went out and hid your talent in the ground. See, here is what belongs to you.

But I want you to look at the second reason why he hid the money and that is found in verse 24:

Then the man who had received the one talent came. "Master," he said, "I knew that you are a hard man, harvesting where you have not sown and gathering where you have not scattered seed."

Verse 25:

"So I was afraid...."

So he had a wrong picture of his master. To him his master was a demanding, exacting master and he was afraid of the man. The real reason he hid that one talent was not because it was not enough but because he did not appreciate his master.

There was a problem with this man and you will find that in verse 26 in the reply his lord gave him (two things):

His master replied, "You wicked [number one], lazy [number two] servant!"

This man was still in his sins. He had not accepted the gift of salvation which is in Christ. He was not only afraid of his master; he was afraid of work, too. (The word "slothful" in some versions means "lazy.") But of all the reasons, the worst of all is that he had failed to understand his master and this is what I would like to say a few words about.

As I read about this third man, I realize immediately that he was a legalist. A legalist always obeys God out fear of punishment or because he wants a reward, not out of love. In other words, legalism has never produced works that are genuine. This man was obviously a legalist. His relationship to God was not a relationship of gratitude and appreciation. He looked at God as a severe judge. The question is: Is this how you look at God, as somebody who is going to ask you some very pointed questions and if you fail the test in the investigative judgment He's going to zap you? Is this your idea of God?

I want you to look at the key word Jesus used in commending the first two servants, or slaves. He did not commend them because they had doubled the talents. That's not what he commended them for. He commended them for being "faithful" and for being "good." To both of the servants he said the same thing. Look at verse 23:

His master replied, "Well done, good and faithful servant! You have been faithful with a few things; I will put you in charge of many things. Come and share your master's happiness!"

He said the same thing about the other man. Now what is this all talking about?

Number one, the gift that God gives every believer is Jesus Christ [John 3:16]:

For God so loved the world that he gave his one and only Son, that whoever believes in him shall not perish but have eternal life.

This gift becomes a reality, a subjective experience, when by faith we experience the new birth. That is the oil. The Holy Spirit brings with Him the gift of salvation but with that gift is found also many other things — talents, abilities. The purpose of those abilities is that, while we are waiting for Christ to come back, we may fulfill His mission for us in the church and in the world. He told His disciples [Matthew 5:14]:

You are the light of the world.

The word "light" is in the singular; it represents Christ. "You" is in the plural; it represents us all, the servants of Jesus Christ.

Then in Matthew 5:16 He says:

In the same way, let your light shine before men, that they may see your good deeds and praise your Father in heaven.

What Christ is saying here is what Paul says also, which is that, for us to maintain the Holy Spirit, for us to maintain our hope in Christ, it is important that we make use of the talents, otherwise, we will lose them. In other words, the fundamental principle in this parable is that we lose what we fail to use. Now I want to give you some examples.

First of all turn to 1 Corinthians 15. I want to give you this as an example. I would like to look at verse 10 but we will read also verse 9 to get the context. This is Paul talking about himself and he makes this statement in verse 9:

For I am the least of the apostles and do not even deserve to be called an apostle, because I persecuted the church of God.

Paul had very low esteem about himself, as far as being a Christian. "But," he says in verse 10:

But by the grace of God I am what I am, and his grace to me was not without effect. No, I worked harder than all of them — yet not I, but the grace of God that was with me.

Now who was Paul and what did he mean "by the grace of God I am what I am"? Paul was recognized as the greatest apostle of the New Testament. But he said, "I am what I am by the grace of God."

...And his grace to me [the talent he received from God] was not without effect. No, I worked harder than all of them — yet not I, but the grace of God that was with me.

Paul used his talent; he was given the gift to take the gospel to the Gentile world and he fulfilled his mission. As he told Timothy [2 Timothy 4:7]:

I have fought the good fight, I have finished the race, I have kept the faith.

The two go together.

I would like to read two more texts both from the books of Timothy because Timothy was a young worker who needed some counsel and that counsel applies to us today. We read in 1 Timothy 4:14-16:

Do not neglect your gift [notice the counsel], which was given you through a prophetic message when the body of elders laid their hands on you. Be diligent in these matters; give yourself wholly to them, so that everyone may see your progress [make use of that talent]. Watch your life and doctrine closely. Persevere in them, because if you do, you will save both yourself and your hearers.

When you discover the truth; when you rejoice in Christ, please share Christ.

The second text is 2 Timothy 1:6-7:

For this reason I remind you to fan into flame the gift of God...

Notice in the previous passage he said, "Don't neglect it." In this passage from one of the last letters he wrote a few years later from prison, he says:

For this reason I remind you to fan into flame the gift of God, which is in you through the laying on of my hands. For God did not give us a spirit of timidity, but a spirit of power, of love and of self-discipline.

Now having said this, I want to take what Jesus is saying in this parable and apply it to our present situation. What is Jesus saying in this parable and the previous one? He is saying, number one, that our hope is in Christ. That's the gift. We receive this gift by faith when the Holy Spirit dwells in us. You want to maintain that, because the devil wants to destroy your faith and, by doing that, drive out the Holy Spirit, so we have to use the talents to God's use. Faith and works together make it possible for us to endure unto the end.

This immediately creates a problem in our midst. One of the greatest problems we have to face as a people is to understand the relationship of faith and works. It has always been a problem in our history. One Sabbath after I presented this study, I quoted a text from Revelation 12 where God says to the last generation of Christians, "Here are My people who have the patience of the saints and the faith of Jesus Christ." Revelation 13:10b:

This calls for patient endurance and faithfulness on the part of the saints.

This dear brother came up to me and said, "You missed — left out — one more statement in that text: 'and they are keeping the commandments.'" Revelation 12:17b:

...Those who obey God's commandments and hold to the testimony of Jesus.

I did not do that because I did not want you to know it. I did it deliberately because I was reserving for this study the explanation of the relationship of faith and works. It is a problem in our midst.

That is why I gave you two quotations. Now we will go to the Bible and lay the foundation from scripture. First of all, what is the relationship between salvation by faith and works? Let's look at two texts. The first one is in Ephesians 2:8-10. Here Paul explains to us in a beautiful, wonderfully clear way the relationship between salvation by faith and the works that Christians produce. Verse 8:

For it is by grace you have been saved, through faith — and this not from yourselves, it is the gift of God — ...

The word "it" refers to grace and not to the word faith. The Greek grammar points primarily to the word "grace." Grace is a gift. Now there are passages where faith is used in the sense of a gift but in this passage the word "it" refers to grace. Salvation is a gift of God.

Now look at verse 9:

...not by works, so that no one can boast.

Salvation is entirely a gift. I want to emphasize that our works do not contribute one iota towards that salvation. Now look at verse 10:

For we are God's workmanship, created in Christ Jesus to do good works, which God prepared in advance for us to do.

God did not save us in Christ only to go to heaven but we were created in Christ to do good works that we should now walk in them. The greatest evidence that we are justified by faith is our works. The works don't save us but they are the evidence. They are the talent put into use.

Let me give you another passage. I'm giving you only two but there are many others. Just before Hebrews and Philemon is the little book Titus. Turn to Titus 3:5:

...He saved us, not because of righteous things we had done, but because of his mercy. He saved us through the washing of rebirth and renewal by the Holy Spirit....

After telling us that we are all sinners, Paul tells Titus that, not because of works of righteousness, not because we have changed or tried to be good but because of His mercy He saved us and gave us the Holy Spirit. Notice that it is out of His love and His mercy that He saved us not because of any works of righteousness we have done. That is how we are saved.

But now look at Titus 3:8. What does verse 8 say to you?

This is a trustworthy saying. And I want you to stress these things, so that those who have trusted in God may be careful to devote themselves to doing what is good. These things are excellent and profitable for everyone.

Notice that genuine faith always produces works. That's what James meant when he said that faith without works is dead. James 2:26:

As the body without the spirit is dead, so faith without deeds is dead.

With this in mind let me give you the picture. I want to turn now to three other texts to get the picture of what happened. The first passage is from Jesus Christ. In John 14:8 we have Philip coming to Jesus. Philip was one of the disciples and he said to Jesus:

Philip said, "Lord, show us the Father and that will be enough for us."

In other words, "We want to see God. We have seen you, Jesus, but we want to see Your Father, who is God." Philip was given this answer [John 14:9-10]:

Jesus answered: "Don't you know me, Philip, even after I have been among you such a long time? Anyone who has seen me has seen the Father. How can you say, 'Show us the Father'? Don't you believe that I am in the Father, and that the Father is in me? The words I say to you are not just my own. Rather, it is the Father, living in me, who is doing his work.

One of the missions that Christ came to this world for besides saving us was to reveal His Father to the world. That is the same desire God has for you. He doesn't only want to save you but He wants to reveal Himself through you because the New Covenant says, "I will dwell in you and I will walk in you." Then Jesus said to Philip, "If you don't believe My words, believe My works, because the works I do; it is not I but it is God who dwells in Me." John 14:11:

Believe me when I say that I am in the Father and the Father is in me; or at least believe on the evidence of the miracles themselves.

In John 14:12 it says:

I tell you the truth, anyone who has faith in me will do what I have been doing. He will do even greater things than these, because I am going to the Father.

Now what has Christ going to the Father have to do with us doing great works? The answer is found in John 16:7 where Jesus told the disciples, "It is necessary that I go to the Father because if I don't go to the Father I cannot send you the Holy Spirit":

But I tell you the truth: It is for your good that I am going away. Unless I go away, the Counselor will not come to you; but if I go, I will send him to you.

In other words, Christ could not dwell in the believers Himself because He took flesh but He was going to send His Spirit which represented Him. The Spirit would dwell in you and because the Spirit dwells in you, you will do great works.

What kind of works will you do? That takes us to the next two texts. Acts 1:8. Jesus tells His disciples:

But you will receive power when the Holy Spirit comes on you; and you will be my witnesses in Jerusalem, and in all Judea and Samaria, and to the ends of the earth.

Don't depend on yourself for witnessing. Or don't say, "I am not capable of witnessing." The work of witnessing is the work of the Holy Spirit through you.

The next text is 2 Corinthians 3:17-18:

Now the Lord is the Spirit, and where the Spirit of the Lord is, there is freedom. And we, who with unveiled faces all reflect the Lord's glory, are being transformed into his likeness with ever-increasing glory, which comes from the Lord, who is the Spirit.

Besides using you to witness Christ, the Holy Spirit does something else. Verse 17 says that, because we have the Spirit of the

Lord, we are free from the problem of self. Verse 18 says that, as we behold the Lord; as we look in the mirror, we become changed from glory to glory even as by the Spirit of the Lord. That Sprit transforms our image to look like the image of Christ.

Having said all this, I still haven't dealt with the problem. After this dear brother came to me and said, "You have left out 'keeping the commandments,'" he gave me a quotation and for your benefit I am including this quotation. This quotation has been bombarded at me many times and everyone who has given me this quotation has taken it out of context. It is found in Welfare Ministry, page 316. This quotation was given in the context of sanctification, not justification by faith. Because we have problems between the relationship of faith and works, we are a confused people.

There are too many Adventists who are standing on the platform that we are saved by faith plus works. That is why I plead with you to study carefully the book of Galatians. We are not saved by faith plus works. That is Galatianism. We are saved by faith that works. I want to read a quotation which shows the balance of Ellen G. White. But before I read to you, let me give you some of the background of this quotation. This quotation is taken from Manuscript #36. I first read this Manuscript, the whole of it, in 1970 at Andrews University when I was studying there. It was in the vault of the E.G. White Estate at Andrews University.

I was so excited because it clarified many problems in my mind that I had but I was very saddened when I was told that I could not share this Manuscript with anybody. Why? Because it is not released. Why was it not released? I have no answer. But five or six years later it was released under Manuscript #371. It was first published in the Review and Herald in March of 1977. Now you can find it in the book Faith and Works, chapter one. Before I read you this quotation I would like to read you the second paragraph in this whole Manuscript but before I do that I want to give you the background of this Manuscript.

This was a talk that Ellen G. White gave to the ministers at Battle Creek [Michigan, U.S.A.] because of the opposition to the message of righteousness by faith given two years before. This talk was given to the ministers over a hundred years ago in 1890. She was pleading with them. "Please study the Bible and see for yourselves that this message is of God." Let me read you the second paragraph because you need to keep this in mind. The "me" refers to Ellen G. White; the One who is presenting the danger is God. Here is the statement.

"The danger has been presented to me again and again [not once, not twice, but many times; what was God presenting to her? What was the danger?] of entertaining, as a people [not the Baptist church, not the Pentecostals but the Adventist church — she is referring to us; she is talking to Adventist ministers], false ideas of justification by faith. I have been shown for years that Satan would work in a special manner to confuse the mind on this point. [I will say 100 years later we are still in the same situation because Satan has worked in a special manner to confuse God's people on this point.] The law of God has been largely dwelt upon and has been presented to congregations almost as destitute of the knowledge of Jesus Christ and His relation to the law as was the offering of Cain."

Yes, Cain did offer a sacrifice but he was offering it as a means of salvation. Abel offered his sacrifice as a confession of faith in the promise of Christ. Two different motivations. They both offered sacrifices. Now let's go on.

"I have been shown that many have been kept from the faith because of the mixed, confused ideas of salvation, because the ministers have worked in a wrong manner to reach hearts [in other words, win souls]. The point that has been urged upon my mind for years [this is the reason why I am emphasizing it] is the imputed righteousness of Christ [not the imparted, the imputed]. I have wondered that this matter was not made the subject of discourses in our churches throughout the land [the word "land" refers to the North American Division], when the matter has been kept so constantly urged upon me, and I have made it the subject of nearly every discourse and talk that I have given to the people."

With this in mind, let us read this quotation because here is where the confusion is.

Salvation as a Free Gift [This is justification by faith]

"There is not a point that needs to be dwelt upon more earnestly, repeated more frequently [so here is the reason for repeating it more frequently], or established more firmly in the minds of all than the impossibility of fallen man meriting anything by his own best good works. Salvation is through faith in Jesus Christ alone....

"Let the subject be made distinct and plain that it is not possible to effect anything in our standing before God or in the gift of God to us through creature merit. Should faith and works purchase the gift of salvation for anyone, then the Creator is under obligation to the creature. Here is an opportunity for falsehood to be accepted as truth [and that's exactly what we are facing today]. If any man can merit salvation by anything he may do, then he is in the same position as the Catholic to do penance for his sins. Salvation, then, is partly of debt, that may be earned as wages. If man cannot, by any of his good works, merit salvation, then it must be wholly of grace, received by man as a sinner because he receives and believes in Jesus. It is wholly a free gift. Justification by faith is placed beyond controversy. And all this controversy is ended, as soon as the matter is settled that the merits of fallen man in his good works can never procure eternal life for him. The light given me of God places this important subject above any question in my mind. Justification is wholly of grace and not procured by any works that fallen man can do."

Have you got it? I am not saying this; Ellen G. White is saying it. But the trouble is we take the second statement and put it in the camp of the first statement.

The second statement is applied to the believers who are justified by faith and who have received the gift of the Holy Spirit. To them she says,

"If we are faithful in doing our part [not to be saved but as believers saved in Christ] in cooperating with Him, God will work through us to do the good pleasure of His will. But God cannot work through us if we make no effort. If we gain eternal life, we must work, and work earnestly. If we lack in spiritual strength, we may know that we have failed of doing our part. Just as soon as the plan of salvation was devised, Satan began to work; and if we hope to stand against him, we, too, must work. We must follow the example Christ has left us, submitting to Him in everything. Our will must be in harmony with His will.

"Other foundation can no man lay than that is laid, which is Jesus Christ.

"Are we placing the right kind of material upon the right foundation? If we lay upon the foundation wood, hay, stubble, sad indeed will be the result! Will that which we are bringing to the foundation endure the fire of the great day of God? Are we using our talents in the Master's service? Are we kind and courteous to all around us? Do we cherish in our hearts, reveal in our lives, the principles of truth?

"The characters we form here will decide our eternal destiny. What kind of material are we using in our character building? We must guard well every point, seeking to gain that purity which will make our lives harmonize with the saving truth we profess to believe. Our part is to put away sin, to seek with determination for perfection of character. As we thus work, God cooperates with us, fitting us for a place in His kingdom.

"If we constantly receive grace from God, we shall be vessels unto honor, sanctified and meet for the Master's use. Daily receiving blessings, we shall daily impart blessings to those around us. But in order to be successful in this work, we must deny self. We cannot at the same time please self and serve Christ. We are not to follow our own inclinations, but look to Jesus, waiting to receive orders from our Captain.

"Our one desire should be to do God's will in a way that He will approve. All our blessings come from Him, and He desires us in return to give Him our glad and willing service. Are we doing this? Are we receiving and imparting His grace? Are we standing under His banner as faithful sentinels? Are we learning precious lessons, that we may teach others? Let us not rob God. All our money belongs to God, and He calls upon us to acknowledge this by paying a faithful tithe and giving willing offerings. The children of Israel were taught that their possessions came from God, and that by the paying of tithe and freewill offerings they were to acknowledge this. Thus we, too, may acknowledge whence our blessings flow. By giving of our means to save those for whom Christ died, we may show our appreciation of His goodness.

"Is it possible that we are robbing God? If so, His blessing cannot rest upon us. This may be the reason why there is not more of the power of God with us. Let each one examine himself, and see whether he is obeying the directions God has given. Remove from your lives everything which separates you from God. Serve Him to the very best of your ability. Show your faith by your works. Cling with living faith to Jesus. Come up to the help of the Lord. Labor earnestly for the Savior. Then the rich blessing of God will be your portion.

"The doing of God's will is essential if we would have an increased knowledge of Him. Let us not be deceived by the oft-repeated assertion, 'All you have to do is to believe.' Faith and works are two oars which we must use equally if we press our way up the stream against the current of unbelief. 'Faith, if it hath not works, is dead, being alone.' The Christian is a man of thought and practice. His faith fixes its roots firmly in Christ. By faith and good works he keeps his spirituality strong and healthy, and his spiritual strength increases as he strives to work the works of God."

— Review and Herald, June 11, 1901

CHAPTER FIFTEEN

THE PARABLE OF THE EMBARRASSED HOST

Luke 11:5-10:

Then he said to them, "Suppose one of you has a friend, and he goes to him at midnight and says, 'Friend, lend me three loaves of bread, because a friend of mine on a journey has come to me, and I have nothing to set before him.'

"Then the one inside answers, 'Don't bother me. The door is already locked, and my children are with me in bed. I can't get up and give you anything.' I tell you, though he will not get up and give him the bread because he is his friend, yet because of the man's boldness he will get up and give him as much as he needs.

"So I say to you: Ask and it will be given to you; seek and you will find; knock and the door will be opened to you. For everyone who asks receives; he who seeks finds; and to him who knocks, the door will be opened."

One of the joys of attending a General Conference session [of the Seventh-day Adventist Church] is that you meet friends, friends that you may not have seen for years. At one General Conference I came across one of my old, old friends that I had when we were together at Newbold [College in England]. He is now the pastor of the Istanbul church in Turkey. The moment I saw him I immediately remembered him for a very special incident.

During our third year the college built a new dormitory for the boys and the girl's club wanted to donate a special gift in remembrance of the opening ceremony for this special occasion. They asked me to design a flowerpot for the main living room. This man from Turkey was a carpenter so they asked him to construct it. The college loaned me its van and I took this man to the lumber yard to buy the lumber for this ornate flowerpot.

We arrived at the lumber yard and he chose the wood. He decided how much he wanted and the salesman, after he had calculated the price, said to him, "That will be six Pounds." (Pounds is an English currency). This Turkish man from the Middle East said, "I will give you four Pounds." This Englishman didn't know what this man was up to and so he said, "I don't think you understood me correctly. I said six Pounds." This Turkish man said, "Yes, I know, but I will give you four Pounds." So I spoke to him and used a few of my Arabic words and I said to him, "In England, we do not bargain."

He totally ignored my statement and he kept on bargaining. This poor Englishman explained to him that in England they sell wood by the foot and that he had bought so many feet at so much per foot and it comes to six Pounds. He said, "If you don't have that much money I would be happy to remove some of the wood so that you could buy four Pounds worth." He said, "No. That's not the issue. I want all this wood but I will give you four Pounds."

I felt like crawling under the table but this Turkish man insisted and this poor Englishman was getting frustrated. He said, "I can't reduce the price because I am simply working here. I am the foreman. The company sets the price." He was trying to explain to him and after he explained to him at great length that he could not reduce the price, this man said, "I appreciate all the explanation but I will still give you four Pounds." I tried to kick him under the table. I said, "Let's go. Give him the six Pounds." We had the money but he wouldn't. He ignored me; he insisted. Finally the Englishman said,

"Take it for four Pounds." As we left he said, "You see, it even works in England."

This parable is very strongly flavored with Middle Eastern culture. Let me give you the background if you have never lived there. Number one, in the Middle East you never telephoned or told people that you were coming to visit. You just arrived at their home and it was against their culture to say, "No." You always had to take them in. No matter how crowded you were or how little you had, you had to take them in and provide them with food and shelter. It was a part of their culture.

In this parable, a man arrives at midnight and he simply says, "Here I am." Of course, this poor fellow had no choice but to let him in. The next thing that you must be aware of is that the women get up very early in the morning and cook the bread. Now their bread is very much like the bread we have here called pocket bread or pita bread. That's the typical bread and she will bake enough bread for the family for that one day.

The average man ate about three loaves a day. The standard procedure was three pita bread for the male, two for the female, and one or two for the children depending on how old they were. Since this was a male visitor, they required at least three loaves and, remember, the request was for three loaves of bread.

Now comes the next problem and this is pretty hard. The peasant Jewish farmer lived in a one-room apartment. That one room was his bedroom, his living room, his kitchen, his everything. But that room was on a split level. Two-thirds of the room was on what they called the ground floor — we would probably call it the first floor — then the other part, the one-third, was on a platform. On the platform was a mat and the whole family slept on that one mat.

When a Jewish family woke up, they would open the door to let in the sunshine and the air because you can imagine that the air must be stuffy. Not only did the family sleep on the platform but they allowed all their livestock to sleep in the lower two-thirds because of stealing. Then there was another problem. I don't know where this came from. The Jews believed in the days of Christ that when the Jewish people reached a certain population, a certain figure, then the Messiah would come. Of course, they were like good Adventists; they wanted to hasten the coming of the Lord. To us, the message must go all around the world; to them, they must have as many children as possible. So the Jewish family was quite large in the days of Jesus Christ primarily so that the Messiah would come soon.

So here you have this man and his wife with a whole lot of children — we don't know how many — sleeping on this one mat, all squashed together. When they woke up, they opened the door, as I mentioned. That door was left open all day long; they never shut it even if they went to the market or they left the house. It was part of their culture that they never stepped in to steal because their neighbors who lived close by watched each other's homes. But when night came and that door was shut and bolted, it meant that everybody had gone to bed. This is the situation.

Jesus takes this typical Middle East incident and He uses it to bring out more than one very important lesson to the disciples. To understand what He is trying to get across, we first have to begin with the context, so please turn to Luke 11:1:

One day Jesus was praying in a certain place. When he finished, one of his disciples said to him, "Lord, teach us to pray, just as John taught his disciples."

The first thing you must take note of is that when Jesus prayed, His prayer was very different from the typical Jewish prayer. The Jews used formal prayers; they had certain words that they would use. Jesus prayed to God as if He was His loving benevolent Father. He prayed crying out His needs and they had never seen anyone pray in this method or form. So one of the disciples said, "Lord, teach us how to pray" and you will notice in verses 2-4 Jesus introduces to them the Lord's prayer:

He said to them, "When you pray, say: 'Father, hallowed be your name, your kingdom come. Give us each day our daily bread. Forgive us our sins, for we also forgive everyone who sins against us. And lead us not into temptation.'"

This was very unique to them because Jesus said, "When you pray, don't address your God with fear." The Jews were very afraid to use the name of God. They were afraid of God but here Jesus tells His disciples, "You address God as 'our Father.' Empty your hearts to Him. Tell Him all your needs. Ask Him for your daily bread. Ask Him for forgiveness of all your sins because He is a God that is concerned about you." Then after introducing them to the Lord's prayer, he gives this parable. The application is in Luke 11:9-13.

First we will look at what He was trying to teach through this parable. Now the parable begins:

Then he said to them, "Suppose one of you has a friend...."

When you look at this statement in the original, it is very interesting. Jesus put it this way, "How many of you would think of pushing your friend away?" He knew that in their culture they would never do this. He is saying, "It is unthinkable when somebody comes to visit you that you would push him away. But instead, if you have no bread, you will go to your friend and ask him for some help."

This is the case we find here.

Then he said to them, "Suppose one of you has a friend, and he goes to him at midnight and says, 'Friend, lend me three loaves of bread, because a friend of mine on a journey has come to me, and I have nothing to set before him.'"

This man arrives at midnight; the host has nothing in the cupboard, which is a little box with a kind of a mosquito net thing made of linen cloth to keep the flies away. He had no bread; they had all eaten the bread. He knows that his friend next door has some bread because they get together in the evening and they gossip and one wife will say, "You know, I have some bread left." So, obviously, he knew that this man — his neighbor — had some bread. So he goes to him at midnight and he pleads with him, "Please, friend, I have a man who has come on a long journey. I have nothing to feed him." You see, it is very impolite to let your visitor go to bed without any food — with an empty stomach — so he's pleading for some bread.

Verse 7 says:

"Then the one inside answers, 'Don't bother me. The door is already locked, and my children are with me in bed [which means I have gone to bed with my family]. I can't get up and give you anything.'"

But verse 8 goes on to say:

"I tell you, though he will not get up and give him the bread because he is his friend, yet because of the man's boldness he will get up and give him as much as he needs."

The "boldness" ("importunity," an old English word, in the King James Version) in the original language means "shameless persistence." When I read the word it reminds me of this Turkish brother. He was "shamelessly persisting" to buy that wood for four Pounds. He would not take "no" for an answer and I was very ashamed. I felt like crawling under the table because I knew in England you don't bargain.

But here was this man who shamelessly persisted. "I will not stop knocking on your door until you give me the bread." The man did not give him the bread even though he was his friend but he finally gave it to him because he was shamelessly persistent. Now this is the situation. Jesus is trying to teach three things. First, our prayers must be earnest. Please remember the context. Jesus is using this parable in the context of praying to God. Jesus says our prayers must be earnest. They must come from desperate needs.

The trouble is we are living in a materialistic world. We don't see our needs but we must constantly remind ourselves what Jesus said in Matthew 5:3 in the Sermon on the Mount:

Blessed are the poor in spirit, for theirs is the kingdom of heaven.

No matter how rich we are, no matter how educated we are, we must constantly remember that, spiritually, we are bankrupt. When we come to God, we must remember that we must come to Him in earnestness. We must pray to Him as one who earnestly seeks His help.

In John 5:30, Jesus, who identified Himself with us, said,

By myself I can do nothing....

In John 6:57 He says,

...I live because of the Father....

In other words, Jesus had learned that He could do nothing, as a man, without His Father. And that is why you will notice He prayed earnestly not only in Gethsemane but all His life. Sometimes He would spend all night long praying earnestly because He recognized that He could not fulfill His mission apart from the grace of God. Jesus tells us in John 15:4-5:

Remain in me, and I will remain in you. No branch can bear fruit by itself; it must remain in the vine. Neither can you bear fruit unless you remain in me. I am the vine; you are the branches. If a man remains in me and I in him, he will bear much fruit; apart from me you can do nothing.

"Without me you can do nothing." And when we come to God we must come earnestly as this young man came to this friend of his. He was not willing to take "no" for an answer. He came earnestly.

Second, from this parable Christ tells us that we must also be persistent in our prayers. This man was persistent. This is typical in Middle East culture. They bargain and they bargain and they bargain until they get what they want and this Turkish man paid four Pounds for wood that was worth six Pounds. Unfortunately, they sometimes project this also on tithe paying. They will say, "God, I thank You that You are such a wonderful, loving God but I am a poor fellow. I have ten children that you have blessed me with." They always blame God for their large families! "And Lord, I don't earn such great money like these foreigners" (meaning Americans). "Can You please forgive me if I don't pay ten percent? Here is fifty cents." They'll give a fraction of their income and say, "Thank you God for still giving me the ticket to heaven."

But Jesus is saying that our prayers must be persistent because our faith must be unshakable. The man did not take "no" for an answer. He knew that even though his friend may not give him bread out of kindness, he would give it to him because of persistence. Now God is not holding back because He wants to hold back but because He wants to develop in each one of us a faith that is unshakable.

I want to give you an example of this. Turn to Matthew 15. Jesus was trying to teach this to His disciples. It is very interesting that Jesus could not find anyone in Israel who had faith that was great and persistent. So what did He do? In Matthew 15 Jesus was preaching by the Sea of Galilee at Capernaum and it tells us that a large crowd was drawn towards Him. They were listening to Him and He was having tremendous success. Then suddenly He tells the disciples, "Let's leave this place and go to Tyre and Sidon." Matthew 15:21:

Leaving that place, Jesus withdrew to the region of Tyre and Sidon.

From Capernaum to Tyre and Sidon is approximately sixty miles. There was no way they could travel by cart or by horseback because they were poor; they belonged to the poorer class. They walked, probably three to four days. They walked sixty miles, Jesus performed only one miracle — that's all — and then they walked back another sixty miles. One hundred and twenty miles just for one lesson. But it was a very important lesson.

Here is the lesson. Matthew 15:22:

A Canaanite woman from that vicinity [a Gentile, a person whom the Jews looked upon as a dog] came to him, crying out, "Lord, Son of David, have mercy on me! My daughter is suffering terribly from demon-possession."

Here is a woman who comes and prays to Jesus, calls Him the Messiah (because the term "Son of David" is a Messianic term), and she says, "Please, I have a daughter who is devil-possessed. I know; I have heard about You; I know You can heal; I believe it. Will you please answer my prayer?"

Listen to what Jesus did. It sounds horrible but He did it for a purpose. Look at verse 23:

Jesus did not answer a word....

He ignored her just like that Turkish man ignored me. I pleaded; I did my best to stop that bargaining; he just ignored me and here was Jesus ignoring this woman. In their culture, when somebody great like Jesus, somebody who is a rabbi, is ignoring someone, then the person will go through his friends or through his disciples. So, obviously, this woman went to the disciples and said, "Please, can you please convince your Master to heal my daughter?"

But the disciples were still victims of Judaism. Here's the rest of verse 23:

...So his disciples came to him and urged him [not to help her, but to], "Send her away, for she keeps crying out after us."

"Please get rid of her; she's a nuisance. She's bothering us." And to make matters worse, Jesus listens to the disciples. Look at verse 24:

He answered, "I was sent only to the lost sheep of Israel."

This was the typical mentality of the disciples, who were still victims to Judaism. In other words, what He was saying to her was: "I am sent to help the Jews not you Gentiles, so I am sorry, I cannot answer your prayers."

Now I don't know what you would have done if you were in her shoes, but I know what she did. Look at verse 25:

The woman came and knelt before him. "Lord, help me!" she said.

Can you imagine? He ignores her, He tells her, "I'm sorry, you don't belong to our group. You're not a Seventh-day Adventist. I can't help you." He ignores her; He listens to His disciples and, instead of getting angry, she comes and kneels before — worships — Him. And she says, "Lord, help me." In other words, "I am not letting You go. You can do what You like but I am not letting You go. I know that You are the only One that can answer (fulfill) my request."

Now He adds insult to injury. Verse 26:

He replied, "It is not right to take the children's bread [that is, that which belongs to the Jews] and toss it to their dogs."

You know, I have seen people leave this [Seventh-day Adventist] church for less reason than this — much less — and that's an evidence of weak faith. But here was a woman who was ignored, who was asked to leave, who was given no promise of help, and now who is insulted.

Listen to how she responds, verse 27-28:

"Yes, Lord," she said, "but even the dogs eat the crumbs that fall from their masters' table." Then Jesus answered, "Woman, you have great faith! Your request is granted." And her daughter was healed from that very hour.

Why did Jesus put her through this terrible experience? For the sake of the disciples. He wanted to show them what it means to have faith that is unshakable, a faith that is persistent and this is exactly what He is teaching in the parable that we are looking at. After the healing, we are told in verse 29:

Jesus left there and went along the Sea of Galilee....

He traveled one hundred and twenty miles to demonstrate to His disciples what it means to have a faith that endures to the end.

Going back to the parable, we have a similar incident with this man. He would not take "no" for an answer. Just like this Turkish man, we were there for almost an hour and the longer he argued with him the smaller I felt. But he was right. He won in the end and he said, in no uncertain terms, "You see, it works." I told his wife. He was not married at that time but years later I met his wife at the General Conference and I said, "Sister, if you see me without any hair on my head it is because of your husband." She said, "What happened?" I had to tell her and she said to me, "He doesn't do it any more. He has lived in the West too long."

Here is a man who was persistent and Jesus says that your prayers must not only be earnest but they must be persistent. With this in mind, turn to James, where he gives us the same counsel in the context of endurance. Let's read the counsel first. James 1:2-4:

Consider it pure joy, my brothers, whenever you face trials of many kinds, because you know that the testing of your faith develops perseverance. Perseverance must finish its work so that you may be mature and complete, not lacking anything.

It is in this context we have the same Greek word, which means "perseverance," or "patient endurance," in the Three Angels' Message of Revelation 14:12:

This calls for patient endurance on the part of the saints who obey God's commandments and remain faithful to Jesus.

Here are people who will endure unto the end, who will not let go of God even though they may feel forsaken; they may feel insulted.

Then in James 1, verse 5 and 6:

If any of you lacks wisdom, he should ask God, who gives generously to all without finding fault, and it will be given to him. But when he asks, he must believe and not doubt, because he who doubts is like a wave of the sea, blown and tossed by the wind.

That is why I spend so much time trying to establish you in the love of God.

Human love is fluctuating. God's love never fluctuates. He loves us with an everlasting love. Therefore, when you pray, pray persistently — not because He wants to hold back blessings from you but He wants you to develop a faith that is unshakable. We are told that after 25 years of waiting, Abraham, against all hope, believed that God still would keep His promise and give him a son. That is what Jesus is saying.

The third thing that I would like to bring to your attention through this parable is that true godly praying is not only asking God for a blessing but that that blessing may be shared with others. Notice this man who persistently, shamelessly asked for that bread did not do it because his stomach was empty but because he did not want his guest to go to bed empty-handed. We must ask God to bless us so that we may be a blessing to others.

In the same book of James, I read these words, in James 4:3:

When you ask, you do not receive, because you ask with wrong motives, that you may spend what you get on your pleasures.

In other words, you ask for your own personal blessing but here is a man who was earnest, he was persistent. He insisted on a blessing not because he wanted something for himself but for his friend who had come from a long journey.

With this in mind, let's go now to the application. You will notice that the application is in harmony with what we have just studied. Luke 11:9. After giving the parable He says:

"So I say to you: Ask and it will be given to you; seek and you will find; knock and the door will be opened to you."

Number one, this man asked. Number two, he asked persistently, and that's what the word "seek" means. He kept knocking until the door opened. What Jesus is doing here is presenting God in contrast to man. If man, who can't be bothered in the night, if man who in the beginning says "no" is able to give good things, how much more is God willing to give us? That's what Jesus ends up with. Verse 10:

"For everyone who asks receives; he who seeks finds; and to him who knocks, the door will be opened."

Now look at the illustration as He goes on. Verses 11-12:

"Which of you fathers, if your son asks for a fish, will give him a snake instead? Or if he asks for an egg, will give him a scorpion?"

These are unthinkable things, says Jesus. Verse 13:

"If you then, though you are evil, know how to give good gifts to your children, how much more will your Father in heaven give the Holy Spirit to those who ask him!"

Notice our prayers must not be for our selfish gratification. We must plead for the Holy Spirit that we may be a blessing to others.

When I take this parable and apply it to the application, number one, I discover especially from John 6:51 that Jesus is the bread of life:

"I am the living bread that came down from heaven. If anyone eats of this bread, he will live forever. This bread is my flesh, which I will give for the life of the world."

That's the kind of bread we should pray for. Number two, that bread becomes mine through the gift of the Holy Spirit. He brings Christ into me, not that I may be full but that I may feed others. We receive Christ that we may share Him with others.

That is why God will bless us if we are earnest; if we are persistent and, of course, for the sake of others, God will bless us that we might be a blessing to others. Here in this parable, Jesus says to, number one, pray to God as if He is your benevolent Father. Number two, pray earnestly, because God doesn't look at your words; He listens to your heart. That's why, in Romans 8:26, Paul says we do not know what to pray for but the Holy Spirit makes our prayers meaningful:

In the same way, the Spirit helps us in our weakness. We do not know what we ought to pray for, but the Spirit himself intercedes for us with groans that words cannot express.

Number three, we must pray persistently, not because God is slow in blessing us but because He wants us to develop our faith so that it is unshakable. And finally, let us pray that we might be a blessing to others. I want this church to be a blessing to others so that we may all grow and reflect Christ and so that our prayers will be a blessing to those around us. May God bless us.

CHAPTER SIXTEEN

THE PARABLE OF THE TWO SONS

Matthew 21:28-32:

"What do you think? There was a man who had two sons. He went to the first and said, 'Son, go and work today in the vineyard.'

"'I will not,' he answered, but later he changed his mind and went.

"Then the father went to the other son and said the same thing. He answered, 'I will, sir,' but he did not go.

"Which of the two did what his father wanted?"

"The first," they answered.

Jesus said to them, "I tell you the truth, the tax collectors and the prostitutes are entering the kingdom of God ahead of you. For John came to you to show you the way of righteousness, and you did not believe him, but the tax collectors and the prostitutes did. And even after you saw this, you did not repent and believe him."

This scripture was spoken by our Lord Jesus during what is known as the Passion week, that is, the last week that Jesus was here just before He was crucified. The day before He had just cleansed the temple. Remember, He took those cords and drove out the moneychangers. This took place the day after.

The chief priests, the elders, the leaders of that temple followed Him and questioned Him regarding His authority and I want you to look at the dialogue that took place because it is in this context that Jesus gave this parable. It is important that we understand the context. So let's look at Matthew 21:23-27. Remember, this is the next day after Jesus had cleansed the temple. In verse 23 we read,

Jesus entered the temple courts, and, while he was teaching, the chief priests and the elders of the people came to him. "By what authority are you doing these things?" they asked. "And who gave you this authority?"

Who gave you the right to do what you did? Who gave you this authority? That's the question they asked.

Jesus could have said, "I have this authority from My Father," but He didn't do that. This was the last week of His earthly ministry. He wanted the leaders of the Jewish church to get one more chance. So He turns to them (verse 24):

Jesus replied, "I will also ask you one question. If you answer me, I will tell you by what authority I am doing these things."

Notice the approach. Now here's the question Jesus posed to the leaders of the church. Verse 25a:

"John's baptism — where did it come from? Was it from heaven, or from men?"

John's baptism was a baptism of repentance. In Acts 19, Paul asked a group of believers if they had received the Holy Spirit. Acts 19:1b-4:

...There he found some disciples and asked them, "Did you receive the Holy Spirit when you believed?"

They answered, "No, we have not even heard that there is a Holy Spirit."

So Paul asked, "Then what baptism did you receive?"

"John's baptism," they replied.

Paul said, "John's baptism was a baptism of reprentance. He told the people to believe in the one coming after him, that is, in Jesus."

Jesus is asking the question, "Did John the Baptist baptize from the authority of God or was he baptizing on the basis of human authority? Was he a self-appointed prophet or was he a prophet of God?" That was basically the question. Verse 25b:

They discussed it among themselves and said, "If we say, 'From heaven,' he will ask, 'Then why didn't you believe him?'"

He put them in a corner. If they admit that John was a prophet of God, they should have believed him. What did John the Baptist come to preach? That Jesus was the Messiah. So they had a problem here.

But they had another problem. Verse 26:

"But if we say, 'From men' — we are afraid of the people, for they all hold that John was a prophet."

So whichever direction they go they are facing a problem unless, of course, they had repented and accepted Christ. Then they would have no problem, but as long as they rejected Christ, they would have a problem saying whether He was of God or whether He was of men. So how did they respond? Verse 27:

So they answered Jesus, "We don't know." [Or, to be more literal to the text, "We will not tell you." They refused to answer.]

Then he said, "Neither will I tell you by what authority I am doing these things."

It is in this context Jesus now turns to these leaders in Judaism and He says to them, "What do you think? I want you to tell me your opinion regarding this parable." He is addressing this parable to the elders and the chief priests of the temple. He's telling them that they have two sons. Now the parable is of a father who asked both his sons to go into his vineyard and do some work today. Now it is very clear that the father represents God, but who is the first son?

The first son is the one who said, "I will not go and work" but later repented and went and worked. If you look at the second part of verse 31, Jesus tells us who that first son was:

Jesus said to them, "I tell you the truth, the tax collectors and the prostitutes are entering the kingdom of God ahead of you."

So the first son who at first said no but then went and worked because he repented represents the tax collectors and the prostitutes who were looked down upon as sinners by the leaders, people who the leaders said were not qualified to go to heaven.

What about the second son? The second son was asked the same question. Verse 30:

"Then the father went to the other son and said the same thing [the same question: go and work today in my vineyard]. He answered, 'I will, sir,' but he did not go."

In the end of verse 32 we are told that this represents the leaders of the church. We read:

"And even after you saw this, you did not repent and believe him."

What is this parable all about? First of all we need to be clear about a statement that Jesus made in the beginning of verse 32:

"For John came to you to show you the way of righteousness...."

What did Jesus mean by that? Remember the question was, "Who was John from? Was he from God or was his baptism by human authority?" The statement is "John came to you to show you the way of righteousness." That phrase, "to show you the way of righteousness" (or "in the way of righteousness" in some translations) may be interpreted in one of two ways and it is possible that both are right. It could mean that what Christ was saying here is that, as it states in some translations, John came to show you the way of righteousness. In other words, "John came to show you that I, Jesus Christ, am the only source of righteousness for salvation."

Or He could mean that, in the thinking of the Jews, John himself followed the way of righteousness in contradiction to Christ. John was a conformist. In other words, John followed all the rules, all the regulations of the Jewish church. The Jews could not accuse John of not fasting. They could not accuse him of breaking the Sabbath. John was a conformist. The Jews could accuse Christ and his disciples of not fasting. They could accuse Him of breaking the Sabbath and they did at least four times.

Whichever way you look at it, John represented righteousness. Either he pointed to righteousness in Jesus Christ or he himself was righteous by his performance. In other words, "You had no excuse for rejecting John and, if you had accepted John and his message, you would have accepted Me." This was His final plea to the Jews.

Why did these leaders, the chief priests and elders, reject Christ? Two reasons. Number one, pride. They did not want to admit that they were wrong. Number two, self-righteousness. They did not want to link themselves with the tax collectors and prostitutes. This parable is dealing with the issue that began way back at the fall of Adam and will not end until the end of time. Do you know the greatest enemy of Christ Our Righteousness is self-righteousness? This conflict began way back at the fall. Do you remember what Adam did when he first sinned and discovered he was naked? He tried to cover himself with fig leaves but God had to cover him up with skins of animals because the fig leaves dried and fell off.

The very next event we read in the Bible is about Cain and Abel. Cain and Abel both offered sacrifices but one did the will of God, the other did not, even though he offered a sacrifice. What did Cain do? He killed Abel and this controversy is going on today. This is what Christ is trying to get across. The first son represents those who are sinners but who recognize that they are sinners. When they are given the gospel, they repent and they accept the gift because they recognize that they are disobedient to God's requirements. They are sinners.

Turn to Matthew 11:20-24 and here you get the same picture of these chief elders and priests. This is in the context of John's message. If you read the previous verses you will notice that Christ gives tribute to John the Baptist. Then in verses 20-21:

Then Jesus began to denounce the cities in which most of his miracles had been performed, because they did not repent. "Woe to you, Korazin! Woe to you, Bethsaida! If the miracles that were performed in you had been performed in Tyre and Sidon, they would have repented long ago in sackcloth and ashes."

Tyre and Sidon were the cities of the Gentiles. They were cities of people that the Jews looked upon as dogs, as sinners. Remember Jesus went to Tyre and Sidon and healed the daughter of the Canaanite woman. Yet Christ is saying, "If Tyre and Sidon had seen what I have shown you, they would have repented." In other words the greatest evidence that Jesus ever gave that He was the Messiah was His works. John 14:8-9:

Philip said, "Lord, show us the Father and that will be enough for us."

Jesus answered: "Don't you know me, Philip, even after I have been among you such a long time? Anyone who has seen me has seen the Father. How can you say, 'Show us the Father'?"

Jesus said, "If you have seen Me, you have seen the Father." In other words, "The works that I do, it is not I who do them, it is the Father." The works of Jesus were works that no other man could do. They were supernatural works. They were evidence that God was in this Man. Jesus is saying in Matthew 11:22:

"But I tell you, it will be more bearable for Tyre and Sidon on the day of judgment than for you."

Then He goes on in verse 23:

"And you, Capernaum, will you be lifted up to the skies? No, you will go down to the depths. If the miracles that were performed in you had been performed in Sodom, it would have remained to this day.

But what happens? Jesus says in verse 24:

"But I tell you that it will be more bearable for Sodom on the day of judgment than for you."

Why? Because God gave greater evidence to the Jews that He was the Messiah than He gave to the Gentiles. Tyre and Sidon did not have the evidence that the Jews had and yet the elders and the chief priests refused to accept Christ as their Saviour.

I would like to look at some more passages to remind you that we are in that same danger. Turn to Matthew 7:21:

"Not everyone who says to me, 'Lord, Lord,' will enter the kingdom of heaven, but only he who does the will of my Father who is in heaven."

The Jews, these elders, these chief priests were famous for giving lip service to God just like the second son. The second son gave lip service, "Yes, sir, I will go and work in your vineyard today," but he was a hypocrite; he did not mean what he said. It did not come from the heart; it was simply outward words to please his father and it was not a heart response. We have this problem all the time.

Now I would like to take this parable which Christ was applying to the elders and the priests of His days and apply it to us, because Jesus is asking the question, "Which of these two sons actually did the will of God, the one who said, 'Yes' but did not go or the one who said, 'No' but repented and said, 'Yes'?" Which of these two sons did God's will? Well, you know what the answer is.

There are two things I want to bring out about the second son, the one who said "Yes" but who did not go. Number one, hypocrisy, which is the typical evidence of a legalist. When God said to the Jews He would give them His law, what did they say? Exodus 19:8a:

The people all responded together, "We will do everything the Lord has said."

The very next day they were worshipping a golden calf around the corner. We know that God hates it when His people give Him only lip service.

Let me give you a text. Turn to Matthew 15:7-9. Here is a statement quoted from Isaiah. Jesus is talking to the Jewish nation and He is saying to the leaders of the church:

You hypocrites! Isaiah was right when he prophesied about you: "These people honor me with their lips, but their hearts are far from me. They worship me in vain; their teachings are but rules taught by men."

Jesus is saying here that when God gave the Jews His commandments, He gave them something that they could not keep. Did He know that? Yes, God knew they could not keep His Ten Commandments. Why? Because the flesh cannot keep God's law. But they did not know it, so they promised God, "All that you say we will do." But when it came to the actual keeping of those commandments, they failed.

Now they had two choices. One was to admit failure, to repent, and say, "God, we have failed miserably." But they chose the second choice. They took the commandments of God which are as holy as

God Himself and they reduced them to human rules that they could keep. They kept those rules and then they deceived themselves because they thought that they were doing the will of God when in actual fact they were not. They refused to admit that they were sinners.

Let me give you one of their rules. According to one of their rules, not working on the Sabbath meant that you could not walk more than three quarters of a mile. But they were very clever because for every rule they had loopholes. If a boy walked three-quarters of a mile and was trying to visit his girlfriend when she lived two miles down the road, he had a problem. He had free time, it was the Sabbath, so what did he do?

If you ate or drank something, then you were allowed to walk another three-quarters of a mile. So he would walk three-quarters of a mile, stop at somebody's house, knock on the door and say, "Please, sir, can you give me a glass of water?" or "Please, ma'm, I need a glass of water?" They all knew about it. They all practiced it and if they were not thirsty they would take only a sip and throw the rest of the water out and say, "Thank you," then walk another three-quarters of a mile and stop at the next house.

What happened if there was no house for the next three-quarters of a mile? Well, they were very clever. They had another loophole. If you drank your spit that was like eating food then you could walk another three-quarters of a mile. This is what Christ is saying, "You hypocrites. Who are you deceiving? Just yourselves."

I have mentioned many times and I will repeat that the formula of the gospel is "Not I, but Christ." The hardest part of that formula is the first part. For you to say, "But Christ," you have to admit that you are one hundred percent a sinner. Most people will admit that they are sinners but to admit that from head to foot there is no soundness, there is nothing good in you is very hard for our human ego.

I was at a college seminar and one of the biggest arguments that came up was the definition of sin. I took one position and my counterpart took another position. He took the position that sin is only a choice and I asked him a question, "I believe when probation closes God will have a people who will not knowingly commit any sins. If, by the grace of God when we reach that position, am I still a sinner in need of grace or am I sinless because I am no longer choosing sin?" The Bible makes it clear.

Once I was at a General Conference session when a young man came up to me and asked me if I had heard his series on "The Sinless but Sympathetic Saviour." I said I had heard about it but I had not heard the tapes. And he said, "Why don't you get a set and listen? I would like your opinion." So I went to buy them and they were $34. Since I had used most of my money helping our African brethren, I could not buy them. When he met me again he asked me if I had them and I told him no, I couldn't afford them. So he said he would give me a set.

I do not agree with his conclusion but I was very impressed with his fourth sermon. This series is addressed to Adventists so the main thrust of his message comes from the Spirit of Prophecy by Ellen G. White and he gave quotation after quotation proving from the Spirit of Prophecy that we are one hundred percent sinners by nature. I am not a sinner because I choose to sin. I choose to sin because I am a sinner. I am not a sinner because I commit sins. I commit sins because I am a sinner.

It is true I can choose not to sin. The Romans 7 man, whoever he is, has chosen not to sin but he calls himself (verse 24),

What a wretched man I am! Who will rescue me [not from my choice but] from this body of death?

Let me put it another way. Every one of us — including this African bush preacher — is one hundred percent sinner from head to foot saved by grace.

Now I do not mean that I am a sinner by performance one hundred percent. None of us are sinners one hundred percent by performance. But given the opportunity and the right circumstances any sin that you have seen committed in this world I will commit. The fact that I have not done it is because of the grace of God. I thank God when Adam sinned that God put restrictions to sin. If He did not put restrictions to sin, this world would have destroyed itself and this human race would have destroyed this world long ago. But I thank God, He has put restrictions.

Now if I look at myself as a one hundred percent sinner, then what is my attitude to others? If I see somebody there committing an act of sin I do not despise him. I say, "There go I but for the grace of God." But if I am a legalist and I am not committing those sins I will look down upon him. That is exactly what these priests and elders were doing. They were looking down upon the prostitutes and the tax collectors.

You have the same problem in Luke 15. There is the background for the prodigal son story. Jesus was eating with tax collectors and sinners. Do you know what the priests were doing? They were murmuring. "Look at him; he's eating with sinners. He's linking himself with sinners. We are self-righteous." These chief priests and elders did not repent because they did not see the need of repenting. "We are not sinners like these prostitutes."

But Jesus told them their righteousness would not take them to heaven. I have spent quite a bit of time trying to explain the issue if you read Psalm 15 out of context. Psalm 15:
Lord, who may dwell in your sanctuary?
Who may live on your holy hill?
He whose walk is blameless
and who does what is righteous,
who speaks the truth from his heart
and has no slander on his tongue,
who does his neighbor no wrong
and casts no slur on his fellowman,
who despises a vile man
but honors those who fear the Lord,
who keeps his oath even when it hurts,
who lends his money without usury
and does not accept a bribe against the innocent.
He who does these things will never be shaken.

The question that Psalm 15 poses is, "Who will be able to live in the presence of God?" That is his basic question. The answer comes, "Those who do righteousness. Those who are blameless." How many of you are blameless? Please read the text completely. The answer is those who are blameless in heart. He is not dealing with performance. He's dealing with heart. A legalist is one who obeys God outwardly but his heart is far from God. That's what Jesus said in Matthew 15:8:

These people honor me with their lips, but their hearts are far from me.

When these prostitutes and tax collectors heard John the Baptist, they recognized they were sinners. When Ninevah heard that they were sinners, they repented, because they did not deny the fact. The man in Romans 7, even though he chose to do righteousness, discovered he could not do it because of sin dwelling in him. So he cried out,

What a wretched man I am! Who will rescue me from this body of death?

But I read in Revelation 3:17 about a people, the last generation of Christians, the Laodiceans:

You say, "I am rich; I have acquired wealth and do not need a thing." But you do not realize that you are wretched, pitiful, poor, blind and naked.

If we would recognize that we are sinners, saved by grace, many things would happen in this church. We would not be critical about others because we come from the same stock. Plant the same apple seeds from the same apple; plant two apple trees (or let it be tomatoes or any vegetable). Take the two seeds from the same stock and plant them in two separate places. Give one a lot of food; deprive the other one of nutrients and give it very little water. The results will be different. One will bear big, juicy fruits; the other will be small and scrawny. It is because of the environment, not because they are different at their very source. They are identical.

We are sinners outwardly in acts based on environment, upbringing, inheritance, but at the very source we are the same.

None of us are better than the other. We are all one hundred percent sinners and when John came and said, "Repent," these elders and chief priests did not. Why? Because they thought they had no need of repentance. "We are sinners," said the tax collectors and prostitutes and they repented.

Christ is pleading with them and this is His final occasion. That is why there is a very important word in the parable. What did the father say to the two sons? He did not say, "Please go and work in my vineyard." He used a very important word. He used the word "today." By "today" He was trying to tell them, "Please, this is your last chance. I am about to be crucified. I am about to leave this earth. Please do not reject the message of John the Baptist. He came to show you the way of righteousness. Repent. Change your ways. Work today."

Matthew 21:28 reads like this:

"What do you think? There was a man who had two sons. He went to the first and said, 'Son, go and work today in the vineyard.'

Please notice the urgency Christ reveals. Now it is true Jesus was speaking to the elders and the chief priests. What about us today? Do you believe the end is near? Do you believe that we are living in the final stages of this world's history and God is saying to us, "Will you please go and tell the others the good news of salvation?" Only those whose hearts have enjoyed the good news, only those who have repented and who realize that they are one hundred percent sinners saved by grace will want to go and work today.

The legalist will say, "Yes, we'll work today." They give lip service but no results. Will you be the first son or the second son? This is a problem that still exists today. By nature we are born legalists. Human beings naturally want to earn their way to heaven. I don't have to teach legalism; all I have to do is leave you alone. I will use the illustration that I have used before: I don't have to do anything to grow weeds. They grow automatically. Don't ask me where they come from but they are there.

When we were in Idaho my daughter had a horse and, when we left Idaho, the stable was full of horse manure. I said to my daughter that maybe we should take some manure with us instead of buying some at our new location. So our roof rack was loaded with horse manure. That was the worse thing I ever did because we had a weed that grew very sharp thorns. It looks like a pea but it has spikes in it and I had not seen it around where we moved but two and a half years later, having been away a month, I came back and saw those weeds growing in my garden. I was horrified that I had imported something that I should never have brought there. So I did my best to pluck them all out before they produced those awful thorns.

I thank God that the gospel of Jesus Christ is that He is the way of righteousness and my part is to repent and say, "Thank You, thank You for saving a sinner like me." I can say with Paul in 1 Timothy 1:15:

Here is a trustworthy saying that deserves full acceptance: Christ Jesus came into the world to save sinners — of whom I am the worst.

It is my prayer that this attitude will change our relationship toward one another; that we will not look down upon each other because all of us are sinners. Given the chance we would do the terrible things that Hitler did, that Idi Amin did. I pray that we will become like the prostitutes because remember in the parable what Jesus said in Matthew 21:31b which was devastating to these elders:

Jesus said to them, "I tell you the truth, the tax collectors and the prostitutes are entering the kingdom of God ahead of you."

I can imagine in the judgment these elders and these priests will say to God, "But this is unfair. Haven't we cast out devils in Your name; haven't we done wonderful works in Your name?" And God will say, "I never knew you." Our works must be the fruits of righteousness by faith.

These very prostitutes and tax collectors who repented did not simply sit down. These were the ones used by God to turn the world upside down after Christ went to heaven. These were the ones who in Acts 8 went all over and preached the gospel to everybody because their hearts were transformed by the love of God. They recognized they were sinners saved by grace.

It is my prayer that you and I will identify ourselves with tax collectors and sinners saved by grace and we will love each other and that we will help each other to walk in the way of righteousness is my prayer in Jesus' name.

THE PARABLE OF THE CLOSED DOOR

Luke 13:24-30:

He said to them, "Make every effort to enter through the narrow door, because many, I tell you, will try to enter and will not be able to. Once the owner of the house gets up and closes the door, you will stand outside knocking and pleading, 'Sir, open the door for us.'

"But he will answer, 'I don't know you or where you come from.'

"Then you will say, 'We ate and drank with you, and you taught in our streets.'

"But he will reply, 'I don't know you or where you come from. Away from me, all you evildoers!'

"There will be weeping there, and gnashing of teeth, when you see Abraham, Isaac, and Jacob and all the prophets in the kingdom of God, but you yourselves thrown out. People will come from east and west and north and south, and will take their places at the feast in the kingdom of God. Indeed there are those who are last who will be first, and first who will be last."

Jesus is traveling towards Jerusalem. He realizes His earthly mission is coming to an end and so He doesn't want to waste any time. As the crowd follows Him on this journey, He is teaching them and this is the setting of this parable of The Closed Door. As they were walking along, you will notice in verse 23 one of the followers turns around to Jesus and asks this question:

Someone asked him, "Lord, are only a few people going to be saved?"

"How many people will be saved?" was his question and I suppose it's a valid question. Jesus does not answer this young man's question directly but, in response, Jesus presents a warning, a very solemn warning. That is found in verse 24:

He said to them, "Make every effort to enter through the narrow door, because many, I tell you, will try to enter and will not be able to."

In the Sermon on the Mount, you have a similar warning. In Matthew 7:13-14, Jesus was telling His disciples:

Enter through the narrow gate. For wide is the gate and broad is the road that leads to destruction, and many enter through it. But small is the gate and narrow the road that leads to life, and only a few find it.

As you read this statement, both in Matthew and in Luke, you get the idea that maybe Jesus is teaching that it is hard to be saved and that it is easy to be lost. Many people feel that way as they read these statements. I used to think that too, but when you analyze this statement in its context and when you realize to whom Christ was making that statement, you know that He is NOT teaching that to be saved is difficult and that we can be lost very easily.

He is dealing with a problem that the Jews faced and unfortunately a problem that we face today. That is why I think this parable is very relevant to us today. That narrow gate represents salvation because the man asked the question, "Will there be few who will be saved?" Jesus response was, "Make sure that you go through that narrow gate." Why is the gate to salvation narrow? Is it because it's difficult? No. It is because you can't take any baggage with you. The only door to heaven is Jesus Christ. Jesus was saying that the only way any human being can be saved is through Him.

You will find this in several statements in the Bible but let me give you one very clear statement. Not long after the church began in Acts 4, one of the very first sermons that was preached by the apostle Peter when John was with him is found in this statement in Acts 4:12. I would like to include verse 11 also so that you are aware who Peter is talking to. He is addressing the Sanhedrin; he is addressing the leading brethren of the Jewish church. He makes this statement in verse 11:

He is "the stone you builders rejected, which has become the capstone."

"This is the cornerstone by which every other stone is measured and you leaders of the church have rejected it." Then in verse 12 we read this very wonderful, clear statement:

Salvation is found in no one else, for there is no other name under heaven given to men by which we must be saved.

The Jews, the crowd that was following Jesus to Jerusalem were taught that salvation is by works. You had to be circumcised; you had to do a whole list of things. They had a string of dos and don'ts and if you didn't do any of them, you would not make it. Jesus said, "No." There are many people trying to go to heaven but they will not make it because the way to heaven is very narrow. You cannot take any of your baggage. I'm not making this up because the parable brings this out. Remember:

The people Christ was addressing in Luke 13 were Jews.

The Jews were walking on that broad road on which every other religion was walking, which is "salvation by works."

If you read Romans 9:31-32, Paul tells us there that the reason why Israel will not make it to heaven is not because they have not tried but because they tried the wrong method, they used the wrong method. Let's read it:

But Israel, who pursued a law of righteousness, has not attained it. Why not? Because they pursued it not by faith but as if it were by works. They stumbled over the "stumbling stone."

Now we are going to look at the parable and, notice, this is exactly what Christ is trying to get across. The question is, "Will there be many?" There's a big crowd following Jesus Christ. "Will many of us be saved?" Jesus says, "Strive to go through that narrow gate." Just as Hebrews 4:11 tells the Jews:

Let us, therefore, make every effort to enter that rest, so that no one will fall by following their example of disobedience.

Let's look at the parable which is found in verse 25:

Once the owner of the house gets up and closes the door, you will stand outside knocking and pleading, "Sir, open the door for us."

But he will answer, "I don't know you or where you come from."

Let me remind you that the Jewish peasants to whom Jesus was addressing this statement lived in a one-room house. It was on two levels. The first half of the house was what we would call ground level or first floor. Then there was a little elevation — maybe two feet — a platform where the people slept. When the family woke up in the morning they stepped off this platform and opened the door to bring in the fresh air and to announce to their neighbors they were awake. That door would remain open all day long. They never closed it; they were not afraid of robbers because there weren't that many in those days. There was a neighborhood watch and nobody stole from their neighbors. It was common to have the door open.

But when night came and it was time to go to sleep, the father — the master of the house — would come to the door after he had brought in all his animals to sleep at the lower level and he would shut the door and bolt it. He was telling his neighbors and everybody around: "Please do not disturb me. I have gone to sleep." Jesus was using this typical practice as a spiritual lesson. He is saying, "When probation closes, when God closes the door, many of you will not be inside but you will be outside." He is not dealing with houses here, He is dealing with salvation, because that is the question.

He is saying, "Many of you will be found not inside the kingdom of God but outside. You will knock on the door and you will cry to me and you will say, 'Lord, Lord, open for us' and I will answer and say to you, 'I do not know you where you are from.'" It is very important that you notice their response. Verse 26:

Then you [the Jews, that is who Jesus is addressing] will say, "We ate and drank with you, and you taught in our streets."

This is a Jewish way of saying, "But, Lord Jesus, we were members of your church in good and regular standing. How come you don't even know us? We were part of Your church!" Notice Jesus is not comparing here between believers and unbelievers. Verse 24:

"...Many, I tell you, will try to enter and will not be able to."

He is talking about people who are trying to go to heaven, who are doing their very best to make it to heaven and who will not make it. He is not talking about unbelievers. He is talking about His chosen people who are trying to go to heaven. They will say to Him, "But Jesus, we were part of Your church. We were part of Your covenant people." He responds in verse 27:

But he will reply, "I don't know you or where you come from. [Then He adds this terrible statement.] Away from me, all you evildoers!"

We have a similar story in the Sermon on the Mount. Turn to Matthew 7:21 where you have an identical incident except here we have more details. We discover that some of these people who were found outside the kingdom when probation closes are not only members in good and regular standing, some of them are actually workers:

"Not everyone who says to me, 'Lord, Lord,' [the same words He uses in Luke 13:25 — these are believers who claim to be followers of the Way] will enter the kingdom of heaven, but only he who does the will of my Father who is in heaven."

Have you ever asked yourself what Jesus meant by that? What is the will of the Father? I'm not going to give you any text but I'm going to give you the statement. I want you to look for the text to see whether I am telling the truth or if I am lying. You will discover that the will of the Father as taught by Jesus Christ and in the New Testament is that you believe on His Son Jesus Christ. Look for the texts. There'll be more than one.

Let's go back to Matthew 7:22:

Many will say to me on that day [that is, when the door is closed], "Lord, Lord, did we not prophesy in your name, and in your name drive out demons and perform many miracles?"

These are not ordinary members; these are people who had offices in the church; these are people who were active in the church. Verse 23:

Then I will tell them plainly, "I never knew you. Away from me, you evildoers!"

Then, after this statement, in Matthew 7 follows the parable of the two men who built houses, one on the rock and one on sand. Remember, the rock stands for Jesus Christ. Let's go back because now we have a problem. Both the passages, the one in Matthew 7 and the one in Luke 13, make this statement, "Away from me, you evildoers!" Jesus was very careful in choosing His words. There are 12 words in the Hebrew language for sin and He chooses one specific word here: iniquity. What does that word mean?

When you read those words, "Away from me, you evildoers [you who do iniquity]!" was Jesus saying, "Yes, I know you prophesied in My name and you did many good thing in My name but your iniquity was more than your good works, therefore, you are weighed in the balances and you are found guilty and therefore you are lost."? Is this what He is saying? The answer is, "No." The context, the grammar will not allow such an interpretation. What He is saying is the good works they were doing was iniquity. The only way for you to understand that is to look at the word and see whether the Bible teaches what I am saying.

The shepherds used a shepherd's rod. If you looked at a shepherd's rod that was used by the shepherds in the Middle East, you would notice that the end of the rod was bent. It was called crooked; it was a U-turn so they could hook the sheep when it was stuck in the bushes or the crevices. It was a tool that the shepherd's used. The Jews use the word "iniquity" when they referred to that bend in the shepherd's rod. That is where the word "iniquity" came from. Iniquity is the crooked part of a shepherd's rod. When it is used spiritually, it applies to man in his fallen condition who is bent towards self.

When God created Adam and Eve, He created them in His image and the Bible tells us that God is love, not the kind of love you and I know but the love that is described in scripture. In 1 Corinthians 13:5, we are told that this kind of love is not bent towards self:

It [Love] is not rude, it is not self-seeking, it is not easily angered, it keeps no record of wrongs.

There is no self in God's love; it's an outgoing love. When Adam sinned, his nature became bent, it became crooked towards self. Read in Steps to Christ, p. 17, by Ellen G. White, the statement that, when Adam sinned, love disappeared and selfishness took its place. Actually what happened was his love bent towards self and became egocentric love. That is the only kind of love you and I can generate naturally. That is what happened to us and that is how we are born.

I read in Isaiah 53:6:

We all, like sheep, have gone astray, each of us has turned [bent] to his own way; and the Lord has laid on him the iniquity of us all.

That "bentness" disqualifies us for heaven. There will be no selfishness in heaven and our nature is bent towards self. But what is Jesus referring to when He says, in this context of our parable, "Away from me, you evildoers [you workers of iniquity]."? I believe, and it's very clear from the passage and the context, that He is referring to self-righteousness.

Do you know that self-righteousness is iniquity? It is not because the acts are bad but because the acts are polluted with self. Everything that man does apart from grace is polluted with self because the essence of our fallen nature is self. Let me give you a couple of texts to show you this. Turn to Isaiah 64:6. Look at this text very carefully:

All of us have become like one who is unclean, and all our righteous acts are like filthy rags...

So Isaiah equates our righteousness with filthy rags. Let's go on [same verse]:

...we all shrivel up like a leaf...

In other words, our righteousness will one day shrivel up like a leaf. When Adam first sinned, he tried to cover his nakedness with fig leaves. What happened when they dried? They dropped off and he was left naked. But look at the next statement [same verse]:

...and like the wind our sins sweep us away.

Here our righteousness is equated with our iniquities. Like the wind, it is here for a moment and it goes as the wind blows it. In other words, our self-righteousness is fig leaves that dry, fall away, and the wind drives off. That is our iniquity. No wonder Paul — the great Pharisee who discovered the gospel — said in Philippians 3:8-9 that when he discovered Christ, he took his self-righteousness and threw it out because it was like rubbish so that he might win Christ and be found in Him:

What is more, I consider everything a loss compared to the surpassing greatness of knowing Christ Jesus my Lord, for whose sake I have lost all things. I consider them rubbish, that I may gain Christ and be found in him, not having a righteousness of my own that comes from the law, but that which is through faith in Christ — the righteousness that comes from God and is by faith.

I was reading a statement one day in Testimonies to Ministers, p. 65, by Ellen G. White. It was quite a devastating statement. We are told in that statement that when the message of Christ our righteousness is clearly presented in this church, many ministers will reject it because they will not be willing to give up their self-righteousness — which is unrighteousness — for the pure truth of Christ our righteousness. What a tragedy!

With this idea that "our righteous acts are like filthy rags" in mind, I am using the principle of the Bible interpreting the Bible.

Turn to Zechariah 3:1-3:

Then he showed me Joshua [Joshua is the Hebrew word for the Greek word Jesus] the high priest standing before the angel of the Lord [therefore Joshua represents God's people standing before God], and Satan standing at his right side to accuse him. The Lord said to Satan, "The LORD rebuke you, Satan! The Lord, who has chosen Jerusalem [the symbol of the church], rebuke you! Is not this man a burning stick snatched from the fire?" [We all belong to the lake of fire but Jesus plucked us out.]

Now Joshua was dressed in filthy clothes [which, as you have seen in Isaiah 64:6, is our self-righteousness] as he stood before the angel.

Will these filthy garments qualify Joshua for heaven? This Joshua has understood the truth and he's not depending on the filthy garments because I read in verse 4:

The angel said to those who were standing before him, "Take off his filthy clothes."

Then he said to Joshua, "See, I have taken away your sin [I have replaced your self-righteousness], and I will put rich garments [of Christ our righteousness] on you."

Now going back to our parable. There are many, many people who will not make it to heaven not because they have not tried but because they used the wrong methods. There is only one way to go to heaven: Christ our righteousness. That doesn't mean you will not do anything. Genuine righteousness by faith produces a lot of works. I don't have to push works. If you have understood justification by faith, the works will come, guaranteed. If it hasn't come, it is because you have not understood or you have not surrendered to justification by faith. The problem is not for me to push it; the problem is because you have not yielded to the truth.

Let us go now to the text. Listen to what Jesus says in Luke 13:27. After He tells them,

"Away from me, all you evildoers!"

notice what He says in verse 28:

There will be weeping there, and gnashing of teeth, when you see Abraham, Isaac and Jacob [the three fathers of Israel] and all the prophets in the kingdom of God, but you yourselves thrown out.

Jesus is not talking to infidels. He is talking to people who claim to be the children of Abraham, Isaac, and Jacob, to people who call themselves the covenant people of God but, in the judgment, they are outside of the kingdom.

In Romans 9, 10, and 11, Paul deals with a very important question which is that the Jews believed that, because they were the descendants of Abraham, Isaac, and Jacob — the three fathers of

Israel — they qualified for heaven. Paul is saying to them, especially in Romans 9:6-8, that not everyone who belongs to Israel, really belongs to Israel:

It is not as though God's word had failed. For not all who are descended from Israel are Israel. Nor because they are his descendants are they all Abraham's children. On the contrary, "It is through Isaac that your offspring will be reckoned." In other words, it is not the natural children who are God's children, but it is the children of the promise who are regarded as Abraham's offspring.

What did he mean by "For not all who are descended from Israel are Israel"? The Palestinians today can claim Abraham as their father because Abraham is their father but they don't belong to Israel. The Amalekites could claim that Abraham and that Isaac was their father because the Amalekites were descendants of Esau but they could not claim to be Israel. You have to have Abraham, Isaac, and Jacob as your father to qualify to be Israel.

But Paul is saying, "No, it is not the natural descendants of these three men that qualifies you to be Israel. It is the qualities of these three men." Let me give you in a nutshell what these three qualities are. The word "father" does not mean the natural father. God did not give Israel three fathers as their natural fathers. He gave three men as the fathers to be the prototype and what he is saying is that you have to have the qualities of these three men to qualify for Israel.

What are the qualities? Let me give you the texts. I'll read only one of them for each because I don't want you to go hungry for too long. I realize I am in America. I wish for the day to come when you will be willing to sit down for hours like Africans do and be willing to study the Word of God. You are willing to sit down for hours to watch TV, six hours a day, according to the national average. Romans 4:11-13 is the first text; Galatians 3:6-9 is the second text and then Galatians 3:27-29 is the third text.

But let me read you Romans 4:11-13 which is very clear. You cannot mix these words. You would have to twist the text to misunderstand it:

And he [Abraham] received the sign of circumcision, a seal of the righteousness that he had by faith while he was still uncircumcised. So then, he is the father of all who believe but have not been circumcised [that is, Gentiles], in order that righteousness might be credited to them. And he is also the father of the circumcised [that is, of the Jews] who not only are circumcised but who also walk in the footsteps of the faith that our father Abraham had before he was circumcised. It was not through law that Abraham and his offspring received the promise that he would be heir of the world, but through the righteousness that comes by faith.

It is not enough to be a natural descendant of Abraham, says Paul. You have to have the faith of Abraham to qualify to be a child of Abraham.

Galatians 3:6-9 says the same thing very clearly:

Consider Abraham: "He believed God, and it was credited to him as righteousness." Understand, then, that those who believe are children of Abraham. The Scripture foresaw that God would justify the Gentiles by faith, and announced the gospel in advance to Abraham: "All nations will be blessed through you." So those who have faith are blessed along with Abraham, the man of faith.

In fact, in verses 27-29, it says that if you have been baptized into Christ you are Abraham's seed and heirs according to the promise:

For all of you who were baptized into Christ have clothed yourselves with Christ. There is neither Jew nor Greek, slave nor free, male nor female, for you are all one in Christ Jesus. If you belong to Christ, then you are Abraham's seed, and heirs according to the promise.

What about Isaac? He is the father of all those who have been born from above, who have experienced the new birth. In Galatians 4:28, discussing under the context of the two covenants — one is salvation by works and salvation by faith or salvation by grace — he makes this statement to those who stand on the platform of salvation by faith:

Now you, brothers [we who are saved by faith], like Isaac, are children of promise.

The Old Covenant is where God gave the law and man promised to keep it. In the New Covenant, God gave the law and God promised to keep it in His Son, Jesus Christ. That's the difference. The difference between the Old Covenant and the New Covenant is not the law; both covenants have the law. The difference is that in the Old Covenant man obeys to save himself; in the New Covenant, God fulfills that obedience as a promise through Jesus Christ. So Abraham was saved by a promise. He will go through that gate and he will sit in that kingdom and all his children because they believed. The moment you believe, God gives you the experience of the new birth. Isaac is that new birth.

Jesus told Nicodemus, who was a member of the Sanhedrin, in John 3:3-7:

In reply Jesus declared, "I tell you the truth, no one can see the kingdom of God unless he is born again."

"How can a man be born when he is old?" Nicodemus asked. "Surely he cannot enter a second time into his mother's womb to be born!"

Jesus answered, "I tell you the truth, no one can enter the kingdom of God unless he is born of water and the Spirit. Flesh gives birth to flesh, but the Spirit gives birth to spirit. You should not be surprised at my saying, 'You must be born again.'"

"Unless you are born from above, you cannot enter the kingdom of God." Unless you walk that narrow way, which allows no room for human performance, you will not enter. In 1 Peter 1:3-4, we are told that we have been born again to a lively hope through the promise of God:

Praise be to the God and Father of our Lord Jesus Christ! In his great mercy he has given us new birth into a living hope through the resurrection of Jesus Christ from the dead, and into an inheritance that can never perish, spoil or fade — kept in heaven for you....

May I repeat, though, that genuine justification by faith always produces works.

What about Jacob? He is the father of all whose faith endures unto the end. In Genesis 32, we have the experience of Jacob. He is fighting with the angel and the angel at the end of the night, in the morning, dislocates his hip and Jacob holds on. The angel in Genesis 32:27 asks the question:

The man asked him, "What is your name?"

"Jacob," he answered.

Do you know what "Jacob" means? "Schemer." "I've been scheming to get my ticket to heaven" because, to Jacob, the ticket to heaven was the birthright. "I've tried every human trick to get it and I have failed. But now I realize it comes from you and I will not let you go until you bless me."

Do you know what the angel said? "From now onwards you will no longer be called a schemer":

Then the man said, "Your name will no longer be Jacob, but Israel, because you have struggled with God and with men and have overcome."

Israel means, "The one who has prevailed."

Jesus tells us in Matthew 10:22:

All men will hate you because of me, but he who stands firm to the end will be saved.

In Hebrews 10:35-39 you have the same message given to the Jews which we must apply to ourselves:

So do not throw away your confidence; it will be richly rewarded. You need to persevere so that when you have done the will of God, you will receive what he has promised. For in just a very little while, "He who is coming will come and will not delay. But my righteous one will live by faith. And if he shrinks back, I will not be pleased with him." But we are not of those who shrink back and are destroyed, but of those who believe and are saved.

Don't ever give up your confidence in Jesus Christ. It has great recompense of reward. The just shall live by faith. "If you draw back, I will have no pleasure in you."

Now let's go back to the parable. Jesus is telling these Jews that Abraham, Isaac, and Jacob and all their children will be sitting in heaven. All those who have the faith of Abraham, who are born from above, and whose faith has endured until the end will enter into the kingdom. Luke 13:29:

People will come from east and west and north and south [from every direction], and will take their places at the feast in the kingdom of God.

The Gentiles will realize that the only way to be saved is by faith. But you Jews, you who are stubbornly resisting the gospel, you who were called first into the kingdom, you will be last, not because you did not try but because you refused the only way God can save you, which is through His Son, Jesus Christ.

When the wicked are lost, I can imagine them saying, "We deserve it." But you have people who have given up many things, who have disciplined themselves, who have gone through many hardships in order to earn their way to heaven and they discover that they haven't made it. Can you imagine the terrible tragedy that we read in this text? "There will be," says Jesus, "weeping and gnashing of teeth." Why? Because they thought that their good works would qualify them for heaven. Whether we talk of justification, our title to heaven, whether we talk of sanctification, our fitness for heaven, or whether we talk about glorification, it has the same formula: "Not I, but Christ."

It must be Christ from beginning to end and our part is faith and faith is saying — not somebody saying to you but you saying to yourself — "Not I, but Christ." In others words, using the language of Galatians 2:20, faith is saying:

I have been crucified with Christ and I no longer live, but Christ lives in me. The life I live in the body, I live by faith in the Son of God, who loved me and gave himself for me.

That is the narrow gate. Jesus is not saying it is hard to be saved and easy to be lost. What He is saying is that there is only one way to be saved and that is through Him.

As we move towards the heavenly kingdom, I want to warn you the road will get narrower and narrower. You will have to take all your baggage and throw it out. The only thing you can take in is the righteousness of Christ. Everything else is dung, says Paul. The message that God is giving to you now is simply the message you find in Revelation 3:18:

I counsel you to buy from me gold refined in the fire, so you can become rich; and white clothes to wear, so you can cover your shameful nakedness; and salve to put on your eyes, so you can see.

The word "buy" means to give up what you have in exchange for what He is offering you.

He is knocking on your door today but if you refuse the gospel, if you refuse the truth of Christ our righteousness in any form, if you want to add even a small portion of your works towards your ticket to heaven, I warn you that you will be out of the kingdom. You will have nobody to blame but yourselves because the Lord will say, "What did you do when you heard that African bush preacher tell you the truth?" May God bless you that you will rest in nothing but Jesus Christ and His righteousness.

CHAPTER EIGHTEEN

THE PARABLE OF THE WISE STEWARD

Luke 12:35-40:

Be dressed ready for service and keep your lamps burning, like men waiting for their master to return from a wedding banquet, so that when he comes and knocks they can immediately open the door for him. It will be good for those servants whose master finds them watching when he comes. I tell you the truth, he will dress himself to serve, will have them recline at the table and will come and wait on them. It will be good for those servants whose master finds them ready, even if he comes in the second or third watch of the night. But understand this: If the owner of the house had known at what hour the thief was coming, he would not have let his house be broken into. You also must be ready, because the Son of Man will come at an hour when you do not expect him.

Many of the parables that Jesus spoke while He was on this earth belong to that category called "the crisis parables" and all of them have to do with the Second Coming of Christ. Christians often sing a beautiful hymn called "We Shall Behold Him." But when Jesus talked of His second coming, He spoke of it as a crisis and we wonder why. It is not possible for us to study all the parables that belong to these crisis parables. We have already covered one and that is the parable of the ten virgins. When the bridegroom came, remember, what were the ten virgins doing? They were sleeping;

they were caught off guard. That's a crisis.

There are four other good parables that belong to this and I have chosen two of those parables for a specific reason. But, first of all, I will mention — at least touch quickly on — the other three for the simple reason that we are living at the time of the end. We believe that the end is very near, therefore, these parables have special significance to us. The first one I have already covered is the ten virgins. The second parable that I would like you to note is the flood in the days of Noah that Christ used as a model for His second coming. There are two passages that deal with this. The first is Luke 17:26-27, but I would like to turn to the second one in Matthew 24:37-39. I want you to notice how Christ uses the flood experience as a parallel to His second coming. (Luke 17:26-27 also deals with the same thing, but Matthew is a little more specific.) Matthew 24:37-39:

As it was in the days of Noah, so it will be at the coming of the Son of Man....

Notice that what took place in Noah's day will be repeated. There will be a similar, parallel experience.

...For in the days before the flood, people were eating and drinking, marrying and giving in marriage, up to the day Noah entered the ark; and they knew nothing about what would happen until the flood came and took them all away. That is how it will be at the coming of the Son of Man.

What is Christ trying to tell us? He's saying that the people in Noah's day were taken off guard. And He says, "That is how it will be at the coming of the Son of Man." This is the crisis. Remember that it was not because the people in Noah's day did not know about the flood. Noah preached about it for 120 years and yet they were caught off guard. The next parable that deals with the same thing is found in Luke 17:28-30 and, this time, Christ, having given them the Noah experience, goes on in Luke's account of the destruction of Sodom and Gomorrah as a model of His second coming:

It was the same in the days of Lot. People were eating and drinking, buying and selling, planting and building. But the day Lot left Sodom, fire and sulfur rained down from heaven and destroyed them all. It will be just like this on the day the Son of Man is revealed.

You have the same experience. They knew, but they did not believe. What Lot was warning them of was unacceptable to their reason. It was unacceptable to their experience. It had never rained in Noah's day; they had never seen fire falling from heaven. They did not believe and they were caught off guard.

The other two parables that are left are found in Mark 13:33-37, in Matthew 24:32, 43-45 and Luke 12:35-40. I have chosen these two parables: the parable of the wise servant or the wise steward who waited for his master who had gone to a wedding and the parable of the man who watched his house knowing that the thief will come at an unexpected time.

Now why have I chosen these two parables in Luke? If you look at the context of the other parables that I mentioned, Christ was primarily dealing with unbelievers, with the world, who heard this about the Second Coming because there is a church that has been preaching about it for over one hundred years. They heard about it but they did not believe it. But this parable is not addressing unbelievers, because as soon as Christ finished this parable that we read in Luke 12 I want you to look at what our good friend Peter did.

Turn to Luke 12:41. After Jesus had given these two parables we read:

Peter asked, "Lord, are you telling this parable to us, or to everyone?"

"To whom are you giving this counsel, this advice, this warning? Is it to us believers, your disciples, or to somebody else, to those other people?" And Jesus responded with these words and I'm going to read verse 42 and onwards and you decide to whom He is talking.

The Lord answered, "Who then is the faithful and wise manager, whom the master puts in charge of his servants to give them their food allowance at the proper time? It will be good for that servant whom the master finds doing so when he returns. I tell you the truth, he will put him in charge of all his possessions. But suppose the servant says to himself, 'My master is taking a long time in coming,' and he then begins to beat the menservants and maidservants and to eat and drink and get drunk. The master of that servant will come on a day when he does not expect him and at an hour he is not aware of. He will cut him to pieces and assign him a place with the unbelievers."

Who was Christ talking to? It's very clear He was talking to the believers. Is it possible for the believer to be caught off guard? Christ is saying, "Yes." Let me go one step further. Is it possible for Seventh-day Adventists who believe in the soon coming of Christ to be caught off guard? The answer is, "Yes." That is why we need to look at these two parables.

The common thread through all these parables that we have looked at, whether we're talking in terms of the world or the believers, is the suddenness of Christ's coming. The coming of Christ will catch us off guard. Let me ask you a question. Were the Jews caught off guard regarding the first coming of Christ? They were the ones who preached the first coming of Christ. They were the first coming Seventh-day Adventists. We are the second coming Seventh-day Adventists. They kept the Sabbath and they believed in the first coming of Christ. Yet they were taken off guard and please don't say, "Yes, the Jews went wrong but we can't go wrong." Remember, they are the cleverest people, when you look at all the prizes, the accomplishments in the world, in music, in art, in all professions, the Jews come number one. If they went wrong, is it possible for us to go wrong? The answer is, "Yes."

What is the emphasis? Why did Christ give these parables? Why did Christ give these parables to His disciples? What was the purpose of these parables? The answer is very simple. He is counseling His disciples, His believers; He is warning them to be ready for the coming of the Lord; be ready for the return of the Lord. Notice how He begins the parable. We began with verse 35 of Luke 12, but if you notice verse 34, He is talking to believers whose treasure is in heaven:

For where your treasure is, there your heart will be also.

Now I am trusting that all your treasure is in heaven.

The first thing He says, as an introduction to the parable, is:

Be dressed ready for service and keep your lamps burning,…

Does it imply the story of the ten virgins? Make sure that you have oil for your light to be burning at a time when you least expect Christ. Some translations say, "Let your loins be girded." This is a Middle East term that may not mean anything to you, so let me explain it to you.

The Middle Easterners wore a long gown just like the Arabs and the Jews do today. The gown went right to their feet and, when they went to sleep, they would curl their feet under their garments to keep their feet warm because, unfortunately, the nights were cold. But the gown was a hindrance when they worked because they would step on it and sometimes fall over. So, when they worked, they raised it up and kept it up by tying a belt round their waist and that is what the phrase "gird up your loins" meant. We don't use it today because it does not make any sense today. But that is basically what Jesus was saying, "Always be prepared for the event."

Now the event here is the lord who is obviously quite wealthy. He has many servants. The word servants in the plural form refers in application to the believers of the Christian community. The lord is Christ. He has gone to a far country. In this parable, He has gone to a wedding. Now I want remind you of the wedding that took place in the Middle East. When we dealt with the Ten Virgins, we discovered that the reception party, the bridesmaids, would have to wait sometimes seven days. They were never sure when the groom would come, because the method of traveling there in those days was very different from ours. Today we may be late and even if the bride is half an hour late sometimes they groan.

But here they would wait sometimes for days before the groom would come. Here is a man who went to a wedding feast. We do not know how far he went and his servants had no idea when he was coming back. Now they had two choices. They could say, "I don't think he will come that soon. So, 'while the cat is away, let us play.'" That's being a foolish steward. The wise one would say, "We have no idea when he will come, so let's be prepared." So I read in Luke 12:36:

...like men waiting for their master to return from a wedding banquet, so that when he comes and knocks they can immediately open the door for him.

In other words, if they were sleeping, what would he do? He would knock again and there would be no reply because they can sleep pretty heavily. Then he would pound on the door, bang on it until the servants would wake up sleepy-eyed and say, "Oh, you are here." But if they were on guard, the moment he knocked the door would be flung open and they would say, "Master, we were expecting you. We have a hot drink for you. We have a meal for you. Just come in."

There is a parallel passage addressed to us as a people. Turn to Revelation 3:20. This is the seventh church of Revelation. This is the last generation of Christians and, in chapter 3, addressing this sleeping church, because Laodicea is lukewarm, He says in verse 20:

Here I am! I stand at the door and knock [in the second parable, Jesus is comparing the second coming as knocking on our door]. If anyone hears my voice [if you are sleeping, you won't be hearing] and opens the door, I will come in and eat with him, and he with me.

Christ is aware that the reason the second coming is a crisis is because it is going to be unexpected. He wants us to be on our guard. Now let's go back to our parable. Luke 12:37. Listen to how Jesus responds to the wise steward:

It will be good for those servants [that is, believers] whose master finds them watching when he comes....

Then, having said that, He deviates totally from Middle Eastern culture. Do you know what He says?

...I tell you the truth, he will dress himself to serve, will have them recline at the table and will come and wait on them.

Notice in the actual life the lord comes to his house, he knocks on the door, the servants are ready, they open the door, they bring him in, they make him sit down and they give him a hot drink. They say, "Do you want a bath?" (They warmed the water; there were no hot showers in those days.) "We are ready to serve you." But, in the parable, we read the very opposite. The "he" does not refer to the servants, which is plural, but to the Lord. The Lord will first gird himself up and he will say, "I want you servants to sit down at my table and I will serve you." That is the difference between the Middle Eastern lord, who will never do that, and the Lord Jesus Christ. What Jesus is referring to here is the great banquet and He wants everyone of you to be there.

Remember, they had watches in the days of Christ. In the Jewish culture, they had three watches a night; in the Roman system, they had four watches. Sometimes when you read your gospels, you will read one account giving four watches, one account giving two watch times, but the Jews had three watch periods. The first one was not hard because it was before midnight and they were awake, but the other two was when most of the watchmen went to sleep.

Christ is implying that He may come at the second or third watch which means that He will come at the time when we are the easiest conduced to sleep. One day our principal at our college in Ethiopia woke up at three o'clock in the morning and he couldn't go to sleep. So he said, "Let me go and see if our watchman is doing his duty." At most of our African institutions, we have to have watchmen because of thievery. So he looked and looked for the watchmen and guess where he found him? Under a eucalyptus tree fast asleep, snoring away at three in the morning which is the second watch.

Now we supplied these watchmen with a very powerful, six cell flashlight so that they could look under the bushes and anywhere where they heard noises. The principal did not wake him up but he took that flashlight away and took it to his house. The next day, just before the watchman began his duty, he came to the principal. He said, "I can't find my flashlight." So the principal said, "Did you lose it?" He said, "I don't know. I took it home and I put it on the shelf and I don't know what happened. Maybe one of my children took it and they lost it."

The principal said, "Are you sure you took it home?" "Yes, sir, I took it home." The principal opened the drawer and told him, "You did not take the flashlight home. I took it away from you at three o'clock in the morning. You were fast asleep." Then came the confession, the apology, and the promise that he would never do it again. Sometimes we do the same thing to the Lord. "Lord, we'll never do it again."

Luke 12:39:

But understand this: If the owner of the house had known at what hour the thief was coming, he would not have let his house be broken into.

When the thief comes, what time does he come? He comes when he knows you are fast asleep. We used to park my car right at the back door where our German shepherd could hear any noise. We kept the dog inside because they would throw poison, kill the dog, and then steal. One day I was so tired I just parked it outside. Jean said, "No, bring it in." I said, "No. No one would steal it. It's an old Peugeot, who will steal it?"

Well, the next morning it wasn't stolen but there were no wheels on it. There were four stones holding the car up and I lost all four wheels. Jesus is saying in Luke 12:40:

You also must be ready, because the Son of Man will come at an hour when you do not expect him.

Even for Adventists, the coming of the Lord will take us by surprise. We had a friend in Rwanda who was from Italy. He was at Newbold with us. He had a habit of taking very long showers. I don't know where he got the water from because we normally used a bucket with holes in it. He would sing at the top of his voice like a good Italian.

One day he was in the shower singing away and the thieves came. They knew that he was too busy and he took his own time. They came with a truck and took his bag, his clothing, his cooker, his fridge, everything. When he opened the door all he had was a towel around him. He couldn't take it. He came back home. He's a dentist in this country today. He was caught off guard.

Now comes the big question. How are we to be ready for the second coming of Christ? Jesus has told us, "You also must be ready, because the Son of Man will come at an hour when you do not expect him." In spite of all our theology, how can we be ready? Because that's the question. I have the answer from the words of Jesus Christ.

I want to take you to another crisis. This is not the second coming, but it is a crisis. Mark 14:38. This is the crisis of the cross and He pled with them to pray for Him because a crisis was coming. The Good Shepherd was about to lay His life down for His sheep and He wanted some support. He came back and He found His disciples sleeping. This is what He said:

Watch and pray so that you will not fall into temptation. The spirit is willing, but the body is weak.

That's where the problem is, the flesh. And we will have this weak flesh until the second coming of Christ.

Now the question is, "How do we watch?" There are three areas that I would like to mention quickly because it is the devil who wants you to be caught off guard. Christ doesn't want you to be caught off guard, which is why He gave these parables. How does the devil get you into the trap? Number one, I call the "wolf-wolf" method. Every time there is a crisis in the world, he uses it to say Christ is coming. "This is the beginning of the war of Armaggedon."

I can go right back to the day I was baptized, 1958, when there was a crisis over the Suez Canal. Nasser had taken the Suez Canal and I remember the evangelist saying, "This the beginning of the war of Armageddon," and my knees began to shake. I was ready for the coming; I was on my knees because, any time now, especially when I was traveling on a motorcycle from Nairobi to London, I might have to face the issue. It fizzled away.

Then something else came and we jumped on the bandwagon. Then came the Six Day war and I heard the same thing. Then came

Cuba during Kennedy's time and I heard the same thing. You know, when you repeat this, the time comes when our people say, "Look, we are tired of all these speculations," and we begin to relax. We begin to say with the foolish servants, "Our master is taking a long time in coming. I have heard that before."

That is why don't you ever say that this is the beginning of Armageddon because of what is happening in the Middle East. Stop speculating, because you are driving our people to get into the "wolf-wolf" mentality. He will come at a time that we do not know. We need to be on our guard all the time. In fact, we read in the Bible that when they say, "Peace, peace," then will sudden destruction come. 1 Thessalonians 5:3:

While people are saying, "Peace and safety," destruction will come on them suddenly, as labor pains on a pregnant woman, and they will not escape.

Peace even may fizzle away. I don't know, but I know one thing, that this is not the war of Armageddon. The war of Armageddon has nothing to do with the Middle East. It is only using the Middle East as a model. It is a war between the world and the church; between God's people and Satan's people around the world. So please, speculations, this "wolf-wolf" mentality has caused a lot of our people to become relaxed.

You have our young people saying, "My grandfather said He's coming and my father said He's coming. We are tired of hearing that He is coming." Well, that is one method and I have a text for that. Matthew 24 is dealing with the second coming of Christ. Look at Matthew 24:11:

...And many false prophets will appear and deceive many people.

Paul tell us in 2 Corinthians 11:3-4, 13-14 that these false prophets will arise within the church itself. These are warnings that come from Paul about the same things. Let me read it for you, 2 Corinthians 11:3-4:

But I am afraid that just as Eve was deceived by the serpent's cunning, your minds may somehow be led astray from your sincere and pure devotion to Christ. For if someone comes to you and preaches a Jesus other than the Jesus we preached, or if you receive a different spirit from the one you received, or a different gospel from the one you accepted, you put up with it easily enough.

Then I read in verses 13 and 14:

For such men are false apostles [false disciples, false prophets], deceitful workmen, masquerading as apostles of Christ. And no wonder, for Satan himself masquerades as an angel of light.

He is trying to deceive the very elect.

The second way that we can be caught off guard is to have a false theology of the second coming. Now we, as a church, to a large degree have been exempted from that. We, as a church, clearly teach that the second coming of Christ will be visible, will be physical, will be literal. But there are many, many Christians, probably more than our church contains, that believe in the secret rapture. They believe in two second comings.

The first one will be a secret rapture for the believers. If you are not part of that, you've had it. The second coming will not be for them, because they have already gone to heaven. If there is no secret rapture and you are not prepared for the literal coming, you will be taken off guard. There is the question of false theology and we need to help our fellow Christians to see that there is no teaching in the Bible regarding secret rapture.

The third thing that we need to watch is, "How should we be ready?" We have all kinds of ways. Note something: before the second coming of Christ will take place, there will be a time of trouble. So the second coming of Christ will be preceded by the time of trouble and the issue in that time of trouble is what we need to be concerned about. What will be the issue? In the time of trouble, Satan will do try to destroy you or to pull you out of Christ so that you will be caught off guard.

There are many who believe the issue is sinless living and I don't find that in scripture. I don't want anyone to misunderstand me, so I'm going to make it very clear. I believe that, by the power of God, men connected to God by faith can overcome every temptation. I believe that the power of God is greater than the power of the flesh.

But I don't believe that is the issue, because victory over sin is not my job; it is God's job. You can puff up your willpower and you can determine to overcome sin but you cannot. "Without Me," said Jesus, "you can do nothing." Our job is to abide in Christ.

Jesus said, in Luke 18:8b:

However, when the Son of Man comes, will he find faith on the earth?

He did not say, "Will I find sinless living people?" He said, "Will I find faith on the earth?" That is the issue. Can God produce a people not only who have faith in Christ but whose faith can endure unto the end even though the heavens fall? Can you hold onto Christ even though you feel forsaken of God? That is the issue.

For that to happen, God has to produce a people whose faith is unshakable no matter what their environment, no matter what their circumstances are. They will be on their guard. They will be walking by faith constantly because they have no confidence in themselves. They have no confidence in what is happening in the world. They do not trust even the false warnings. They realize that Christ may come any time. They must be on their guard constantly.

I want to turn to my closing texts. The first one is Romans 8:24, which lays the foundation for the other two texts. I have three texts. First of all I want to make the foundation clear. Listen to what Paul is saying in Romans 8:24a:

For in this hope we were saved.

There are two kinds of salvation — salvation by hope and salvation by reality. The first is called "justification by faith." That is salvation by hope. The second is called "glorification." That is when salvation will be a tangible reality and there's a space of time in between the two. In between that space of time is the salvation of sanctification, which is an ongoing process.

But Paul is saying here we are saved by hope. Here's all of Romans 8:24:

For in this hope we were saved. But hope that is seen is no hope at all. Who hopes for what he already has?

When the reality has come, you will no longer say, "I am looking forward to my salvation," because you already have it. Now look at verse 25:

But if we hope for what we do not yet have, we wait for it patiently.

While we are living under the umbrella of justification by faith, which is salvation by hope, do we wait for a period and then say, "We give up"? No.

That brings me to the second text, James 1. One of the hardest things for us is to have patience. I have more patience in the mission field than I have here and I'll tell you why. Many missionaries think that when God sends them to the mission field it is to help the natives, but I have discovered something. Very often God sends you to the mission field to help you. One of the things I learned in the mission field is patience. I had to wait for buses. I had to wait even to cash a check. I once timed how long it took to cash my check. I went to the bank and waited a whole hour.

But when I came to this country, I discovered that this is a country that does not know how to wait. We want everything now, not tomorrow, and it is ruining me. I am becoming like that. When I come to the supermarket, I look for the shortest line. We may not have to wait for supermarkets in this country; we may not have to wait for the banks to cash a check. In this country, I can use a card and get the money by punching a few buttons.

But when it comes to the second coming of Christ, this applies to the whole world. We have to learn to wait. And waiting is the hardest thing for us to do. So here is the counsel. James 1:2:

Consider it pure joy, my brothers, whenever you face trials of many kinds...

The context is, "Count it all joy when the devil tries to pull you out of Christ either through crisis, persecution, or through many problems." Why? Not because you enjoy these things. Verses 3-4:

...because you know that the testing of your faith develops perseverance. Perseverance must finish its work so that you may be mature and complete, not lacking anything.

Jesus said in Matthew 10:22 (last part):

He who stands firm to the end will be saved.

My final text is applying to us. Revelation 14:12. It is my prayer that this text applies to you and that every part of this text is yours. The first thing this text says is:

This calls for patient endurance on the part of the saints....

Here are people who a have hold on Christ and will not let Him go, not even during the time of trouble. Remember Jacob. Do you know what it means to have your leg dislocated? Do you know the pain involved? I know what I'm talking about. I have had that experience playing soccer in Africa. It is excruciating and Jacob would not let go until the angel blessed him.

Do you know what he was told? Genesis 32:28:

Then the man said, "Your name will no longer be Jacob, but Israel, because you have struggled with God and with men and have overcome."

Israel is all those who have prevailed. Here's all of Revelation 14:12:

This calls for patient endurance on the part of the saints who obey God's commandments and remain faithful to Jesus.

All three are related. Don't take one without the other. Don't just say keep the commandments. You cannot keep the commandments without the faith of Jesus and you cannot have patience without the faith of Jesus. The faith of Jesus is the foundation.

It is my prayer that, in spite of all our theology, in spite of all our teachings, be warned that the coming of Christ may take us off guard. He may come at a time and in a way that we least expect, even though we have it quite clearly in our minds. But whatever way He comes, whatever time He comes, it is my prayer that the parable will be applied to you, that you will have your loins girded, that you will be ready, because at such an hour that you know not, He shall come. May God bless us as a people. Amen.

CHAPTER NINETEEN

THE PARABLE OF THE SOIL

Luke 8:4-8:

While a large crowd was gathering and people were coming to Jesus from town after town, he told this parable: "A farmer went out to sow his seed. As he was scattering the seed, some fell along the path; it was trampled on, and the birds of the air ate it up. Some fell on rock, and when it came up, the plants withered because they had no moisture. Other seed fell among thorns, which grew up with it and choked the plants. Still other seed fell on good soil. It came up and yielded a crop, a hundred times more than was sown."

When he said this, he called out, "He who has ears to hear, let him hear."

This is commonly known as "The Parable of the Sower," but you'll notice that I have changed the name. I am calling it "The Parable of the Soil." The reason I have done this is because we are told nothing about the sower in this parable except what he did which is sow seed. But we are told a great deal about the soil and I am convinced that the whole purpose of this parable is to press home how the seed, which is the Word of God, not so much how it is sown or who sows it, but how it is heard, responded to, and the results it produces in the life. That is why Jesus ended the parable with these words, "He who has ears to hear let him hear."

Now the big question that we must ask ourselves as we are confronted with this parable is, "Has the Word that has been sown in my life born any fruit?" Because the Gospel is not a theory. It is not some great or grand idea that somebody invented. The Bible describes the Gospel as the power of God unto salvation. If it is so that the gospel is the power of God unto salvation, then there has to be some evidence in our lives. There has to be a salvation that issues out in holy living. There has to be a salvation that issues out in effective witnessing and service. This is the clear teaching of the New Testament.

Let me give you a couple of texts to show you how this is taught by two writers of the New Testament. Turn to 1 Peter 1:13-16:

Therefore, prepare your minds for action; be self-controlled; set your hope fully on the grace to be given you when Jesus Christ is revealed. As obedient children, do not conform to the evil desires you had when you lived in ignorance. But just as he who called you is holy, so be holy in all you do; for it is written: "Be holy, because I am holy."

The gospel must produce holiness of living.

Then turn back to 1 Corinthians 15 and you will discover that the Gospel must also produce effective service. I read in 1 Corinthians 15 these words of the apostle Paul. He is talking concerning himself. In 1 Corinthians 15:9-10, Paul says,

For I am the least of the apostles and do not even deserve to be called an apostle, because I persecuted the church of God. But by the grace of God I am what I am, and his grace to me was not without effect. No, I worked harder than all of them...

And then he adds,

...Yet not I, but the grace of God that was with me.

Of course, these two cannot be separated.

We will look at the parable, expound on it, and then see what God is trying to tell us today living in the 20th Century, which is the same as what Christ was telling to that great multitude which gathered to hear Him 2,000 years ago. The first thing we see as we look at the parable is that the common denominator is the seed.

You will also notice that the seed was sown in four different kinds of soil. What is that seed to which Jesus was referring? He tells us what that seed is in Luke 8:11 because, after He gave this parable, in Luke 8:9, the disciples came to Him and they said, "What does this parable mean?" Beginning at verse 11 in Luke 8:11-15, Jesus expounds on this parable. Not only do we have the parable, but we have Jesus' interpretation of the parable.

In verse 11 He says,

"This is the meaning of the parable: The seed is the word of God."

And God sows that seed by various means. He uses the radio; He uses the preaching of the word, He uses witnessing, but the seed is the Word of God. I read in John 1:1:

In the beginning was the Word, and the Word was with God, and the Word was God.

Then in John 1:14a, we read,

The Word became flesh and made his dwelling among us.

So the Word of God is Jesus Christ, and if you turn to Hebrews 4:12 we are told something about the power of this Word. I want you to listen to this one:

For the word of God [which is Jesus Christ] is living and active. Sharper than any double-edged sword, it penetrates even to dividing soul and spirit, joints and marrow; it judges the thoughts and attitudes of the heart.

This is why I said that the Word of God is not some theory. It is living and powerful and sharper than any two-edged sword.

Of course, in the days of Paul, in the days of the New Testament, they didn't use machine guns; they used swords to fight, and this was a two-edged sword so that you could use it both ways. And the Word of God is like a two-edged sword that "penetrates even to dividing soul and spirit, joints and marrow," dividing what is of God and what is of man, what is of the Spirit and what is of the flesh. That is what the Word does, because it discerns and separates the two. So the seed that Jesus was referring to here in this parable is the Word of God.

The soil that is spoken about here represents the hearts of men. Look at the context. This was almost like an evangelistic effort, because in Luke 8:4 we read that a great multitude came to hear Him, plus people from all the various cities around that area. The soil represents the hearts of the hearers, and you will notice that He divides the hearts of men who hear the Gospel, the Word of God, into four camps. I have classified each of these camps as follows:

The first one is found in the second half of Luke 8:5:

A farmer went out to sow his seed [which is the word of God]. As he was scattering the seed, some fell along the path; it was trampled on, and the birds of the air ate it up.

I call this heart a hard heart and you will see why in a few moments.

The second soil is in verse 6:

Some fell on rock [or on stony ground], and when it came up, the plants withered because they had no moisture.

I call this the shallow heart.

Then there is the third soil which is in verse 7:

Other seed fell among thorns, which grew up with it and choked the plants.

This is the divided heart.

Finally we come to the good heart, the responsive heart, the open heart in verse 8:

"Still other seed fell on good soil. It came up and yielded a crop, a hundred times more than was sown." When he said this, he called out, "He who has ears to hear, let him hear."

As we come to the end of the parable, we see a field of wheat without any weeds. During one summer, just before the harvest, you could see several kinds of wheat fields. Some of them were pure wheat. Others had green clumps sticking out. Do you know what they were? They were weeds. That's the divided heart. But at the end of the parable, we see a wheat field or a corn field, and the stalks are full and fat with grain. They tell me they had a bumper harvest that year. The soil is well tilled and watered, and what a beautiful sight for the farmer.

Now what is Jesus trying to tell us? Well, before we arrived at this interpretation, it is clear that what Jesus is looking for from those who hear His word is fruit, because Jesus is comparing the sowing of the gospel as the sowing of seed, just like a farmer who plants seed, is looking for fruit. But before we come to the fruitfulness that He is looking for, He gives us three main reasons why a Christian is unfruitful, why human beings who have heard the Gospel are unfruitful. We will look at each one of these hearts.

We will begin with a hard heart which is verse 5, and the interpretation is verse 12. We have already read verse 5. Let's read verse 12:

Those along the path are the ones who hear [the gospel], and then the devil comes and takes away the word from their hearts, so that they may not believe and be saved.

The first thing I want to remind you of is the common denominator. Notice that the same kind of seed was sown in four different kinds of soil, so there is no difference in the seed. It is the same gospel. What Christ is dealing with here is our response to that gospel. This first soil, the hard heart, is the seed that falls by the wayside. I need to explain this because it is a little bit different than how we do it today. In America, the farmer first plows the field. He prepares the soil and then he plants the seed.

That is not how it was in Palestine in Christ's day. During the off-growing season, during the time when the fields were not used, normally during winter, the fields were often used by the people as short-cuts going to the market place. So the fields were full of 15 inch paths that went across the field. When it came to planting time, they did not first plow the land like the farmer does here. They sowed the seed first, and maybe two or three days later they plowed the land. Then they waited for the rain to come and the seed would germinate. So here is the farmer, he sows the seed and some of it fell on the 15-inch pathway that was the result of people walking on it. Two things happened to that seed:

Notice in verse 5, it was trampled down. Before the plowing took place, people still used it and it was trampled down.

The birds came and devoured those seeds.

To what are these two things referring? Well, it tells us that this heart is a stubborn heart. It is a heart that is resisting the Word of God. I would like to give you a couple of texts because this refers to the impenetrable heart, a heart that the seed is not allowed to go in. We will look first of all at Mark's account of this parable. All three Gospels have recorded this parable. In Mark 4:15, which is an interpretation of this first soil, Jesus uses a word here that Luke does not use:

Some people are like seed along the path, where the word is sown. As soon as [in some translations, "immediately"] they hear it, Satan comes and takes away the word that was sown in them.

Now we have discovered that the seed is the Word of God, which is Jesus Christ and Him crucified. When this gospel is preached, some hearts immediately respond in a negative way and I want to tell you how Paul describes this in 2 Corinthians 4. How does the devil, who is represented by the birds, immediately remove the seed? Paul tells us how he does it in 2 Corinthians 4:3-4:

And even if our gospel is veiled [prevented from germinating], it is veiled to those who are perishing [or who are lost]. The god of this age has blinded the minds of unbelievers [remember, the mind and the heart are synonymous terms in the Bible], so that they cannot see the light of the gospel of the glory of Christ, who is the image of God.

In other words, the devil comes and says, "No, this is a bunch of lies. Salvation isn't an easy thing. You have to earn it."

I had a phone call once from a man who wanted to put a cartoon in one of the magazines he edits. He said, "One of your parishioners from your previous church told me that you had a very special cartoon that you hung in your office, and I would like you to send me a copy." Well, I left it there, so I don't have it. But it was a cartoon that I cut out from Christianity Today. It was based on a bank ad which said, "Put your money in our bank, because we do it the old-fashioned way. We earn it." In the cartoon, a group of Pharisees were telling Jesus Christ, "We believe in salvation the old-fashioned way. We earn it." Their hearts were hard to the gospel. They did not want to respond because the devil had blinded their eyes so that they may not see the good news.

We are told that not only would the birds devour, which means the devil takes away the good news from them by deceiving them, but we are told that the seed is also trampled on the ground. I want to give you another text about trampling. Turn to Hebrews 10:26, a verse that is greatly misunderstood by many. What does the text say?

If we deliberately keep on sinning...

This is a misunderstood statement because to us the word "sin" normally means transgression of the law, but the writer of Hebrews is not discussing the law here. He is discussing the gospel. He is discussing what He said in Hebrews 10:14:

...Because by one sacrifice he [Christ] has made perfect forever those who are being made holy [or those who have accepted Him].

How do I know? Because the context says so (Hebrews 10:26):

If we deliberately keep on sinning after we have received the knowledge of the truth [or have heard the truth], no sacrifice for sins is left...

That's the gospel. All that is left is (Hebrews 10:27):

...but only a fearful expectation of judgment and of raging fire that will consume the enemies of God.

Here Paul is writing to the Jewish Christians, using Hebrews 10:28 as an example because they are so familiar with the book of Moses, the book of the law:

Anyone who rejected the law of Moses died without mercy on the testimony of two or three witnesses.

Here is a person who knows the law of Moses, he breaks it and he is punished. He might have some excuse and say, "I did it because I am weak." But look at Hebrews 10:29:

How much more severely do you think a man deserves to be punished...

You may have an excuse for breaking the law, but you have no excuse for rejecting the gospel because it is a gift, and if you deliberately, willfully reject the truth after you have heard the gospel,

How much more severely do you think a man deserves to be punished [listen to the next words] who has trampled the Son of God under foot, who has treated as an unholy thing the blood of the covenant that sanctified him, and who has insulted the Spirit of grace?

Notice the past tense.

"That blood sanctified you, but you counted it as something useless. You trample underfoot the gospel, you count it as a common thing and insult the Spirit of grace." I hope there is nobody reading this with a hard heart, who has rejected the gospel.

But now we must move to number two, back to Luke 8:6:

Some fell on rock [or on stony ground, in some translations], and when it came up, the plants withered because they had no moisture.

Now notice there is a difference here. In the first heart, the seed was snatched away immediately. In the second heart, the shallow heart, there was germination. The soil was there but it was very thin. The seed germinated but the roots were not allowed to go down deep because there was a thick layer of rock just below that thin layer of soil, and the roots could not go down. The result was that, suddenly, that seed which had germinated, withered away.

Look at Christ's interpretation of this parable. Verse 13:

Those on the rock [or the stony ground] are the ones who receive the word with joy when they hear it, but they have no root. They believe for a while, but in the time of testing they fall away.

Notice they receive the Word with joy. I would like to read both Matthew's and Mark's account. Let's start with Matthew 13:21. Let's see how Matthew puts the same parable:

But since he has no root, he lasts only a short time. When trouble or persecution comes because of the word [because you have accepted the gospel you are facing crisis, you are facing opposition, you are facing criticism], he quickly falls away.

This is what Matthew tells us. He gives us a little more detail. In Mark 4:16-17, we read Mark's account of this parable:

Others, like seed sown on rocky places, hear the word and at once receive it with joy. But since they have no root, they last only a short time. When trouble or persecution comes because of the word, they quickly fall away.

In other words, the moment you become a Christian, the moment you rejoice in Christ, I can guarantee you, the devil will make life hard for you. The question is, can you endure it? Will you hold on? Unfortunately, this group — the shallow heart — does not hold on. Outwardly, they look all right. For a while there's a great response, but that response is only a covering. Beneath is solid rock which cannot stand persecution and opposition so you give up.

That moves us to the third soil. I would like to emphasize the third soil because I believe the greatest danger we face as Christians is the third soil. Look at Luke 8:7:

Other seed fell among thorns, which grew up with it and choked the plants.

Verse 14, the application:

The seed that fell among thorns stands for those who hear, but as they go on their way they are choked by life's worries, riches and pleasures, and they do not mature.

Have you seen the progression? Jesus is describing not only four groups of people but he's describing a progression. The first soil, which is the hard heart, the seed is snatched away immediately. The second soil the seed germinates, but it does not last very long; it dies suddenly. The third seed goes one step further. It germinates; it shows life; it even shows some development. There is a promise but it never reaches maturity. The seed got in; the seed went down but it could not develop fully and produce fruit, because there was a rival crop. Something came in and choked the good news out of that person.

One day a young boy, 13 or 14 years old, a young teenager, was returning home from school. This is up in the highlands of Kenya, called Keyse. He was dissatisfied with his religion. He was a Roman

Catholic and he was dissatisfied with the rituals. It brought him no joy, no peace, no hope. He was returning home at sundown. The sun set and it was getting dark. He looked up and he prayed, "God, is there not something better than this? Is this the way that You want me to go, simply following rituals or is there a better way? Can you lead me to it?" He was praying while he was walking, and suddenly as he was walking out in the country there on the pathway, he saw a little piece of paper torn away from a magazine. He looked at it and he picked it up. It was just a small piece of paper and all it had was an address on it. He did not know what that address meant, but it was the address of the Review and Herald. How that paper got there, he does not know to this day, because the nearest Adventist church was 50 miles away. There were no Adventists living there.

But there was this little piece of paper torn from the Review with the address, and he felt impressed that God was answering his prayer so he wrote a letter to the Review and Herald. He said, "I don't know who you are or what you publish, but I have a great burden," and he explained his story. "Could you help me if you have any material or books that will teach me how to walk the way of God and give me some Bible lessons?" The Review and Herald published his letter, and you dear people from this country flooded him with literature: Signs of the Times, Message Magazines, Bible Readings for the Home — all kinds of books. So much so that the officer at the post office called this boy and said, "Would you please tell these people to stop sending? You're cluttering our post office." It was a small post office in a little village out there.

Well, he took this material and he read it and he studied his Bible and gave his heart to the Lord. He accepted the teachings of this church. Then he began to teach others, and within a year he had 50 people who had joined him and they were worshipping every Sabbath. Then he discovered that there was an Adventist church in that district and he got the address of the headquarters. He wrote to them saying, "Can you send a pastor? We have 50 people to be baptized." The President said to one of the pastors, "You go, and please check. I don't think they are ready for baptism." But when the pastor came and examined them, they knew their Bibles; they knew everything. So he had a great baptism service.

The young boy went to his father just like the prodigal son, and said, "Father, I want my inheritance now." The Keyses are mainly farmers and the parents divide the land among the sons, so this boy got the piece of land that was designated for him. He did not sell it and spend the money on himself. He took this land and he built a church and donated it to the cause of God. Then when he finished his primary education he came to our secondary school and then he went to college. That's where I met him. He took theology and he graduated. He came to Uganda because our theology course was offered at our college there. Very sincere; I won't say very highly academic, but he was very sincere and very dedicated. He was determined to be a great worker for God. What wonderful promises.

Just after he graduated he saw an ad in the newspaper from the University of Nairobi, offering scholarships even in the department of theology. He said, "Now I can get some more education free of charge." So he saw me one day and he said, "Do you think that I should apply?" And I said, "No." He asked me why. I said, "Because I happen to know the professor of the department of theology there, and he is very liberal." But he did not understand what I meant. He thought I did not want him to progress in education, so he applied and got the scholarship.

There he was exposed to what is hitting a lot of our young people: the historical, critical method of studying the Bible, where the mind is elevated above revelation, where human experience is made the measuring stick of truth. Gradually, he became intellectual and he began to look at the Bible as written by some poor old people thousands of years ago who did not have much intelligence and did not live in the scientific age.

He began throwing his books away, one by one. He left the church and worked for the government as a teacher. I visited him and he said, "Ah, this is something for my mother and father who are uneducated, who cannot read and write. You are now talking to an educated man." What a tragedy! The seed had been sown; it had germinated; it had developed. But sad to say, something came in and choked out the life of the gospel in this young boy.

Do you read what the text says? Cares, riches, and pleasures. We are living in a country where we are always bombarded with this. Young people, you are always bombarded. Once I took a week of prayer and four girls came to see me. They were all seniors and they said, "Pastor, this is the first time in our four years at this academy that we've had a week of prayer where the speaker spoke from the Word of God." I asked, "What did the others do?" "Well, they tried to entertain us." I am not here to entertain you, because the devil is here to entertain you. There is nothing wrong enjoying or having a good time but it is wrong when you allow the cares, the pleasures, and the riches of this world to snatch away the life of the gospel in you.

We are told in the Bible (Ephesians 4:30):

And do not grieve the Holy Spirit of God, with whom you were sealed for the day of redemption.

This is one of the greatest temptations in this country. We don't have these temptations in communist countries where your life is in danger all the time, where you struggle to survive. But in a country where we have lots of material things, there is great danger.

I am going to be honest with you. According to a very conservative report, it is estimated that there is a minimum of two million former Seventh-day Adventists living in the North American Division. They were once members of the church, and this, of course, is true, unfortunately, of all other denominations. People are leaving the churches. They are leaving Christ because they think the world is a better place. Their life is choked out and this is the greatest danger we face in this part of the world.

Now I want to go to the fourth soil. The same seed is sown in the good soil. Here we have a wonderful picture of the good soil. We have seen the first soil is a hard heart. The second soil is a shallow heart. The third soil is a divided heart, where the seed lacks room for growth. But now we have an open heart that is receptive, a heart that is teachable, a heart that is submissive.

Here is the difference between legalism and the gospel. Legalism is only concerned with outward conformity and outward performance. The gospel does not begin with the outward performance. It goes deep down to the very core of your being, the heart, the inner man, and it transforms the heart. And then it begins to grow, and eventually, outwardly it produces the fruits of love, joy, peace, longsuffering. That is what Christ is looking for in every believer.

Let's look at the words of Jesus Christ. Turn to John 15. Christianity is not simply a mental assent to truth. Christianity is the power of God in your life. Christianity demands that, if it has taken a hold in you, and is growing in you, and controlling you, it has to bear fruit. There is no "maybe." Of course, Luke says a hundredfold, but if you look at the other accounts of this parable you will notice that it says thirtyfold some, sixtyfold others, and some a hundredfold.

In John 15:5, Jesus is speaking:

I am the vine...

Remember, Christ is the Word of God, the seed that is sown.

I am the vine; you are the branches. If a man remains in me and I in him, he will bear much fruit...

This is the open heart. Such a believer bears "much fruit." It may be thirtyfold, it may be sixtyfold, it may be a hundredfold but it will always bear much fruit.

...apart from me you can do nothing.

In other words, "Without Me, you cannot bear fruit, for without Me, you can do nothing."

Now look at John 15:6:

If anyone does not remain in me, he is like a branch that is thrown away and withers; such branches are picked up, thrown into the fire and burned.

This is the tragedy of the third soil because it germinates, it develops, but it never grows to maturity. It ends up in the fire. John 15:7:

If you remain in me and my words remain in you...

The question is not whether you have heard the Word. The question is not whether you have received the Word. The ultimate question is: "Is the Word abiding in you? Is it controlling you? Are you saying, 'Not I, but Christ'?" That's the question.

If you remain in me and my words remain in you, ask whatever you wish, and it will be given you.

And by the way, when the Word abides in you, you will never ask anything for yourself, or for egocentric concern. You will ask what David asked (Psalm 51:10):

Create in me a pure heart, O God, and renew a steadfast spirit within me.

"God, give me Your grace that I may witness for You. Give me Your love that I may reflect Your love."

Those are the kind of desires that come into you when the Word abides in you. Ellen G. White tells us His desires will be our desires, His thoughts will be our thoughts, His ambitions will be our ambitions. Why? Because the Word of God is abiding in you. John 15:8:

This is to my Father's glory, that you bear much fruit, showing yourselves to be my disciples.

Jesus said in John 13:35:

By this all men will know that you are my disciples, if you love one another.

This is what Christ is looking for. He is looking for a people who are manifesting a life that is fruitful. When God gave the gospel first to the Jews, it was His plan and His desire that the Jews would lighten the earth with the knowledge of the God of Heaven. But after 1,500 years, Jesus could say to them (Matthew 23:37-38),

O Jerusalem, Jerusalem, you who kill the prophets and stone those sent to you, how often I have longed to gather your children together, as a hen gathers her chicks under her wings, but you were not willing. Look, your house is left to you desolate.

Then He gave the gospel commission to the early Christian Church. We are now living 2,000 years later, and yet Revelation

18:1 has not been fulfilled. What does it say there?

After this I saw another angel coming down from heaven. He had great authority, and the earth was illuminated by his splendor.

I want to conclude with what God's plan is for each one of us. This is God's desire for this church. I would like to read two texts, both from the Old Testament, both pointing to God's ideal for each one of us, and for His church but which was never fulfilled among the Jews. It is my prayer that it will be fulfilled in the Christian church. The first one is Ezekiel 20:41. Listen to this:

I will accept you as fragrant incense when I bring you out from the nations and gather you from the countries where you have been scattered, and I will show myself holy among you in the sight of the nations.

The Amplified Bible version brings it out so clearly:

I will manifest My holiness among you in the sight of the nations [who will seek Me because of My power displayed in you].

Isn't that wonderful? That is what God wants to do. He wants this Church to bear fruit, and to display His power to a perishing world.

The other text is found in Micah 4:1-2:

The Mountain of the LORD.

In the last days the mountain of the LORD's temple will be established as chief among the mountains; it will be raised above the hills, and peoples will stream to it.

Many nations will come and say, "Come, let us go up to the mountain of the LORD, to the house of the God of Jacob. He will teach us his ways, so that we may walk in his paths." The law will go out from Zion, the word of the LORD from Jerusalem.

The Living Bible translations also puts it nicely:

But in the last days, Mount Zion, [which is the symbol of the Church] will be the most renowned of all the mountains of the world.

What Micah is saying is that the Christian Church will be the most noted one, the most famous one among all the other religions of the world. They will be praised by all nations. They will be renowned; they will be known and they will be praised.

Do you know why? Because the request that was made by the famous pagan philosopher Nietzche, will finally be fulfilled. Nietzche was the son of a Lutheran pastor who gave up Christianity to become an atheist. He was a great philosopher. Do you know what he said to the Christian church? "If you expect me to believe in your Redeemer, you Christians will have to look a lot more redeemed." As long as there is jealousy, as long as there is distrust, as long as there is backbiting, we are not displaying the power of the Word in our lives.

The question that I am asking you today is: Which soil do you belong to: the hard heart, the shallow heart, the divided heart, or the open heart? Remember that when Jesus said, "He that has ears let him hear," He was saying, "You hearers can decide which of the four soils you would like to be. You can choose."

If you have been the first three in the past, may God give you the grace to say, "Now I don't want to be the hard heart; I don't want to be the shallow heart; I don't want to be the divided heart. I want to be the open heart because the open heart is the one whose Christianity endures unto the end." If you read the parable, if you read Luke 8:14-15, you will notice, "it bears fruit with patience." When people accept the gospel, don't expect to see a transformation outwardly immediately. It takes time for the Word to come out to the top. Give them a chance to grow. But ultimately it is my prayer that this church will lighten the world with the glory of Jesus Christ. Amen.

CHAPTER TWENTY

THE PARABLE OF THE MUSTARD SEED

Mark 4:30-32:

Again he said, "What shall we say the kingdom of God is like, or what parable shall we use to describe it? It is like a mustard seed, which is the smallest seed you plant in the ground. Yet when planted, it grows and becomes the largest of all garden plants, with such big branches that the birds of the air can perch in its shade."

Among this crowd that came to listen to Jesus were some scribes and Pharisees who had, unfortunately, perverted the whole purpose and mission of the Messiah. They had taken the ideas, the philosophies, the system of the world and applied it to the kingdom of God. Then Jesus came. He was poor, uneducated, and, in their eyes, insignificant. How could He be the One to fulfill that great mission of the Messiah, who was supposed to come as a conquering ruler and get rid of the Romans and establish the kingdom of God? In response to this false theology, Jesus spoke this parable of the mustard seed (and the following parable of the leaven, where the woman put a little leavening into the dough and it leavened the whole bread).

All three of the synoptic Gospels — Matthew, Mark, and Luke — record the parable of the mustard seed. But somehow Matthew omits the first statement which is a question and which is extremely important in order to understand the parable. Turn to Mark 4. We are going to study this parable from Mark where we have the full parable. It is recorded in Luke, too, but we will look at Mark. Notice that Jesus began this parable by asking two questions. Mark 4:30:

Again he said, "What shall we say the kingdom of God is like, or what parable shall we use to describe it?"

The Pharisees were trying to compare the kingdom of God to a typical kingdom of this world, except it would be stronger, it would be greater, it would be richer. Jesus was simply saying by these questions, "There is nothing in secular history, there is no earthly kingdom with which I can compare the kingdom of God because the kingdom of God is in complete opposition to anything that is human." I was very interested to notice the observation that is found in Christ's Object Lessons by Ellen G. White. I would like to read it to you because it involves something here that we need to apply to our own situation. Listen to this from Christ's Object Lessons, page 77 [brackets indicate my comments]:

"Earthly governments prevail by physical force; they maintain their dominion by war; but the founder of the new kingdom [the kingdom of God] is the Prince of Peace. The Holy Spirit represents worldly kingdoms under the symbols of fierce beasts of prey [you will find this in the books of Daniel and Revelation]; but Christ is 'the Lamb of God, which taketh away the sins of the world.' John 1:29. In His plan of government there is no employment of brute force to compel the conscience. The Jews looked for the kingdom of God to be established in the same way as the kingdoms of the world. [This is the part I want you to listen to.] To promote righteousness they resorted to external measures. They devised methods and plans. But Christ implants a principal. By implanting truth and righteousness He counteracts error and sin."

There are some here who would like me to follow the same methods as the Jews did: impose upon you rules and regulations and tell you, "If you don't shape up, you won't make it." That is a worldly method. Like one Russian Marxist told me in Ethiopia, "We don't believe in five day non-smoking programs. That doesn't work. We believe in authority. When we pass a law, 'No smoking,' nobody smokes, because, if they do, they will have to swallow lead." God doesn't use that method. There was nothing in the worldly kingdom Christ could use for comparison.

So what did He do? He took a little seed from among the different spices they used in the Middle East, He took the smallest of the spices, a little round seed approximately one-thirty-second of an inch in diameter, and He used that as a comparison. Why? Because the kingdom of God works in a completely different system. It does not work on the basis of rules and regulations. He implants in the life of the believer a new life, a new principal. When that life is released by germination and is allowed to develop it produces a bush that is bigger than any other tree. The mustard seed, the smallest of small seeds, Jesus says, produces a bush that is so big compared to the other herbs that the birds can to rest on it and find shade.

I don't know how many of you have seen a mustard seed. The Jews ate what is known as kosher meat. Have any of you tasted kosher meat? One day we were returning from furlough and the airline forgot to bring four vegetarian dishes, they had only three. So the stewardess said to me, "I'm sorry, we have only three. Do you mind if we gave you a kosher meal?" So I said, "Fine."

I can't remember if it was my wife or I who had it but all I remember is that it looked awful. What they do is take the meat and scrape all the fat which, by the way, is one of the tastier parts. Then they soak the meat in salt water until all the blood is drained. They squeeze all the blood out until you have a piece of flesh that looks like overchewed chewing gum or shoe leather and it tastes awful. So to make it tasty they put spices in it and one of the key spices was mustard.

Any of you who come to my home and have rice and curry, mustard is one of the key ingredients for making curry, too, because it's a very important spice. In America they make a paste called mustard, but that is not the way to use mustard because it has to be cooked. Otherwise, it is abrasive.

The mustard seed was a small seed. It looked like a grain of sand. When Jesus spoke this parable, there were bushes of mustard because it is a common plant all over the area. They could see this mustard bush towering above all other herbs because, even though the seed was small, it produced a huge bush, as Jesus says in this parable. Jesus is comparing the kingdom of God with this mustard seed. Christ is saying that the kingdom of God does not begin by force. God doesn't take the kingdom of the world by force. He implants in the life of individuals, in the life of the church, a new life, a new principle. As long as that mustard seed sits in a bottle it is useless as far as reproducing. But the moment you sow it — and that's what the parable is talking about — verses 31-32:

It is like a mustard seed, which is the smallest seed you plant in the ground. Yet when planted, it grows and becomes the largest of all garden plants, with such big branches that the birds of the air can perch in its shade.

When you sow the mustard seed into the ground something happens, because in that mustard seed is a life principle. There's a germ in it which has life in it. That life is dormant until the seed is sown. When does that seed spring to life? That's one of the questions we are going to answer. Because when it does, it begins to grow and it grows it grows so big, Jesus says, that it covers the whole earth. Now Jesus, of course, was primarily referring to the establishment of the kingdom of God as part of the Christian church.

The Christian church began with a very small, insignificant group — twelve disciples. They were fishermen; they were peasants; they had no PhDs; they had no technology behind them; they had no budget; they were poor; they were insignificant; they counted for nothing in the eyes of the Pharisees and the scribes. But when I turn to Acts 17:6, which was only a few years later, that seed had germinated and grown so mightily that the enemies of the gospel accused the Christian church and the disciples of turning the world upside down:

But when they did not find them, they dragged Jason and some other brothers before the city officials, shouting: "These men who have caused trouble all over the world have now come here...."

Small beginning, but what a great growth.

Then by the third century A.D., the Christian church had become so strong, so influential, so powerful that the emperor of Rome, the greatest emperor in those days of the greatest empire, realized that the only way he could survive as an emperor was to become a Christian. So, for political diplomacy, and out of wisdom from a fleshly point of view, he decided to become a Christian.

Constantine was baptized into the Christian church because he realized that there was no way to destroy the Christian Church. The Roman Empire did try, for three centuries, to destroy the church by martyrdom, by persecution. That great church father Tertullian made this statement, "The more you kill us; the more you mow us down, the more we spring up." He made this famous statement now found also in The Great Controversy: "The oftener we are mown down by you, the more in number we grow; the blood of Christians is seed." The blood of the martys is the seed of the church. The more you kill us and sow us into the ground, the more Christians come up.

That is the secret of the kingdom of God. God doesn't want your budget; He doesn't depend on your budget. He doesn't depend on technology, and we are making the mistake of trying to borrow from the world, its resources, its culture, its policy, its philosophy. It will not work. In the end of the 16th Century, the world moved in a new direction. It is called the Scientific Method. By the 18th century, we had arrived to the Age of Enlightenment. The Holy Bible, especially in France, was chucked out. No longer would we accept this Book, the Revelation of God.

But the scientific method created a problem in the Christian church. "How can Christianity be acceptable to a scientific world?" was the biggest question the theologians of the 17th and 18th Centuries faced. They came up with a solution, a solution that did not come from the Word of God. The solution came from their own ideas and it was, "We need to make Christianity conform to the scientific method." They developed what is known today as the historical critical method of interpreting Scripture, by which they made the human mind the measuring stick of truth so that they would be acceptable to their peers, the scientific minds.

The Christian Church has been going down and down. It is only when we restore the Bible as the life of the church, only as we make Christ the Source of the power of the church (like Martin Luther and the Reformation did and turned the world upside down, or like John Wesley did and turned England upside down) that we will solve the problems that we facing today. There is a prophecy in Revelation 18:1 that has to do with the last generation of Christians. Do you know what the prophecy says?

After this I saw another angel coming down from heaven. He had great authority, and the earth was illuminated by his splendor.

Before the end comes, God is going to lighten this earth with His glory by the last generation of Christians. That is us and we need to discover the principle of the mustard seed and what it is that caused that small seed to produce such a big bush.

The life in that seed had that ability, just like the life of Christ has the ability to produce a church that is dynamic, that is powerful, and that is able to bring shelter and shade and peace and hope to the world around us. But that life in that mustard seed cannot produce that big bush unless it first dies. The principle of any seed — whether it be mustard seed or corn seed or any other seed — is life out of death. That seed has to be sown; that seed has to die before life can come out and produce that big bush.

But, first of all, let me give you a couple of texts to show you clearly that God does not depend on human resources to fulfill His mission. Turn to 1 Corinthians 1. Remember that Corinth was the most sophisticated church in the New Testament time. It was famous for all kinds of philosophy, of all kinds of humanistic ideas which, unfortunately, were creeping into the church itself. Paul in the very first chapter is trying to tell them that the power of the church is not in human resources. It is in the cross of Christ. He begins in 1 Corinthians 1:17-18 by saying:

For Christ did not send me to baptize, but to preach the gospel — not with words of human wisdom, lest the cross of Christ be emptied of its power. For the message of the cross is foolishness to those who are perishing, but to us who are being saved it is the power of God.

Now I go to verses 23-29:

But we preach Christ crucified: a stumbling block to Jews and foolishness to Gentiles, but to those whom God has called, both Jews and Greeks, Christ the power of God and the wisdom of God. For the foolishness of God is wiser than man's wisdom, and the weakness of God is stronger than man's strength. Brothers, think of what you were when you were called. Not many of you were wise by human standards; not many were influential; not many were of noble birth. But God chose the foolish things of the world to shame the wise; God chose the weak things of the world to shame the strong. He chose the lowly things of this world and the despised things — and the things that are not — to nullify the things that are, so that no one may boast before him.

Do you realize that we can turn this place upside down? But it will take the life of Christ.

How should that life be manifest in us? Let's start with Romans 6. Many of you have already been baptized, but the question is, "Do you know what your baptism was all about?" This is the question, not, "Have you been baptized by immersion?" The question is: "Do you know what it all stands for?" Paul tells us in Romans 6:3:

Or don't you know that all of us who were baptized into Christ Jesus were baptized into his death?

Now look at verse 4:

We were therefore buried with him through baptism into death in order that, just as Christ was raised from the dead through the glory of the Father, we too may live a new life.

That is the mustard seed that must grow in you and become a big bush. Let me put it in the words of Jesus. Turn to John 12:24. Jesus puts it very beautifully. Here is the principle. Jesus is talking here and He says:

I tell you the truth, unless a kernel of wheat falls to the ground and dies, it remains only a single seed. But if it dies, it produces many seeds.

That is the secret of the seed, and you will notice that Christ often used the seed as the principle of His kingdom. The seed must first die before it can unleash all that is in it, which is the power to grow and to develop. If it abides alone it does nothing, but if it dies, it brings forth much fruit. Then, in verse 25, Jesus applies this to our personal lives:

The man who loves his life will lose it, while the man who hates his life in this world will keep it for eternal life.

Turning back to 1 Corinthians 15:36, Paul brings out the same idea and he uses strong words here. He is saying to the Corinthians:

How foolish! What you sow does not come to life unless it dies.

Turn to 2 Corinthians 4:11:

For we who are alive [the "we" refers to believers who have died in Christ, but now are alive in Him] are always being given over to death for Jesus' sake, so that his life may be revealed in our mortal body.

Do you realize what Paul is teaching? The life that you were born with, the life of the flesh, cannot grow into the kingdom of God; it has to die. It is the life of Christ that is implanted by the new birth experience that must grow. It must grow, it must develop until it overshadows everything else. But the only way it can grow is if we follow the principle of the cross. Jesus said in Luke 9:23:

Then he said to them all: "If anyone would come after me, he must deny himself and take up his cross daily and follow me."

The world does not need to see how good we are. The world needs to see God manifested in the flesh, and that is the kingdom of God.

Now I want to turn to my final text, and I want to relate to you a story that I have already told you before but it is so pertinent that it deserves repetition. I was conducting a week of prayer at the Seventh-day Adventist college in Ethiopia. Among that student body was a young Egyptian, a senior student taking mechanized agriculture and he had a problem because, when he graduated, he could not remain in Ethiopia, because his permit would not allow him. He had to go back to Egypt where he would be required to do two years of military service. There was no choice or option like we have here in this country and during those two years he had to carry a rifle and he had to shoot any Jew that he saw. Those were the days when reconciliation had not taken place between Egypt and Israel.

His teacher in his Bible class told him that it is a sin for Christians to carry arms. Now during the week of prayer I gave them time for questions. He wanted to see whether I would support his teacher or else support him, because he felt it was not wrong to fight for his country. His argument was that in the Bible we read about how God told Israel to fight against the other nations. So he asked me the question, "Is it a sin for Christians to carry arms and to kill?"

I gave him an answer that he was very pleased with. I said, "Darwit, any Egyptian who does not fight for his country should be ashamed of himself." He said, "Thank you." I said, "But I am not finished. I would like to ask you a question." He said, "What's that?" I said, "Have you ever seen a dead Egyptian fight for his country?" He said, "No." I asked, "Why not?" He said, "It's impossible." I said, "Why is it impossible?" He said, "Well, it's obvious. He is dead." "Are you a Christian?" I asked. He said, "Yes." I said, "Then you are dead, too, and your life is hid in Christ, and, by the way, Christ was a Jew." He didn't like that.

He said, "No, Pastor, I am not dead. I am Darwit. I am an Egyptian." "Then you are not a Christian," I told him. "Oh, yes, I am a Christian. I am an Egyptian Christian," he responded. I said, "There is no such thing in the Bible because the Bible tells me there is no Jew; there is no Greek; there is no male; there is no female; there is no rich; there is no poor; there is no educated or uneducated; we are all one in Christ." He did not agree with that so I said to him, "That's your problem, not mine."

Two weeks later he was testing a John Deer tractor with his instructor. They had a terrible accident. The tractor capsized and pinned him under, crushing his body. It took them 20 minutes to bring another tractor and raise the tractor and pull him out. There was a hospital three kilometers away owned by the Sudan Union Indian Mission. Two nurses and two doctors examined him. Both doctors pronounced him dead. The nurse came with a bed sheet to cover his body, and, as she was covering his head, his eyes blinked. She shouted, "He is alive!" Sure enough, he was alive because the students were praying for him and God performed a miracle. He did come back to life!

The hospital there was a bush hospital so they did not have equipment. They phoned us in Addis Ababa and we had to send the mission plane because the roads were terrible, too bumpy for him to go by car. We flew him to our Addis Ababa hospital. This was before the Marxists took it over. He was unconscious for two, maybe three weeks. I can't remember exactly how long. Then when he recovered consciousness I went to visit him. His body from waist up to head was in bandages; his chest was crushed; his jaw was broken; he was in a terrible mess. All that was open were his eyes. He looked like an Egyptian mummy but a live one.

I bent down to his ears and I whispered, "Darwit, how are you?" and I shall never forget what he said. He said, "Darwit is dead! You are talking to a Christian." It was a whisper, but it was something that he had discovered the hard way. He never carried arms. He had to flee for his life. They would have shot him in Egypt. He went to Sweden, married a Swedish girl, and I think he is still there now. The only way that new life can spring up in your body and produce a mighty Christian is for the old life to die so that the new life may spring up.

The famous German martyr who died under Hitler at the age of 29, in his favorite book, The Cost of Discipleship, made this statement: "When God calls you to be His disciple, He calls you to die." When all of us die and let the Holy Spirit take over, I can guarantee you that, small as we are, insignificant as we are, we will turn this place upside down."

But as long as the majority refuse to die, the rest of us are struggling because the fact is this, that God wants the body, which is the kingdom of God, to grow, and He wants each one of us to die. I can warn you: if you refuse to die, you will end up dying yourself because Jesus said, "He who does not hate his life will lose it," but if you surrender this life to the cross of Christ, that seed that was sown at Calvary — one life — will spring up and produce a great tree. Men and women will come and say, "What a wonderful tree. How did you manage it?" and you will say, "Not I, but Christ."

One seed died on Calvary's cross and the history of that one seed is found in the first four books of the New Testament, called the Gospels. But that seed sprang up into life in the Christian church and produced a mighty work so that the whole world was shaken at its very foundation. The record of that tree that grew out of that one seed is called the book of Acts. Read the book of Acts. That's the history of the seed that germinated and produced a great tree: the Christian church.

Unfortunately, the devil came in and perverted the gospel, from "Not I, but Christ" to "I, plus Christ." That mixture, which began with the Galatian church, destroyed the power of the church and the church was plunged into darkness. Ever since the 16th and 17th Centuries, God has been trying to revive the church by restoring the Gospel. He began with Martin Luther, and then came the Scientific Method which swept everything, including the Lutheran church, back into Liberalism. Then He raised John Wesley, and, for a time, the tree began to grow and develop and then it fizzled away again. Finally, I believe He raised the Advent Movement to lighten this earth with His glory. We have been in this world too long.

The world is waiting desperately. I want to give you the sad facts. When I left East African Union in 1982, the membership there was 150,000. Four years later, when I went to visit my Mother in Kenya, the membership had risen to 275,000. Then, only a year later, at the General Conference, the report was that they had reached 300,000. The church in the North American Division is on the decline, and all our money and all our budget and all our technology will not solve the problem. The only solution is that we must die and let the Holy Spirit take over. We will grow and I don't mean only grow numerically. My greatest concern is not numerical growth. My greatest concern is spiritual growth, the fruits of which is numerical growth.

It is my prayer that we all will be willing to die and let Christ take over. It is a costly business but I want to remind you of our study. You may have to suffer in this world, but, in the end, the wicked will be exterminated and the believers will be established. Until then, let the Lord live in us and may we all have one goal, "For me to live is Christ."

For that to happen we must confess with Paul (Galatians 2:20):

I have been crucified with Christ and I no longer live, but Christ lives in me. The life I live in the body, I live by faith in the Son of God, who loved me and gave himself for me.

This is the kingdom of God. It is like a little mustard seed. It begins small but, when it grows and develops, it overshadows everything else in this world. This is my prayer for this church, in Jesus' name. Amen.